Postcolonial Reconfigurations

Postcolonial Reconfigurations

An Alternative Way of Reading the Bible
and Doing Theology

R. S. Sugirtharajah

scm press

British Library Cataloguing in Publication data

A catalogue record for this book is available
from the British Library

0 334 02932 5

First published in 2003 by SCM Press
9-17 St Albans Place, London N1 0NX

www.scm-canterburypress.co.uk

SCM Press is a division of
SCM-Canterbury Press Ltd

Printed and bound in Great Britain by
Creative Print & Design, Ebbw Vale

Contents

Acknowledgements

I am grateful to several people without whose help and encourage-
ment this volume would not have been possible. I thank Anna
Hardman, previously the Senior Editor of SCM Press, for her enthusiastic support for the project from its inception, and Alex Knights
for his expertise and sensitivity in shepherding the volume. I am
particularly grateful to Dr Dan O'Connor, with whom I have had
many conversations about these essays, and am indebted to him for
his uncanny skill in refining many of my incoherent ideas. Finally to
my wife Sharada for her unflagging support and love without which
I wouldn't have been able to complete any of my research projects.

R. S. Sugirtharajah

Introduction
Repositioning Christian Discourse

This collection brings together essays on biblical and theological themes and the application of postcolonial criticism to these disciplines. It tries to provide a compelling case for the value of postcolonialism and its serviceability for these fields. It is designed to encourage a reconsideration of many of the assumptions and critical practices of the biblical and theological disciplines and to indicate the beneficiary and energizing effects of postcolonialism on them.

The major phase in the development of hermeneutics in the colonies began with the anti-colonial and national rehabilitation movements of the nineteenth century. On the one hand, the early interpreters had to resist colonialism, for which they profitably raided their past cultural and philosophical heritage. But on the other hand, they had to reexamine that very heritage itself. Though their ancient resources provided ammunition to withstand the colonial onslaught, the interpreters, to their horror, discovered that the indigenous heritage they so eagerly turned to contained several contaminated aspects, customs and practices such as untouchability, caste distinctions, polygamy, female circumcision, and widow-burning. This realization prompted an ambivalence common to the discourse of this period, where interpreters simultaneously commended and condemned their cultural heritage. Later, when the West's hermeneutical methods became preeminent, Third World[1] interpreters both recognized their power and at the same time repudiated them. European reading practices were borrowed in order to gain acceptance and were often nativized and interspersed with vernacular methods. A

---

[1] The term 'Third World' continues to trouble many. It is used here not in its geographical but in its rehabilitated political sense. It is employed as a lexical metaphor to encapsulate the political, economic and cultural imbalances that exist between the powerful and the powerless. For the origin and the deployment of the term, see the *Dictionary of Third World Theologies*, ed. Virginia Fabella and R. S. Sugirtharajah, Maryknoll: Orbis Books, 2000, pp. xxi and xxii.

number of critical theories, both foreign and local, were tried and discarded. It was in this dialectical tension between the colonized and the colonizer, recuperating and rejecting one's own culture, and both imported and indigenous methods, that Third World hermeneutics was fashioned. This volume continues this dialogue and tries to move the debate beyond its current binary entrapments.

A brief word about the current status of the three hermeneutical elements which preoccupy this volume – the Bible, Christian discourse, and postcolonialism.

First, about the Bible and its interpretation. The Bible we possess today is the result of relatively recent cultural and ecclesiastical factors – Protestantism, the Enlightenment, modernity and print culture. Today we not only have a different Bible, but we mint meanings which were not anticipated by the original writers/tellers/hearers/ readers of the narratives. Illuminated by centuries of human experience, intellectual enquiry and cultural fluidity, we question its retrogressive elements – such as the support of slavery, patriarchal control, corporal punishment of children, and homophobic and xenophobic attitudes – which the dominant thinking of the time would have been comfortable with. At the same time, we embrace and transpose the ancient texts, and propel them to yield new meanings unenvisaged by the authors of the narratives, in order to meet our contemporary needs. We use the Jubilee Laws in Leviticus 25 to write off Third World debt, we cite the Nazareth Manifesto to critique global capitalism, and we employ the Exodus motif whenever we find ourselves in an oppressive context. We continue to examine, expose, explain and transcreate meanings. The question is: Why should an ancient text matter today? Or to put it more tendentiously, why should we turn to a distant and obscure era and to figures like a rural Galilean or an urban Roman for illumination for a world which is becoming increasingly global, multi-textual and secular. The answer lies with those who are busily using biblical texts to define a narrow vision of biblical faith, especially in the aftermath of September 11. This includes a Scripture-spouting president of the world's only superpower who combines patriotism with a sense of divine mission. In Bush we have an overtly pious Christian leader whose vision of the world is determined and restricted by a single and simplistic reading of the Bible, thus erasing its indeterminacy and ambiguity. It is precisely this which makes it worthwhile to turn to its pages to make it clear to all those who adhere to a narrow understanding of the Bible that it is a book not with one message but with many, and that biblical texts often emit conflicting signals.

Secondly, Christian theological discourse in the Third World continues to be directed and constrained by two discourses – theology as an experiential enterprise, and identity-hermeneutics. Great claims have been made for Third World theologies as experiential discourses which reflect the feelings and pains of people. The Western academic approach has been dismissed as irrelevant and ivory-towerish. Such a dismissal came as a contextual necessity, to resist the abstract and universalizing tendencies of the Western academic theologies which invaded the Third World. Though Third World theologies offered a necessary corrective to the regnant Western theologies, their over-emphasis on involvement and engagement has led to the notion that they do not have a rational and credible basis to undergird their proposals. 'Third World', when referring to theologies, has come to be synonymous with 'spiritual', 'practical' and non-rational. Such a perception reinforces the orientalist notion of the 'other' being emotional and sentimental, and does a grave injustice to the analytic and logical traditions developed especially in Indian and Chinese hermeneutical practice. Third World theologies need to reclaim these rational traditions, not with a view to parading them to score points, but to demonstrate that these analytical traditions wrestle with questions which are not addressed elsewhere and, more importantly, how they endeavour to work out solutions to them.

The other narrative which preoccupies Third World theological discourse is that of identity-hermeneutics. Generic and pan-Asian, pan-Latin American and pan-African theologies of the 1960s have given way to localized-identity and issue-specific theologies. The result has been the emergence of feminist, Dalit, Burakumin and tribal theological discourses. These theological articulations are largely attempts to grapple with subaltern status and to recover identity and authenticity. In this process communities have been reimagined, and reconceptualized. Metanarratives such as that of unity in diversity have been celebrated but then discredited. Paradoxically, identity-based theologies are in danger of reifying their own subjecthood and contexts. What began as a startlingly original discourse is now rife with theological clichés, and as a result the discourse both undermines and plays into its own stereotypes. Identities and contexts change. Once this happens, to keep on parroting uncritically the old catchphrases is to run the risk of turning these once emancipatory concepts into ossified absolutes and paper-tiger triumphalism.

Finally, the term 'postcolonial'. It emerged in the 1990s as a descriptor for a wide array of discursive and praxiological exercises which earlier went under the rubrics of 'Third World', 'Non-Western

World', 'Minority Studies'.[2] The term postcolonial has come into prominence not because these labels were seen as tainted, but because it has become increasingly a fundamental universal category along with 'race, and class, and caste, and age, and gender' (Moore 2001: 124). The term generates at least three meanings. First, in a historical sense, it encapsulates the social, political and cultural conditions of the current world order, bringing to the fore the cultural, political and economic facts of colonialism, and aiding recognition of the ambiguities of decolonization and the ongoing neocolonization. Secondly, as a critical discursive practice, postcolonial criticism has initiated arresting analyses of texts and societies. It provides openings for oppositional readings, uncovers suppressed voices and, more pertinently, has as its foremost concern victims and their plight. It has not only interrogated colonial domination but has also offered viable critical alternatives. Thirdly, the term implies the political and ideological stance of an interpreter who is engaged in anti-colonial and anti-globalizing theory and praxis. Applied to biblical studies, it seeks to uncover colonial designs in both biblical texts and their interpretations, and endeavours to read the text from such postcolonial concerns as identity, hybridity and diaspora. Unlike the current biblical scholarship produced, invigorated and contained by virtuous aspects of the Enlightenment and modernity, postcolonialism concentrates on the vicious aspects of modernity – colonialism and how its legacy influenced and informed the promotion of the Bible and the development of biblical interpretation.

About this Volume

The volume is organized under two interrelated headings – 'Relocating Biblical Studies' and 'Remapping Christian Theological Discourse'. These divisions, as anyone in the field will know, are contrived, and as disciplines, they often overlap and are interconnected. In spite of what some of the practitioners of these disciplines would aver, Biblical Studies and Systematic Theologies need each other for their survival and credibility.

The first chapter, 'A Postcolonial Exploration of Collusion and

---

[2] The literature is too vast and ever-growing to be listed here. For a useful introduction to methods, history and debates about postcolonialism, see McLeod 2000; for its application in biblical studies, see Sugirtharajah 1999; 2001; 2002; Dube 2000; Dube and Staley 2002; Segovia 2000a; 2000b; and Boer 2001.

Construction in Biblical Interpretation', celebrates the inauguration of postcolonial theory. As an exercise in postcolonial reading, it looks at two biblical narratives, the Matthean missionary command at Matthew 28.19, and the Pauline missionary-tours narratives recorded in Acts, and demonstrates how reactivation of these texts during the territorial expansion of the European nations provided scriptural sanction for and legitimized the colonial enterprise. The essay ends with an interrogation of the theory itself with a view to confirming its significance.

Chapter 2, 'Son(s) Behaving Badly: The Prodigal in Foreign Hands', investigates Luke's well-known account of the parable of the Prodigal Son, and maps out its hermeneutical kismet as it sojourns outside its natural Christian environment, and is put to use profitably by interpreters who belong to religious traditions other than Christian, and writers of secular fiction. These writers, in our case Kiran Nagarkar and Thomas Palakeel, reconfigure the Lukan parable, to further their literary, ideological and hermeneutical projects. In scrutinizing these literary pieces, I try to place them within the postcolonial trope of irony, and demonstrate how, in their appropriation of the gospel parable, Nagarkar and Palakeel end up replicating the very values they seek to repudiate. The essay also deals with the hermeneutical implications of outsiders raiding stories which are not part of their cultural and theological inheritance.

'Marketing the Testaments: Canongate and their Pocket-Sized Bibles' looks at one of the publishing sensations of the last century, the Canongate Bible. An Edinburgh publishing firm, Canongate brought out parts of the King James Version of the Bible in the form of single books. Each volume has an introduction by a famous person from the literary, pop or scientific world not normally renowned for their Christian faith, and persons from Jewish and Buddhist traditions. The purpose was to attract new Western readers for whom the Bible had become an 'archaic monument'. The writers include P. D. James, Bono, and the Dalai Lama. In looking at these introductions, the essay examines the following: the beneficial aspects of the Pocket Canon; the merchandising of the Bible, and employment of religious themes by commercial and secular firms; the resurrection of the Bible through the King James Version; the colonial corollaries in redacting, producing and promoting the Bible; the function of the interpreter's personal voice in reading a narrative; and the debate surrounding the application of personal-voice criticism to biblical studies.

'Loitering with Intent: Biblical Texts in Public Places' continues the theme of the last chapter – the effect of the Bible in the public arena –

this time by exploring the fate of biblical texts as they find themselves in the popular press. Newspapers are not the natural place to look for biblical citations, but they are occasionally being bandied about to either promote or proscribe cases ranging from asylum-seekers to the use of corporal punishment for children. In a culture where biblical allusions and imagery have been all but eclipsed, the sporadic appearance of sacred texts in the secular print media is an indicator that the scriptures still have some hermeneutical purchase. The essay looks at four areas – international conflict, sexual orientation, law and order and bringing up children – where biblical texts are being summoned either to endorse or to repudiate. This raises hermeneutical issues such as how biblical texts are used in print media, the nature of the texts employed, the interface between popular and professional reading, and the role of the common reader as a biblical commentator, and concludes with consideration of the status and influence of the Bible outside its own comfortable constituency.

The subject matter of 'A Modern Tool-Shed for a Global Village' is simultaneously linked to the use and abuse of historical critical tools and biblical interpretation in an international context. While conceding the liberative nature of historical criticism when it first emerged on the hermeneutical scene, the chapter maps out its subsequent oppressive and colonizing tendencies when it was introduced to the Third World. The essay urges that, instead of rather complacently declaring itself the court of appeal, criticism should overcome the considerable distance it has created between the academy and the general public and be at the service of ordinary people. The second part of the essay addresses the fate of Third World hermeneutics in the face of the globalization of biblical interpretation and the serious implications for its practitioners. This chapter was originally written in response to Heikki Räisänen's paper and delivered at the 1999 International Meeting of the Society of Biblical Literature held in Helsinki. Since the reader may not have benefit of Räisänen's paper, I have reworked mine, cutting out explicit references to his in order to facilitate smooth reading. I beg Räisänen's pardon.[3]

The last chapter in Part I, 'Getting the Mixture Right: Promises and Perils of Postcolonial Criticism and Biblical Interpretation', addresses the following: the renewed need to establish a case for the relevance of postcolonialism in the twenty-first century at a time when territorial

---

[3] Those who wish to follow the full debate should see Heikki Räisänen et al., *Reading the Bible in the Global Village: Helsinki*, Atlanta: Society of Biblical Literature, 2000.

colonialism has almost come to an end; the potential reasons for its little impact on biblical scholars and their hesitancy to employ post-colonialism as a critical tool; the areas where postcolonialism and biblical studies can productively engage with each other; some future concerns of postcolonialism, one of which is the troubling question of the role of belief in a post-Enlightened era if the discourse is to continue to maintain its relevance as a potential tool, and the chapter ends with a conundrum which those in the business of reading and interpreting constantly face.

Beginning Part II, 'Remapping Christian Theological Discourse', 'Postcolonialism and Indian Christian Theology' is concerned with the creation of cultural stereotypes in theological writing and the danger of venerating the vernacular in an attempt to avoid Euro-centrism and create an indigenous Indian theology. This chapter challenges the hitherto maintained orthodoxies of Indian/Asian theological discourse which have treated people as having singular identities, and regarded cultures as discrete, fixed and exclusive entities. What the chapter argues is that in the postcolonial context Christian theological reflection needs to take on board not an imagined homogeneity but a plurality of identities and coalescing of cultures. As a way forward, the chapter goes on to propose the post-colonial category of hybridity as a potential tool for working out a theology.

Chapter 8, 'The Magi from Bengal and their Jesus: Indian Construals of Christ during Colonial Times', brings to the fore the often neglected Indian contributions to scholarly debates surrounding Christology. It discusses the work of three Hindus, Raja Rammohun Roy, Keshub Chunder Sen and P. C. Mozoomdar, in terms of re-imaging Jesus against the problematic of a colonial ethos, and demonstrates how these Hindus unwittingly re-orientalized the Orient and drew on and went beyond the modernizing tendencies introduced by colonialism.

'Complacencies and Cul-de-sacs: Christian Theologies and Colonialism' looks at the reluctance of Christian theologians to address the implications of colonialism for the discipline. While other academic disciplines have grappled with the implications of European empire, colonialism has not been a popular subject for systematic theology. As samples of this negligence, the essay investigates the theological discourse of two Western theologians, Niebuhr and Warren, and demonstrates how they project a native-friendly empire, and overlook the predatory nature of colonialism. The chapter is equally critical of the Indian Christian response to empire, and concludes with a proposal that 'vernacular cosmopolitanism' provides a possible discursive space for doing theology in a postcolonial context.

The last chapter, 'Textual Takeaways: Third World Texts in Western Metropolitan Centres', problematizes teaching and introducing theological texts from Third World countries in Western academies. This chapter emerges out of my experience of brokering texts from other cultures when they are treated as objects of scrutiny and analysis, their cultural features flattened and their cultural origin and context erased. The chapter suggests that one way to overcome such misreading is to engage in a Saidian contrapuntal reading. The chapter also explores the role of the Third World academic in presenting such texts to Western audiences when the distance between presenter and subject is often blurred, and the presenter is perceived as subject matter as much as the subject he or she presents. It also draws attention to the enormous power and responsibility conferred upon the Third World interpreter, and the seduction he or she faces.

These chapters are by no means all-inclusive in their scope, nor do they embody a homogeneous approach. Inevitably, in a collection like this, one is liable to refer to the same material more than once, but in each such case I have been trying to make a different point. What they all share, however, is a resistance to the devaluation of colonial ideologies in the mainstream biblical and theological discourse. What they try to do is to critique colonialism and neo-colonial tendencies in biblical hermeneutics and theological discourse, and view postcolonialism as a potential energizer of these disciplines by providing conceptual tools and an analytical framework for such a critique. Above all, these chapters attest the continuing force of colonialism as a potential threat and see postcolonial criticism as a fruitful tool in understanding both the colonial past and the contemporary world order. In advancing postcolonialism, these chapters do not shy away from interrogating postcolonial discourse itself.

Where do we go from here? One thing is certain: there is no return to the past, as some revivalists and reformers would like us to do. There is no harking back to the beginning either; as the Indian literary critic Satchidanandan has said, 'there are no beginnings, there is only a constant renewal of our sources of desire and memory, of search and discovery, a ceaseless encounter with new points of recognition within representation, a linking in the chain of being and becoming' (1999: 25). What postcolonialism implies is that there is no recourse to a time when tradition was pristine, identity was pure and immaculate, or cultures were uncontaminated. What postcolonialism signifies is that the future is open and the past unstable and constantly changing. If the essays assembled here reflect and resonate this mood, and point to different ways of engaging with the Bible and working out a theological discourse, then I would be more than pleased.

References

Boer, Roland, 2001. *Last Stop Before Antarctica: The Bible and Postcolonialism in Australia*, The Bible and Postcolonialism, 6, Sheffield: Sheffield Academic Press.

Dube, Musa W., 2000. *Postcolonial Feminist Interpretation of the Bible*, St Louis: Chalice Press.

Dube, Musa W., and Jeffrey L. Staley (eds), 2002. *John and Postcolonialism: Travel, Space and Power*. London: Sheffield Academic Press.

McLeod, John, 2000. *Beginning Postcolonialism*, Manchester: Manchester University Press.

Moore, David Chioni, 2001. 'Is the Post- in Post-Colonial the Post- in Post-Soviet? Toward a Global Postcolonial Critique', *PMLA* 116.1.

Satchidanandan, K., 1999. *Indian Literature: Positions and Propositions*, Delhi: Pencraft International.

Segovia, Fernando F. (ed.), 2000a. *Decolonizing Biblical Studies*, Maryknoll, N.Y.: Orbis Books.

Segovia, Fernando F. (ed.), 2000b. *Interpreting Beyond Borders*, The Bible and Postcolonialism, 3, Sheffield: Sheffield Academic Press.

Sugirtharajah, R. S., 1999. *Asian Biblical Hermeneutics and Postcolonialism: Contesting the Interpretations*, Sheffield: Sheffield Academic Press. (US edition, Maryknoll, N.Y.: Orbis Books, 1998.)

Sugirtharajah, R. S., 2001. *The Bible and the Third World: Precolonial, Colonial and Postcolonial Encounters*, Cambridge: Cambridge University Press.

Sugirtharajah, R. S., 2002. *Postcolonial Criticism and Biblical Interpretation*, Oxford: Oxford University Press.

Part I

Relocating Biblical Studies

1

A Postcolonial Exploration of Collusion and Construction in Biblical Interpretation

'Easy win, monkey,' Ganesh said. 'The old fellow's education is so much deeper.'
'Ah, yes, but the Bengali's reading is so much wider,' Hanuman said. 'He has an MA in colonial literature.'
'True, true, but that will apply only peripherally, if at all.'

Vikram Chandra, *Red Earth and Pouring Rain*

I set out to do three things in this chapter. First, to trace the emergence of postcolonialism as a critical discourse and then to try to define postcolonialism. Second, I shall examine the collusion between colonialism and exegesis, and contest the Eurocentric construction of Christian origins. To illustrate the former, I shall revisit two key mission narratives, the Great Commission (Matthew 28.19) and Paul's missionary tours (Acts 13–14; 15.40–18.22; 18.22–21.16) and demonstrate how the Matthaean verse was reactivated and the Pauline missionary-journey pattern was fabricated at the time of Western colonial expansion with the busy involvement of Western mercantile companies. Third, and to elucidate the latter, I shall look at the formation of the gospel tradition and the reluctance and shyness on the part of Western biblical critics to admit any interfusion of Eastern conceptual categories into the gospel materials. In conclusion, as an exercise in clarification, for those who are engaged in postcolonial reading practice, I should like to set out some of the issues we now need to address.

Postcolonialism emerged as a critical activity within what is known as Commonwealth or Third World Literature Studies. As the Indian critic Harish Trivedi claims, it was the first time that the colonized other was placed at the centre of academic discourse:

Unlike with feminism or post-structuralism or even Marxism, the discourse of post-colonialism is ostensibly not about the West where it has originated but about the colonised other. For the first time probably in the whole history of the Western academy, the non-West is placed at the centre of its dominant discourse. Even if it is in part a sort of compensation for all the colonial material exploitation, the academic attention now being paid to the post-colonial is so assiduous as to soothe and flatter. (1996: 232)

He also goes on to warn that this new attention, a grudging favour granted by the West, could well be a new form of colonialism.

Since the 1960s, most of the literary productions which emerged during and after colonialism in the former colonies in Asia and Africa, were accorded the title 'Commonwealth Literature'. The term 'Commonwealth' not only kept alive the notion of British cultural influence, but also perpetuated the notion that the empire had been a willing association of free people. Recently, the term 'postcolonialism' has been used increasingly to signify the text and context of these writings. Postcolonialism got its imprimatur when the publishers Routledge, at the last minute, changed the name of a volume which had been under preparation for more than a decade from *The Encyclopedia of Commonwealth Literature* to *The Encyclopedia of Post-colonial Literatures in English* (M. Mukherjee 1996: 5). A further impor-tant moment in postcolonial discourse was the production of the Indian series Subaltern Studies: Writings on South Asian History and Society. This dissident project, in keeping with the efforts of the radical movements of the 1970s to write history from the underside, has been successful in scrutinizing, challenging and transforming how the subaltern was constructed in the dominant models of Indian historiography.[1] We also need to recognize the outstanding work of C. L. R. James, Frantz Fanon, Aime Cesaire, Amilcar Cabral, Albert Memmi, Chinua Achebe and Ngũgĩ wa Thiong'o, to name a few, whose writings, though emanating from diverse cultural and histori-cal locations, offered precursory intellectual stimulus to the current postcolonial thinking.

Initially, postcolonialism was seen as a convenient pedagogical tool rather than as advancing particular theoretical concepts. It was later that cultural critics like Edward Said (1985, 1993), Spivak (1988, 1990) and Homi Bhabha (1994) gave postcolonialism its theorization and practice. This trio speaks from different sites, and mobilizes different philosophical and conceptual categories. Their writings resist any neat summary, yet there is a certain central aspect and unifying force

---

[1] So far there have been nine volumes published, under the editorship of different authors, by Oxford University Press, Delhi.

in their approach, namely, to investigate and expose the link between knowledge and power in the textual production of the West. One can detect at least two meanings and usages of postcolonialism emerging from their writings – postcolonialism as reading strategy, and as a state or a condition. Said and Spivak treat postcolonialism as a reading strategy. Bhabha, on the other hand, sees postcoloniality as a condition of being. He foregrounds the contemporary subjectivities in literary and epistemological terms, at the same time highlighting the issues of ambivalence and hybridity.

Postcolonialism is not simply a physical expulsion of imperial powers. Nor is it simply recounting the evils of the empire, and drawing a contrast with the nobility and virtues of natives and their cultures. Rather, it is an active confrontation with the dominant system of thought, its lopsidedness and inadequacies, and underlines its unsuitability for us. Hence, it is a process of cultural and discursive emancipation from all dominant structures whether they be political, linguistic or ideological.

Postcolonialism, it has to be stressed, has a multiplicity of meanings, depending on location. It is seen as an oppositional reading practice, and as a way of critiquing the totalizing forms of Eurocentric thinking and of reshaping dominant meanings. It is a mental attitude rather than a method, more a subversive stance towards the dominant knowledge than a school of thought. It is not about periodization. It is a reading posture. It is a critical enterprise aimed at unmasking the link between idea and power, which lies behind Western theories and learning. It is a discursive resistance to imperialism, imperial ideologies, imperial attitudes and their continued incarnations in such wide-ranging fields as politics, economics, history and theological and biblical studies.

An anti-colonial mode of critique is not new. There were earlier attempts during the colonial days. In confronting the colonizer, the earlier colonized in the Raj era made use of the Western constructions of the colonizer and the colonized, of centre and periphery. The earlier colonized were largely shaped by, and remained in many ways locked into, the very structure they were keen on demolishing. What is new in the current anti-imperial contestation is that it goes beyond the essentialist and contrastive ways of thinking, East–West, us–them, vernacular–metropolitan, and seeks a radical syncretizing of each opposition. Where the current postcolonialism differs from the earlier form is that while challenging the oppressive nature of colonialism it recognizes the potentiality of contact between colonizer and colonized. Distancing itself from both the reverent admiration of native values and a cringing attitude towards all that is Western, the present postcolonialism tries to integrate and forge a new perspective by critically and profitably syncretizing ingredients from both vernacular and metropolitan centres.

Postcolonialism as a critical enterprise is, in Samia Mehrez's view, an 'act of exorcism' for both the colonized and the colonizer. 'For both parties it must be a process of liberation: from dependency, in the case of the colonized, and from imperialist, racist perceptions, representations, and institutions which, unfortunately, remain with us till this very day, in the case of the colonizer' (1991: 258). In other words, in the process of decolonization, the imperializer and the imperialized are inevitably locked together. In the case of the former, it means re-examining their collusion with the empire and imperialism, and reassessing a Western ethnocentricism which was passed off as universalism. In the case of the latter, it means reviewing internal colonization, virulent forms of nationalism and excessive nativism.

One of the hermeneutical agendas in this liberative role of post-colonialism is to encourage what Edward Said calls 'contrapuntal reading'. This is a reading strategy advocated by him with a view to encouraging the experiences of the exploited and the exploiter to be studied together. In other words, texts from metropolitan centres and peripheries are studied simultaneously. Contrapuntal reading paves the way for a situation which goes beyond reified binary characterizations of Eastern and Western writings. To read contrapuntally means to be aware simultaneously of mainstream scholarship and of other scholarship which the dominant discourse tries to domesticate and speaks and acts against. In Said's words, 'we . . . re-read it not univocally but contrapuntally, with a simultaneous awareness both of the metropolitan history that is narrated and of those other histories against which (and beyond which) the dominating discourse acts' (1993: 59). Translating this into the biblical field, it means to read Hisako Kinukawa's *Women and Jesus in Mark* with Bas van Iersel's *Reading Mark*; Karl Barth's *Romans* with Tamez's *The Amnesty of Grace: Justification by Faith from a Latin American Perspective*; Bultmann's *John* with Appasamy's *Christianity as Bhakti Marga*; and Neil Elliot's *Liberating Paul: The Justice of God and the Politics of the Apostle* with Jaswant Raj's *Grace in the Saiva Siddhantham and in St Paul*. By linking such works to each other, and juxtaposing neglected texts with the mainstream, we can highlight gaps, absences and imbalances.

Mandating Mission and Imperialism

Both as a state or a condition, and as a reading strategy, postcolonialism is a useful critical concept for New Testament studies. In this regard, a preliminary task will be to disrupt some of the prevailing assumptions about the New Testament. As an example, I should like to reinvestigate some of the texts and exegetical practices which undergirded and colluded with colonialism and colonial mission. I am particularly interested in looking again at the Matthaean missionary commission (Matthew 28.19) and the missionary journeys of Paul (Acts 13–14; 15.40–18.22; 18.22–21.16). These were profitably used in the missionary efforts of the church in the colonial period. Commentaries for Indian students written during both the colonial and the post-independent periods mobilized Matthew's text as a biblical warrant to missionize the natives, and utilized the mission-journey narratives as a model for their Christianizing work. These texts had been dormant and were largely disregarded by the reformers, yet were reinvoked in the eighteenth and nineteenth centuries during the evangelical revival which significantly coincided with the rise of Western imperialism. At this time, the Matthaean text came to be used as a template to institutionalize the missionary obligation, and Luke's alleged recording of Paul's missionary undertaking was fabricated as a way of perpetuating the myth that it was from the West that the superstitious and ignorant natives received the essential verities of God's message.

Before the eighteenth century, Matthew's command 'Go ye and preach' was an unfashionable, under-exegeted, often even absent, text. It was William Carey (1761–1834), the Baptist missionary pioneer, who reactivated it as a missionary command for the modern period.[2] The earlier missionaries seem to have appealed to and sought endorsement from other texts. Robert de Nobili (1577–1656) found the Pauline axiom 'to the Jews I have become a Jew' spurring him on in his missionary endeavours in South India (Neill 1934: 56). Frederick Schwartz (1726–98) recuperated another Matthaean verse: 'Come unto me all ye that labour and are heavy laden, I will give you rest' (11.25) (Page 1921: 56), and the first English mission agency, the Society for the Propagation of the Gospel in Foreign Parts, founded in 1701, sent its first missionaries to America on the basis of the appeal in Acts, 'Come over . . . and help us' (Thompson 1951: 19). David Bosch furnishes a further list of texts exemplifying the missionary thrust in

---

[2] See Boer 1961: 16, 17.

different periods of history. The patristic understanding of mission was based on John 3.16, whereas the medieval Roman Catholic missionary impulse was animated by Luke 14.23: 'Go out to the highways and hedges, compel people to come in, that my house may be filled.' The Reformers looked to Romans 1.16–17. The Enlightenment era produced its own host of preferential texts. The aforementioned Acts 16.9 had been prominent among Western Christians who saw their task as rescuing the peoples in distant lands who were in darkness. The premillenialists mandated their mission in the words of Jesus: 'And this gospel of the kingdom will be preached throughout the whole world, as a testimony to all nations; and then the end will come' (Matthew 24.14); and the Social Gospellers appealed to the Johannine saying: 'I came that they may have life, and have it abundantly' (John 10.10) (Bosch 1991: 339–40).

Carey, on the other hand, in his pamphlet *An Enquiry into the Obligations of Christians to Use Means for the Conversion of the Heathen* (1792), resurrected the Matthaean commission as the proof text for compulsive preaching of the gospel in distant lands. The *Enquiry*, a curious text for its time, resembles the prospectus of a modern-day multinational company, with elaborate statistical details reminding Christians of their inescapable obligation to preach the gospel to distant lands. The pamphlet was not only a missionary apologetic but provided a strategy as well. Central to all this was Matthew 28.19. Since then, this verse has exercised a considerable influence on the institutionalized missionary efforts of the Christian church.

The phenomenal expansion of Christianity in the first few centuries seems on the whole to have come about with little institutionalized mission and little formal preaching. Alan Kreider, who has investigated the growth of the pre-Christendom church, is of the view that organized mission played little part in its expansion:

[T]here was, as Arthur Darby Nock has emphasised, 'little, if any direct preaching to the masses'; it was simply too dangerous. Or organizing the congregations for mission: according to Georg Kretschmar, 'the recruitment to the faith was never institutionalized' . . . How about prayer for the conversion of pagans? According to Yves Congar, 'the Christians prayed for the prosperity and peace of people, but scarcely for their conversion'. Most of the very few prayers for conversion which survive from the early centuries, eight out of eleven in all according to my count, are in fact prayers in obedience to Jesus' command to pray for enemies and persecutors. As to theologizing of an explicitly missionary nature, the only

word which for Norbert Brox will adequately describe 'the scarcity
of reflection about mission' is 'astonishing'. To this list of surprising
omissions I would like to add one more. In my reading of early
Christian materials with a missionary's eyes, I have been amazed at
the absence of pastoral admonitions to evangelise. A sample of this
is *Ad Quirinum* by the North African bishop and martyr Cyprian.
The third book of this work is a manual of 120 'heavenly precepts'
to guide catechumens in the Christian life. These 'precepts' cover a
whole range of areas of Christian concern – 'that brethren ought to
support one another', or 'that we are to be urgent in prayers' – but
none, not one of the 120, urges the believers to evangelise. (1994: 8)

He goes on to furnish the actual reasons for the growth of the early
Jesus movement. The movement grew in the early days not because
there was organized oral dissemination of God's word, but through
public demonstration of the faith. This was mediated by a number of
means. For instance, martyrdom, which brought not only notoriety
but also admiration for a people who valued their new-found faith
and were willing to die for it. People also came to know about the new
faith in less dramatic ways. Exemplary behaviour of individual
Christians at workplaces and in neighbourhoods attracted attention.
Exorcism, too, played a vital evangelistic part: 'in an age of competi-
tive miracle-working, the Christian God seemed stronger than other
Gods' (Kreider 1994: 12). In Kreider's view Christianity also spread in
the pre-Christendom phase because of the extraordinary characteristics of Christian worship, which nurtured and prepared Christians to
face the outside world: 'The worship was shaping a people whose life,
and whose response to the world, were distinctive' (28).
    In contrast with the movement described by Kreider, Protestant
Christianity was strikingly inert in Carey's England. Indeed, it was a
Roman Catholic argument against the Reformation that it had failed
to inspire mission. The title of the first section of Carey's pamphlet
'An Enquiry Whether the Commission given by Our Lord to his
Disciples be not still binding on us' is an indication of the hermen-
eutical mood of the time:

> There seems also to be an opinion existing in the minds of some,
> that because the apostles were extraordinary officers and have no
> proper successors, and because many things which were right for
> them to do would be utterly unwarrantable for us, therefore it may
> not be immediately binding on us to execute the commission,
> though it was so upon them. (Carey 1961: 8)

Carey, in summoning Matthew's closing verses, was countering
the prevalent hermeneutical convention of his time. For instance, the
view among the Danish clergy of the time was that no further world-
wide mission was called for. This, they based on their reading of
Romans 10.18 and Colossians 1.23. These verses were interpreted to
mean that the apostles had preached the gospel to 'every creature
under heaven' (Sandgren 1991: 83). Thus, for the Reformers and for
the ecclesiastical thinkers of Carey's time, the commission had been
binding only on the apostles and had lost its efficacy with their death.
The Reformers did not envision an organized missionary programme,
and took it for granted that they did not have a mandate to preach
the gospel and to establish churches in distant places. Such a perception was based on the Reformers' understanding of ecclesiastical
duties. They distinguished between two kinds of office – apostles and
pastors. It had been the task of the former to preach everywhere they
went, and the latter's role was to serve the local churches, their
authority limited to the area of their ministry. Calvin encapsulated
this thinking when he wrote:

> . . . for the Lord created the apostles, that they might spread the
> gospel throughout the whole world, and he did not assign to each
> of them certain limits or parishes, but would have them, wherever
> they went, to discharge the office of ambassadors among all nations
> and languages. In this respect there is a difference between them
> and pastors, who are, in a manner, tied to their particular churches.
> For the pastor has not a commission to preach the gospel over the
> whole world, but to take care of the Church that has been com-
> mitted to his charge. (cited in Boer 1961: 19)

Luther, too, held similar views.[3] Though he rediscovered the power
of the Word, he continued to subscribe to the received notion that
missionary preaching was a privilege of the apostles. Carey, a Baptist
and Calvinist, was reacting against this Reformation understanding
when he reappropriated the Great Commission.

Carey's hermeneutical challenge to the received missiological
orthodoxy of the earlier phase of European colonialism and imperialism invites a further postcolonial reconsideration, and a first question
might be whether the Matthaean church was true to the great commission or whether there is any sign of its members having engaged
in missionary activities. The popular perception of the Matthaean
community has been that it had a positive Gentile bias and was

---

[3] See Boer 1961: 19.

actively involved in evangelizing them. A fresh investigation by David C. Sim contests such assumptions (1995). He has shown that there is internal and external evidence to suggest the contrary. The Gospel of Matthew contains a number of unsympathetic statements about the Gentiles (5.46–7; 6.7–8, 31–2; 18.15–17). It is not always generous to those who were not part of the Jewish race. They are called 'dogs' and deemed not worthy to eat the bread that belonged to the children of Israel. The strongest contempt for Gentiles was expressed in Matthew 18.17, where Matthew's Jesus instructed the followers that if a wrongdoer failed to accept the correction of the community then that person should be treated 'as a Gentile and a tax collector'. The disciples are also instructed not to follow the example of the Gentiles in seeking position and power (10.25). The writer of Matthew's Gospel did not think much of Gentile piety either. In his reckoning the prayer of the Gentile was a vain noise (6.7). These negative perceptions indicate that for Matthew the Gentile world is a foreign and godless place which must be avoided and, more importantly, whose practices must not be imitated by his readers. The reason for this stance could be attributed to the persecution the Matthaean community faced at the hands of the Gentiles during and following the first Jewish war against Rome. Matthew's discourses on mission (ch. 10) and apocalypticism (chs 24–5) corroborate this.

What is interesting is that Carey's call to win the souls of the unbelievers in foreign lands and his reactivating of the Matthaean command happened at a time of unprecedented territorial conquest by the West. Historians of colonialism have come up with different periodizations of the imperial advance of the West. Carey's call to evangelize distant lands falls within what Marc Ferro categorizes as colonialism of a new type, yoked to the Industrial Revolution and to financial capitalism, and marked by expansionist policies (1997: 19). It is highly significant to a postcolonial hermeneutic that Carey's fascination with this dormant verse arose at a time when Europe was engaged in just such a colonialism.

This leads us nicely to the missionary tours of Paul, and it will become clear as we go along that the reconfiguration of the tour scheme, too, had interlocked with the imperial advance of Europe.

Missionary Tours and Mercantile Trading Companies

The emergence of many missionary societies in the eighteenth and nineteenth centuries led exegetes to impose a missionary-journey structure on the Acts. This missionary-tour scheme has been used to sustain and legitimize mission activity. Generations of Indian students studying for the Serampore theological degree[4] have been asked to answer a question which runs like this: 'Describe the missionary journeys of Paul and draw out the implications for the missionary task in today's India.' The textbooks available offered ample scholarly help to the hapless students. There were two commentary series specifically written for Indian students – the Indian Church Commentaries and the Christian Students' Library.[5] The commentaries on Acts in both series contain a plan of the book. In this, the commentators make the three journeys central to Luke's volume. Harold Moulton, one of those who contributed to the Indian Christian Students' Library, wrote: 'Most of the remainder of the book is taken up with the account of the missionary tours designed to plant the Gospel in the places where it can have most effect if it strikes root' (1957: 40). He persuades the students: 'the same strategic sense is necessary for the full development of the Christian enterprise everywhere' (41). A similar view is expressed by T. Walker, who contributed a volume for the other series: '[Acts is] in the main, a record of mission work in distant lands' (1919: lii). He goes on to say that the very divisions of the book emphasize this fact, and 'follow the lines of the Saviour's last command' (lv). Moulton also concocted a missionary headquarters, Jerusalem/Antioch, to which Paul keeps returning and reporting (55, 57).

Like the missionary command, the tour scheme had been paid little attention by either the pre-Christendom church or the Reformers. The first reference to the journey pattern, according to John Townsend, appeared in J. A. Bengel's *Gnomon Novi Testamenti* (1742). Even here Bengel mentioned it only in his preface and failed to follow this up in his commentary or in the chronology of Paul that he published separately. The commentaries which followed the work of Bengel also adopted the mission-journey pattern. Surveying the commentarial writings on Acts in early and medieval times, Townsend concludes that the writers were silent about the missionary pattern. Ancient writers such as Irenaeus, Jerome, Ephraem, John Chrysostom and Bede observe a hermeneutical reticence on this topic: 'The fact that these writers . . . are silent about a missionary-journey pattern in Acts

---

[4] Serampore College, the first Western-style college in Asia, is the only Protestant institution which has a charter to confer theological degrees in India. It is proud of the fact that it got its charter from Denmark in 1818, even before the University of Calcutta was instituted.

[5] For a postcolonial critique of these series, see Sugirtharajah 1998a: 9–10; 1998b: 283–96.

would certainly cast doubt on any argument that the pattern was originally intended by the author of Luke–Acts' (1986: 102). This is equally true of those who belonged to a later time, Erasmus, Calvin and Theodore Beza, who failed to detect in Acts the missionary itinerary.

A rereading of the textual evidence in Acts raises a serious challenge to the accepted view that the author conceived a triple journey plan for Paul, with Antioch or Jerusalem providing the base for departure and return. Of the three journeys, only the first (chs 13–14) has some semblance of a missionary tour, originating from Antioch. It takes Paul through Cyprus and a series of towns of Southern Asia Minor – Pisidian Antioch, Iconium, Lystra and Derbe – and then he goes back by the same route but missing out Cyprus. The 'second journey' seems to have been unplanned, and Paul simply drifts from one Roman city to another, until he reaches Corinth and settles down there for a while, getting involved in a fracas with the local Jewish community. He decides to leave, and the 'third' tour begins at once, at 18.23. It is a misnomer even to call it a journey because Paul spends three years in Ephesus (20.31) – three months in the synagogue (19.8) and two years in the school of Tyrannus (19.10) debating. It was during this time that he was involved in the Corinthian correspondence, and, according to 2 Corinthians 13.2, in an unhappy and unprofitable trip to Corinth. He returns to Ephesus and then moves up to Macedonia and then to Greece, or probably Corinth, where he spends three months, followed by a short stay in Troas (20.6–12); and then journeys down the west coast of Asia Minor, finally reaching Jerusalem. Interestingly, the *Acts of Paul*, an early Christian text which describes Paul's work and travels, does not seem to be aware of such a tour pattern, but instead sees his travels through various Roman cities as a 'single continuous journey without a return to some sponsoring Church' (Townsend 1986: 101). Roland Allen, too, who drew on Paul and worked out a model for conducting missions in the foreign field, is doubtful about a planned scheme: 'It is quite impossible to maintain that St Paul deliberately planned his journeys before hand, selected certain strategic points at which to establish his Churches and then actually carried out his designs' (1912: 15).

Why, then, was a missionary pattern imposed on the Acts during the colonial period? The likely answer is that the commentators were swayed by the momentous territorial changes taking place at the time, and were reading these events back into Apostolic times. The eighteenth century witnessed the rise of Western Protestant missionary activity and the establishment of a plethora of denominational missionary agencies. From the Protestant side, the Society for Promoting Christian Knowledge was founded in 1698; the Baptist Missionary Society in 1792; the London Missionary Society in 1795; the Church Missionary Society in 1799; the Wesleyan Methodist Society in 1813; and the Netherlands Missionary Society in 1797. Roman Catholic mission activity in the modern period goes back to the formation of the Sacra de Propaganda Fide in 1662, and further impetus was given by the founding of the Association for the Propagation of the Faith in 1822.

> Unlike the earlier missionaries, such as Francis Xavier (1506–52), who had wandered about fairly much on their own, missionaries of this period looked to their home societies for support and guidance in their work. Since it was standard missionary practice for evangelists to operate out of a home base, one should not be surprised at the exegetical assumption that Paul, the great missionary of the New Testament, had done the same. (Townsend 1986: 104)

It is no coincidence that the founding of all these missionary societies took place contemporaneously with the activities of trading companies like the East India Company and the Dutch East India Company. The East India Company initially resisted the presence of the missionaries. It feared that the interference of missionaries in local religious customs and manners might be counter-productive to its mercantile interests. However, with the renewal of the Company's charter in 1833 and the abolition of its monopoly, missionary enterprise received a boost. It was further helped by the British Indian Government's legislature, which set out to protect the rights of the Christian converts. Once the impediment to missionary work was removed, the missionaries themselves became willing supporters of commercial expansion. William Ward (1769–1823), the colleague of Carey at Serampore in India, lamented the 'extraordinary fact' that the British goods purchased annually by India were 'not sufficient to freight a single vessel from our ports'. But he hoped that once Indians were enlightened and civilized they would 'contribute more to the real prosperity of Britain as a commercial people, by consuming her manufactures to a vast extent'. He went on: 'But let the Hindoost'han receive that higher civilization she needs, that cultivation of which she is so capable; let European literature be transfused into all her languages, then the ocean from the ports of Britain to India, will be covered with our merchant vessels . . .' (1820: liii). When the Opium War ended and the Nanking Treaty favoured Western trade and missions to China, a Swedish pastor who was monitoring the news in the East wrote: 'Trade shall be a vehicle for mission' (Sundkler 1965: 121). Mission and mercantile interest often overlapped.

In concluding this section, some reflections. The trouncing of the Spanish Armada by the English had a major impact on geopolitics and mission. Previously, mission could be carried on only under the auspices of one or other of the colonial powers; these, however, were all Catholic (Sundkler 1965: 97). With Catholic maritime control loosened, the way was cleared for Protestant England and Holland, with their newly rediscovered Bible, to enter the fray. Along with the scramble for territories arose also a sense of missionary obligation (Sundkler 1965: 97), while, significantly, as we have seen, conditions created by Protestant Europe's maritime access to overseas colonies informed biblical interpretation. The rise of Protestant countries as colonial powers, the vigorous mushrooming of Protestant mission-sending agencies, and the recuperation of missionary texts, were all inextricably mixed.

The story of the expansion of the Church as it is told through Paul's journeys in Acts is selective and partial. It documents only the spreading of the Church in the West and totally ignores the Eastward movement of the Church. It celebrates and privileges only the Hellenistic expansion of the Church, namely, from Jerusalem to Rome, and the Jewish mission to Gentiles in the Roman Empire. What the author of Acts fails to record is that there was another history of the founding of the Church east of the Euphrates and throughout the Persian Empire, whose territorial control extended to the borders of India. While Paul and other Christians were engaged in mission among Greeks, Romans and barbaric tribes in the West, the people of the East, especially in Edessa, Persia, Arabia and Central Asia, China and India, were also being presented with the message:

> It is a surprise to most people to learn that there was a large and wide-spread Christian community throughout the whole of Central Asia in the first centuries of the present era and that such countries as Afghanistan and Tibet which are spoken of to-day as lands closed to the gospel message were centres of Christian activity long before Mohammed was born or the Krishna legend had been heard of. (Stewart 1928: xxix–xxx)

The missionary impulse for the spread of Christianity in Asia, according to T. V. Philip, came not from Hellenistic but from Jewish Christianity (1997). As with the case of the westward expansion of the Church, the eastward spread too was achieved not through institutionalized preaching but through the effective presence of Christians.

The monastic movement and its ascetic ideals played a considerable role:

> The monks were popular with the masses . . . The masses knew that the monks had particular compassion to those who suffered and the monks were always willing to help the people spiritually as well as materially. The monasteries became congregating centres of the poor and those who suffered. (Philip 1997: 12)

Traders, craftspeople, migrants and refugees from religious persecution all carried the gospel. It is this story of the eastward expansion which has been totally ignored in the narration of Luke–Acts. Philip reminds historians of mission to look again at *The Odes of Solomon*, *The Gospel of Thomas*, *The Acts of Judas Thomas*, *Didascalia Apostolorum*, and the writings of Ephraem, Aphrahat and Narsai, to understand the movement of Christianity to the East (1997: 8).

The imposition of a missionary-tour pattern on Acts has other hermeneutical implications in addition to bolstering a westward expansion of the Church. It reinforces the view that the churches in Asia and Africa have been recipients of the gospel as a gift from a benevolent West to enlighten the heathen. It largely ignores the Christian presence in these parts of the world before the arrival of the modern missionary movement. John England in his recent book *The Hidden History of Christianity in Asia* (1996) has traced the often-ignored and seldom-discussed complex and diverse histories of the Church in Asia. He attributes such neglect to, among other things: 'Outdated assumptions regarding orthodoxy and heresy, along with culturally-confined criteria in scholarship . . . [which] often prevent any adequate study of eastern Christianity in terms of its own historical and cultural setting' (2, 3). Drawing on a variety of evidence ranging from manuscripts to coins and paintings, he has demonstrated that it is possible to establish the presence of Christians from 'Syria in the west to Japan in the north-east and as far as Java in the south-east by the first half of the eighth century' (8). The perception held hitherto of the post-Nicene history of European peoples as normative is, in England's view, now, with the availability of the 'equally rich history of east of Antioch', unsustainable.

The hermeneutical concoction of a missionary headquarters to which Paul keeps returning after completing an assignment is a critical one. Since most of the modern movement's missionaries worked with and through a home base in Europe, and were constantly in touch with them regarding the running of the native churches, the origins of such an exegetical conjecture are clear (Townsend 1986:

104). But the implication for churches in Asia or for that matter Africa or the Pacific is significant. The idea of a headquarters, be it in London, Halle or Geneva, takes on a different shading. Besides the suggestion of the organizational power and institutional might of the gospel, encoded in the word 'headquarters', is the idea that there is over there a large and controlling decision-making machinery. Anything these churches do has to be checked and validated by an external authority.

Carey's contemporaries were Tom Paine and Mary Wollstonecraft. Wollstonecraft's *The Vindication of the Rights of Women* appeared in the same year as Carey's *Enquiry* and interestingly they had a common publisher and bookseller in Joseph Johnson, a nonconformist and holder of radical political views. While Paine and Wollstonecraft were writing about and engaged in radical political causes, popular protests, independence for nations and the rights of women, Carey was silent and did not raise his voice against colonial expansion or the evils of imperialism. Dharmaraj, who has studied the interrelation between colonialism and mission, concludes:

> In spite of Carey's lofty social and moral ideals in delivering the innocent victims from cruel religious practices, Carey had miserably failed from raising his voice against European political and economic oppression in India. His fight against Hindu social and religious evils had evangelistic and missionizing goals. Carey's unwillingness to speak against the political and economic evils of the colonial government had missional and monetary aims. (1993: 53)

From a postcolonial perspective it would be difficult to sustain the missionary import of Matthaean and Lukan texts which were made to serve the political and commercial interests of the West. The foregoing rereading contests the textual features both of these and of past interpretative practices. It invites a reorientation in both our missiological assumptions and our exegetical conclusions. At a time when there are widespread virulent forms of religious fanaticism, a discourse with an intense missionary thrust and proselytizing tendencies will not only add confusion to an already bewildering situation, but will be difficult to sustain.

Moving Beyond the Mediterranean Milieu

In my introductory remarks on postcolonialism, I referred to the liberative possibilities of contrapuntal reading in the biblical field. A further postcolonial exercise is to reclaim the New Testament writ-

ings, re-establishing them as bearers of conceptual aspects of Eastern
literature. The tendency of biblical scholars to impose Christianity as
the interpretative template has often blurred their vision. They have
successfully promoted the belief that the New Testament writings
were the product exclusively of Hellenistic and Hebraic thinking.
When looking at the New Testament period and the literary productions which emerged at that time, biblical scholars maintain a
deep-seated Eurocentric bias, asserting that anything theologically
worthwhile can only be supplied by Greco-Judaeo traditions. In other
words, Greece provides the intellectual and philosophical roots, and
the Judaic heritage furnishes the religious base. In thus failing to
widen their hermeneutical base, these scholars also invent a Christianity successfully insulated from any contact with Indic religions.
Biblical scholars ignore the possible presence, impact and contribution of Eastern religions in the Mediterranean region during the time
when the Christian faith emerged. G. B. Caird sums up the position: 'I
should have thought that the Indian notion of NT dependence on
Buddhism was due simply to a deficient historical sense. I certainly
know of no NT scholar outside India who would give such an idea
credence for a minute.'[6] But the Christian faith grew up in a cultural
and literary milieu which was indeed influenced by Indian, Buddhist
and Hindu thought patterns. The trade links between India and
the Mediterranean Roman Empire were busier than has often been
credited. Along with merchandise, religious ideas travelled both to
and from the Mediterranean world. The edicts of the Emperor Asoka
inform us of the presence of Buddhist missionaries in Western Asia
(thirteenth edict *c.*256 BCE). Theravada Buddhist monks had long been
active in Alexandria before the birth of Christianity. Another, named
Zarmanochegas, was sent by King Porus to Rome in 37 BCE as a
member of the Indian political mission. At Athens he performed the
religious act of voluntary self-immolation, and a monument was
erected there in his memory. Paul, in his epistle to the Corinthians,
refers to voluntarily burning himself to death: 'If I give away all I
have, and if I deliver my body to be burned, but have not love, I gain
nothing.'[7] Puzzled at this verse, Western Christian exegetes try to find
a Judaic background, however tenuous; or they dismiss or deny that
the Athens monument to the Buddhist could have had any influence
on Paul (for instance, see Barrett 1968: 302–3; Bruce 1971: 125–6 and
Thrall 1965: 93).

---

[6] Quoted in Derrett 1967: 34.
[7] I owe this point to Mackenzie 1928: 41.

The Indian presence in the Mediterranean world, especially during the formative years of Christianity, and the possible percolation, especially of Buddhist ideas into Christian thinking, were widely acknowledged by earlier Indologists and those from the History of Religions School. The interest slackened after the First World War. One reason for this was the pressure exerted by the Vatican. Henri de Lubac was one who was silenced and reprimanded by Rome for his advocacy of Buddhist influence on Christianity.

Building on earlier comparative studies, three recent works have once again demonstrated the textual and conceptual affinities between Buddhist writings and the Gospels. Interestingly, these studies were not undertaken by biblical scholars but by historians of religion and an English literary critic. There are so many teachings and stories about Buddha and Jesus which are remarkably similar. So, too, are the ethical teachings of the two leaders, on non-violence and purity of mind. Even before the study of Q became fashionable in biblical circles, R. C. Amore argued that the Q source or the Sayings Gospel used by the first three Gospel writers, might well have been a Buddhist text. He reckons that the Gospel writers, drawing on both Jewish and Buddhist traditions, could well have refashioned them to suit the contextual needs of their time. He writes:

> There are several indications that Luke and Matthew were drawing upon a source or sources that in addition to sayings about the end of the era also contained sayings that were in effect Jewish-Christian versions of Buddhist teachings. The Sermon on the Mount has the highest concentration of these Buddhist sayings, but they are also found in quantity in later chapters of Luke and Matthew. (1978: 178)

Later he goes on:

> The doctrines of the preexistence of Jesus, the stories about his birth and infancy, and the belief in his return to heaven followed the Buddhist model. This avatar pattern was combined with other interpretations of Jesus derived from Jewish expectations . . . I suggest that the Buddhist avatar model helped Christianity transform the Jewish messiah concept into a saviour figure that was understandable to the gentiles. Among the non-Jews of the West it enabled Christianity to compete successfully with the old Hellenistic and Roman cults as well as with the old Mithra religion of the Roman Empire. Among the non-Jews of the East it enabled Christianity to supplant old Iranian religions and ironic-

ally, block the rapid westward expansion of Buddhism itself. (1978: 185, 186)

The provenance of Matthew has been a vexing problem among biblical scholars. There have been proposals which locate the origin of the Gospel variously in such disparate places as Antioch and the coastal towns of Phoenician Syria. Robert Osborne, scrutinizing the special M materials in the Gospel, offers the suggestion that Edessa could be the place for the origination of Matthew's Gospel. The conceptual nature of the material in M leads Osborne to postulate Eastern influence. Since Edessa was strategically placed on the famous Silk Route that linked East and West, it is possible that M materials could have been influenced by Mithraism, Zoroastrianism and Buddhism. Examining five of the six sayings (omitting the one on divorce) in Matthew 5.21–48, which all begin with 'You have heard that it was said . . . but I say to you', Osborne detects striking parallels between these and the teaching of Buddhism:

> These rules represent the arterial directions in which Buddhist self-control is to be exercised. Jesus' teaching 'on murder' (Mt. 5.21–26), 'on adultery' (Mt. 5.27–30), 'on swearing' (Mt. 5.33–37), and 'on retaliation' (Mt. 5.38–42), to use customary headings, are closely paralleled in Buddha's prohibitions 'on anger, lusts of the flesh, untruthfulness and desire for material possessions'. Moreover the essential spirit of each places great emphasis on the inward intention. (1973–4: 224)

He also finds echoes of Buddhist teachings in Matthew 5.29 and 11.28–30 and draws out the similarity between Peter walking on the water and Buddha's disciple Sariputta attempting the same.

Moving on from the Synoptics and focusing on the Johannine writings, Edgar Bruns is of the opinion that 'Johannine thought is structurally closer to that of Madhyamika Buddhism than it is to either Judaic or Hellenistic thought' (1971: vii). He also postulates a theory that the beloved disciple in John's Gospel could have been modelled on the Buddhist tradition. Ananda, the disciple of Buddha, could have been the counterpart for John. Though there were other master–disciple relationships (Plato–Socrates, Moses–Joshua, Elijah–Elisha, Jeremiah–Baruch), they were faithful secretaries or in some cases authentic successors, but 'none of these were guarantors of a religious message' (1973–4: 237).

More recently, marshalling current literary methods such as deconstruction, Zacharias Thundy has demonstrated that materials from other cultures have provided ingredients for the Gospel narratives. In his view, many Indian stories were woven into the Gospel texts and contemporary apocryphal literature. He has shown that a number of stories about the childhood of Jesus correspond in many details with those about the Buddha. Thundy has also demonstrated that the Buddhist scriptural texts and traditions are older than the comparable Christian writings. Borrowings, in the majority of cases, were from the East to the West. He comes to the conclusion that non-Jewish traditions provided the sources for stories about Jesus' childhood. In pointing out the intertextual nature of the New Testament and Buddhist writings, he concludes that there is a 'concealed presence' of Indian ideas and motifs in the Gospel tradition:

> I add(ed) my voice to this growing critical chorus to proclaim that the New Testament is not Western literature, pure and simple, but rather still very much Eastern. This is not because the gospels were composed in the East by Orientals but because they were extensively influenced by their Oriental sources of which India and its religions were an integral part. (1993: 272)

Such an acknowledgement and appropriation will enable us to go beyond the traditionally exclusive missionary claims regarding the Christian story. More importantly, it will celebrate the hybridized and eclectic nature of religious stories. It will refuse to be limited by religionist and preservationist imperatives, and ascribe fluidity to the texts.

Cautionary Markers

In conclusion, I would like to raise some of the questions that keep coming up as we engage in postcolonial discourse. My purpose is to bring some clarification into our thinking and practice. Postcolonialism may be a trendy substitute for what is known as Third World Theologies, and a convenient label for lumping together all Asian, African, Latin American, Caribbean and Pacific theologies. The caution that the Indian critic Satchidanandan raised in another context is equally valid for us. Postcolonialism could become 'another fashion in the international methodological market', or another 'new tool shaped in the West's critical foundry'. He also goes on to warn that 'postcolonialism can be neocolonialism with or without a hyphen, the empire assigning a role to former colonies and commanding them once again to speak its language' (1996: 6).

We need to pay attention to the fact that over the years the Master himself has changed, and, along with him, his language of discourse, too, has changed. The master discourse no more talks about civilizing mission. At a time when market forces are sweeping across the world in the form of globalization, the new lexicon is not about rescuing the benighted natives but concerns the universal ethics of human rights. In our discursive resistance, we tend to take a high moral ground. We employ the language of moralism, and use in our vocabularies words such as truth, responsibility, guilt, which we acquired mainly through mission and convent-school education. Hence our preoccupation with grand theorizing about how Europe underdeveloped Asia or Africa. The West we are addressing now is not familiar with such a vocabulary. Recently, through its postmodernist culture, the West has been telling us that the language of guilt, truth and responsibility are foreign to present-day multinational capitalists, international power brokers, transnational bankers and military strategists. They speak a different language – the language of success, efficiency, performance and profit. The moral agenda has moved on. Failure to note this moral shift may mean, according to Denis Ekpo, that we are barking up the wrong tree: 'We may be thinking that we are still striking at the West when in fact we may be boxing a straw West entirely of our making' (1996: 12).

The other question we need to address is whether in our writings we, the native orientalists, are replicating orientalist tendencies. Like Ali Behdad, I, too, am haunted by the question whether I am a post-colonial orientalist perpetuating the European representations of the orient within the space provided by the academy. In foregrounding the colonial constructions of the past, we may evade any discussion of the place of a postcolonial critic within the academy, and of the way we have been implicated in its power relations. As Ali Behdad says, no critic is outside the power relations of the academy, and we need to 'inquire into the implications of our critical predicaments' (1994: 138).

Postcolonialism may give the impression that the sole preoccupation of the colonized after territorial independence is colonialism. There are grave ramifications in such a postulation. Excessive interest in colonialism can cause us to ignore our histories before colonialism, and also conveniently to overlook indigenous annexations and anni-hilations of our people and their history. Although postcolonialism is an important political and cultural agenda, we have other equally important issues to grapple with, such as poverty, nationalism, com-munalism, casteism, patriarchy, internal exiles, all of which may or may not be linked to colonialism. In our eagerness to produce a resist-ance theory, we may ignore the minorities within our societies –

dalits, women, tribals and Burakumin. Conferring subaltern status on all these who are under-represented in our countries, we may have fallen victim to the very colonizing tendencies we seem to resist. Said warned long ago of the 'dangers and temptations . . . to formerly colonized peoples . . . of employing this structure upon themselves or upon others' (1985: 25).

Ultimately, the question is not about what to do with the hapless hyphen, or whether our project is seen as colonial or postcolonial, modern or postmodern. When we come to decide the questions that affect our communities and our people, such as housing, health care, social security, education or homeland, the relevant questions will be about how they affect the lives of the people, rather than whether the proposal is modern or non-modern, colonial or anti-colonial. The task of postcolonialism is to ensure that the yearnings of the poor take precedence over the interests of the affluent; that the emancipation of the subjugated has primacy over the freedom of the powerful; and that the participation of the marginalized takes priority over the perpetuation of a system which systematically excludes them.

A postcolonial critic's role is not simply limited to textual dealings or literary concerns. Postcolonial hermeneutics has to be a pragmatic engagement, an engagement in which praxis is not an extra option or a subsidiary enterprise taken on in the aftermath of judicious deconstruction and reconstruction of the texts. Rather, this praxiological involvement is there from the outset of the hermeneutical process, informing and contesting the whole procedure. If we neglect this, we may become ridiculous figures like the Lavatri Alltheorie portrayed in Rukun Advani's novel, *Beethoven among the Cows*. In the longest chapter of the book, entitled, 'S/he, or A Postmodern Chapter on Gender and Identity', Lavatri Alltheorie is described as a 'Postmodern theoretician, boa deconstructor, discourse analyst, poststructuralist critic, feminist historian of subalternity, colonialism and gender' (1995: 145–6). A diasporic Indian academic, she offers courses to packed audiences of white students on 'the semiology of Deconstruction and the Deconstruction of semiology' (1995: 146). The danger is that we will be seen as deliberately using catchphrases and buzzwords as a form of posture and power play. As Arun Mukherjee says, it is not enough to fight the colonizer with the 'textual weapons of irony and parody' (1996: 19). If we do so, we may, like Lavatri Alltheorie, become renowned for 'specialization in Complete Bunkum' (Advani 1995: 165).

This chapter was previously published in R. S. Sugirtharajah (ed.), *The Postcolonial Bible*, Sheffield: Sheffield Academic Press, 1998, pp. 99–116. Reprinted with permission of Continuum.

References

Advani, Rukun, 1995. *Beethoven among the Cows*, Delhi: Ravi Dayal Publisher.

Allen, Roland, 1912. *Missionary Methods: St Paul's or Ours. A Study of the Church in the Four Provinces*, London: Robert Scott.

Amore, Roy C., 1978. *Two Masters, One Message: The Life and Teachings of Gautama and Jesus*, Nashville: Abingdon Press.

Barrett, C. K., 1968. *A Commentary on the First Epistle to the Corinthians*, London: A. & C. Black.

Behdad, Ali, 1994. *Belated Travels: Orientalism in the Age of Colonial Dissolution*, Cork: Cork University Press.

Bhabha, Homi K., 1994. *The Location of Culture*, London: Routledge & Kegan Paul.

Boer, Harry R., 1961. *Pentecost and Missions*, Grand Rapids: Eerdmans.

Bosch, David J., 1991. *Transforming Mission: Paradigm Shifts in Theology of Mission*, Maryknoll, N.Y.: Orbis Books.

Bruce, F. F., 1971. *1 and 2 Corinthians*, London: Oliphants.

Bruns, Edgar J., 1971. *The Christian Buddhism of St John: New Insights into the Fourth Gospel*, New York: Paulist Press.

Bruns, Edgar J., 1973–4. 'Ananda: The Fourth Evangelist's Model for "the disciple whom Jesus loved"', *Studies in Religion* 3(3): 236–43.

Carey, William, 1961 (1792). *An Enquiry into the Obligations of Christians to Use Means for the Conversion of the Heathen*, facsimile edn with an introduction; London: Carey Kingsgate Press.

Chandra, Vikram, 1995. *Red Earth and Pouring Rain*, London: Faber & Faber.

Derrett, J. Duncan M., 1967. 'Greece and India: The Milindapanha, the Alexander Romance and the Gospels', *Zeitschrift für Religions- und Geistesgeschichte* 19: 32–64.

Dharmaraj, Jacob S., 1993. *Colonialism and Christian Mission: Postcolonial Reflections*, Delhi: ISPCK.

Ekpo, Denis, 1996. 'How Africa Misunderstood the West: The Failure of Anti-Western Radicalism and Postmodernity', *Third Text: Third World Perspectives on Contemporary Art and Culture* 35: 3–13.

England, John, 1996. *The Hidden History of Christianity in Asia: The Churches of the East before the year 1500*, Delhi: ISPCK.

Ferro, Marc, 1997. *Colonization: A Global History*, London: Routledge & Kegan Paul.

Kreider, Alan, 1994. 'Worship and Evangelism in Pre-Christendom', The Laing Lecture 1994, *Vox Evangelica* 24: 7–38.

Mackenzie, Donald A., 1928. *Buddhism in Pre-Christian Britain*, London: Blakie & Sons.

Mehrez, Samia, 1991. 'The Subversive Poetics of Racial Bilingualism: Postcolonial Francophone North African Literature', in Dominick LaCapra (ed.), *The Bounds of Race: Perspectives on Hegemony and Resistance*, Ithaca, N.Y.: Cornell University Press, pp. 255–77.

Moulton, Harold K., 1957. *The Acts of the Apostles: Introduction and Commentary*, Madras: Christian Literature Society.

Mukherjee, Arun P., 1996. 'Interrogating Post-colonialism: Some Uneasy Conjectures', in Harish Trivedi and Meenakshi Mukherjee (eds), *Interrogating Post-Colonialism: Theory, Text and Context*, Shimla: Indian Institute of Advanced Study, pp. 13–20.

Mukherjee, Meenakshi, 1996. 'Interrogating Post-colonialism', in Harish Trivedi and Meenakshi Mukherjee (eds), *Interrogating Post-Colonialism: Theory, Text and Context*, Shimla: Indian Institute of Advanced Study, pp. 3–11.

Neill, Stephen, 1934. *Builders of the Indian Church: Present Problems in the Light of the Past*, London: Edinburgh House Press.

Osborne, Robert E., 1973–4. 'The Provenance of Matthew's Gospel', *Studies in Religion* 3(3): 220–35.

Page, Jesse, 1921. *Schwartz of Tanjore*, London: SPCK.

Philip, T. V., 1997. 'The Missionary Impulse in the Early Asian Christian Tradition', *Programme for Theology and Cultures in Asia Bulletin* 10(1): 5–14.

Said, Edward, 1985 (1978). *Orientalism*, London: Penguin Books.

Said, Edward, 1993. *Culture and Imperialism*, London: Chatto & Windus.

Sandgren, Ulla, 1991. *The Tamil New Testament and Bartholomaus Ziegenbalg*, Uppsala: Swedish Institute of Missionary Research.

Satchidanandan, K., 1996. 'The Post-Colonial Questions', *Indian Literature* 175: 5–6.

Sim, David C., 1995. 'The Gospel of Matthew and the Gentiles', *Journal for the Study of the New Testament* 57: 19–48.

Spivak, Gayatri Chakravorty, 1988. *In Other Worlds: Essays in Cultural Politics*, London: Routledge & Kegan Paul.

Spivak, Gayatri Chakravorty, 1990. *The Post-Colonial Critic: Interviews, Strategies, Dialogues*, London: Routledge & Kegan Paul.

Stewart, John, 1928. *Nestorian Missionary Enterprise: The Story of a Church on Fire*, Edinburgh: T. & T. Clark.

Sugirtharajah, R. S., 1998a. *Asian Biblical Hermeneutics and Postcolonialism: Contesting the Interpretations*, Maryknoll, N.Y.: Orbis Books.

Sugirtharajah, R. S., 1998b. 'Biblical Studies in India: From Imperialistic Scholarship to a Post-colonial Mode of Interpretation', in Fernando Segovia and Mary Ann Tolbert (eds), *Teaching the Bible: The Discourses and Politics of Biblical Pedagogy*, Maryknoll, N.Y.: Orbis Books.

Sundkler, Bengt, 1965. *The World of Mission*, London: Lutterworth Press.

Thompson, H. P., 1951. *Into All Lands: The History of the Society for the Propagation of the Gospel in Foreign Parts 1701–1950*, London: SPCK.

Thrall, Margaret E., 1965. *The First and Second Letters of Paul to the Corinthians*, Cambridge: Cambridge University Press.

Thundy, Zacharias P., 1993. *Buddha and Christ: Nativity Stories and Indian Traditions*, Leiden: Brill.

Townsend, John T., 1986. 'Missionary Journeys in Acts and European Missionary Societies', *Anglican Theological Review* 68: 99–104.

Trivedi, Harish, 1996. 'India and Post-colonial Discourse', in Harish Trivedi and Meenakshi Mukherjee (eds), *Interrogating Post-Colonialism: Theory, Text and Context*, Shimla: Indian Institute of Advanced Study, pp. 231–47.

Walker, T., 1919. *The Acts of the Apostles*, Madras: SPCK.

Ward, William, 1820. *A View of the History, Literature, and Methodology of the Hindoos: Including a Minute Description of their Manners and Customs and Translations from their Principal Works*, 3 vols., London: Black, Kingsbury, Parbury & Allen.

2

Son(s) Behaving Badly

The Prodigal in Foreign Hands

> Above all, sacred texts supply the illusions that suit the powers that be and calm the fears of the general population.
>
> William H. Gass (2000)

Two critical categories that are causing turbulence in an already crowded and congested arena are postmodernism and postcolonialism. Judgements about critical theories have always been notably belligerent. In the case of these categories, the debate is still fierce because of the mixed and scattered nature of their origins. This is further complicated by a virtual absence of any irrefutably agreed-on precise understanding of what these terms stand for. On the face of it, both categories look as though they were made for each other and could well be natural partners in their mission to destabilize hegemonic hermeneutical practices. However, the alliance is not as unproblematic as it appears.[1] Those who work in the field have discerned two types of postmodernism: the postmodernism of complicity and the postmodernism of revolt. The first is exemplified by a cynical recovery of used-up modes and a compliance with predominant cultural agencies. The second is characterized by its irreproachable political agenda, theory, and agency, which unsettles various dominants like classism, racism, and sexism (Woods 1999: 131). It is with the second – oppositional, critical, and praxiological activity – that postcolonialism wishes to be associated.

One of the emblematic marks of postmodernism has been its employment of irony as a counter-discursive practice. Basically, what irony does is to disrupt 'the taken-for-granted meaningfulness of utterance and writing', and expose its artificiality (Edgar 1999: 199). This discursive practice, as Linda Hutcheon has argued, is not confined to postmodernism alone; 'postcolonial and the feminist

---

[1] For a discussion on the interface between postmodernism and postcolonialism, see Adam and Tiffin 1993; Quayson 2000: 132–55.

enterprises, among others, have also often turned to irony' (Hutcheon 1994a: 210). However, like many other tropes, when irony is put to use by practitioners of both postcolonialism and postmodernism, it assumes different incarnations and comes with its own diverse nuances and variations, reflecting different social and cultural contexts of production.

Having forged a critical but productive collocation between postmodernism and postcolonialism, let me spell out the aim of this chapter. What I am proposing to do is to look at one of the iconic narratives of Luke recorded in chapter 15, universally known as the Prodigal Son, and to study its interpretive fate as it travels outside its natural Christian habitat and falls into the hands of interpreters – especially expositors who belong to other religious traditions and writers of secular fiction. These writers, who are conversant with the story, retell it to meet their own ideological and hermeneutical agendas. I will confine myself to the Indian literary landscape and look at Kiran Nagarkar's novel *Ravan and Eddie* (1995), where a character employs the Lucan parable to thwart its inherited centuries-old interpretation. A parable that is defined and circumscribed by its Christian and colonial association is now being used to harass the very people who first employed it for ideological and propagandistic purposes. The second example is a fiction, 'The Serpent and the Master' by Thomas Palakeel (1994), where the writer attempts to rewrite and subvert the Lucan parable from the prism of the son's balked attempt to gain freedom from his father's emotional and material grip. In interrogating these writings, I will try to place them within the postcolonial/postmodern trope of irony and demonstrate how, in their appropriation of this trope, they end up falling prey to the very values they sought to unmask. I will also investigate the hermeneutical purposes and implications of such an appropriation of a Christian story.

The Prodigal Son in Khaki Shorts

The retelling of the Prodigal Son in Nagarkar's novel occurs when one of the eponymous heroes, Eddie Coutinho, a Christian, unwittingly enrolls himself as a member of a Hindu religious organization in his neighbourhood. Although the parable is not pivotal to the plot, it is narrated at an important stage in the development of the character. Briefly, the novel is about sons of two Indian families – one is Hindu, the Pawars, and the other is Roman Catholic, the Coutinhos. It concerns their self-discovery in postcolonial India. They live on different

floors of the same Central Work Department *chawl*[2] number 17 in
Bombay. Despite being thrown together in the congested housing
estate, they might well have lived in parallel worlds. They come
from different states in India, the Pawars from Maharashtra and the
Coutinhos from Goa. They speak different languages at home and
celebrate different religious festivals. Eddie goes to an English-
medium school run by Roman Catholics, and Ravan attends a munici-
pal school where English is taught as a second language. They are not
only separated by religion, culture and language but also divided by
a different colonial heritage – one British and the other Portuguese. To
all intents and purposes, though Eddie was born and bred in India, as
with all Indian Catholics, his 'umbilical cord was stretched all the way
to Lisbon' (Nagarkar 1995: 16). Where the worlds of Eddie and Ravan
collide is the most unlikely place of all, *sabha* – a Hinduist organization
involved both in educational and in mobilizational work in the *chawl*.
Its description 'of white shirts and flared khaki half-pants fame'
(Nagarkar 1995: 17) alludes to the Rashtriya Swayamsvek Sangh
(RSS), a paramilitary and militant Hindu organization with strong
nationalistic undercurrents. The *sabha* was active in the *chawl*, and
under the leadership of Lele Guruji, it vigorously recruited members
from all communities to save India from non-Hindus. In one of his
rousing speeches to his sharply attentive *sabha* boys, Lele Guruji
thunders:

> For centuries, Muslims, Catholics and Protestants have converted
> Hindus. It is time we turned the tide. What we need is a wild
> bushfire that spreads across the country and brings back the lost
> souls to Hinduism. Anyone who enrolls a non-Hindu in our Sabha
> will get a Wilson fountain pen. And the new member will be
> given not only a Wilson fountain pen and ball-point set but also a
> beautifully illustrated and abridged copy of the *Stories from the
> Mahabharata and Shri Krishna's Life* in Hindi, English or Marathi. Go
> into the world and light fires, the fires of Hinduism. Jai Hind.
> (Nagarkar 1995: 20)

Ravan was already a member of the *sabha*, but he did not join with a
view to save India from non-Hindus. That was the last thing he had in
his mind. He was forced into it by his mother, Parvathi, whose objective was purely pragmatic – to keep Ravan out of mischief. She did not
have any inkling of the politics of the *sabha*. Enticed by the idea of

---

[2] *Chawl* is a low-cost housing estate inhabited by the low-income families of
bus conductors, peons, and petty government officials.

getting a Wilson pen for bringing new members, Ravan embarked on
a recruitment campaign. He had a couple of disasters initially. On one
occasion he was thoroughly beaten up for associating with an outfit
that was allegedly linked with the group that killed the father of the
nation, Mahatma Gandhi. Then one fine day, he ran into Eddie and
casually mentioned the *sabha*. This was the very first time they had
spoken to each other. Eddie, to everyone's surprise, turned up at the
founder's day of the *sabha*. Elated by Eddie's arrival, Appa Achrekar,
the elderly firebrand of the *sabha*, in celebration of a new catch and a
Christian at that, told the story of the Prodigal Son in a perverse way.
In a delightfully mischievous ironic reversal, Achrekar dubbed the
Christian Eddie as the Prodigal who had now come back to his rightful home. After centuries of missionary preaching that branded
Indians and those who were outside the Christian framework as
prodigals, Achrekar ironically inflated and at the same time punc-
tured the roles. Listen to the way the leader ended the story:

> Eddie Coutinho is our prodigal son. How many centuries have
> passed since he and his people were converted and left us? I have
> lost count. But he is back amongst his own and we rejoice at the
> return of our prodigal. (Nagarkar 1995: 33)

What happened when Eddie's mother and his Catholic priest discovered his conversion (to their horror) and called him the prodigal a
second time round is another matter and need not detain us here.

The Yielding Son

Palakeel's story, in keeping with the Indian way of storytelling, is full
of plots and subplots and is inhabited by a whole host of characters.
It is essentially a primordial parable that retells the tale of a young
person's failed attempt to leave home and lead a life of his own, free
from parental control and the pressures of the extended family. It is
about a Christian family in Kerala in South India who fast and pray
during Holy Week and brood about the death and resurrection of
Jesus. It points out the futile effort of the son, Appu, to live literally
and imaginatively away from home and his father's expectation. The
son's desire is to study Malayalam literature and become a writer, but
his father's plan is to send him to medical school and make him the
first medical doctor in the family. As a way of counteracting the resistance of the son, the father sends him to spend time at a secular
monastery run by a master whose fame included, among other things,
producing a fake Bible. Eventually, when the father and the master

urge him to undertake the self-quest he is pining for, and offer money, the son, unlike the son in the Lucan story, becomes frightened of the impending journey. When he thinks about the prospect of the hazard- ous long rail rides, deserts, and strange languages, he decides to return to the family, much to the joy of his father. Whereas, in the Lucan narrative, taking the money is seen as the son's right, in Palakeel's story it is seen as a failure. In the eyes of his granduncle, the moment Appu took the money, he had come a cropper: 'You took money. You failed' (Palakeel 1994: 182). The son – egoistical, insecure, and underconfident – realizes that star-gazing alone is not sufficient. He starts hearing voices: 'Turn back. Go home. Return to your begin- nings. Go home' (Palakeel 1994: 182).

The Prodigal Going Native

These retellings acknowledge the background and the influence of Judeo-Christian elements, but, at the same time, they redirect that influence by opening and nativizing or Hinduizing it. Indigenization is achieved either through writing in additional materials or by excis- ing awkward elements in the texts. In Nagarkar's retelling, the elder son, who stood steadfast by the family, was aghast at the celebration, and he asked what was to be his reward. The father's reply was literally from the *Bhagavad Gita*: 'Duty well done is its own reward, my son' (Nagarkar 1995: 33). Unlike the Lucan father, who reminded the elder son that all that belonged to the father belonged to the son as well, the Indian retelling propounds the message of the *Bhagavad Gita*. Disinterested service, one of the spiritual tenets of the *Bhagavad Gita*, which has become the gospel of Hinduism, is injected into the text.

These accounts are more inclusive than the source-text in that they are gender inclusive. By contrast, in the Lucan parable, the narrative centres around the father, and the role of the mother is written out, inexplicably in a drama set in a West Asian context. These retellings restore the mother to the text and give her a part, however restricted it may be. In Nagarkar's narration, it is the mother, seeing a dot at the very edge of the horizon, who asks, 'Who could it be?' (Nagarkar 1995: 32). And unlike the Lucan story, where only the father embraces the son, here the mother, too, puts her arm around him. The mother is accommodated, though her role is circumscribed by patriarchal norms. For instance, in Palakeel's story, Appu, agonizing over his decision, shares it with his mother. Instead of understanding her son's dilemma, the mother identifies herself with patriarchal beliefs and disapproves of her son's quest. Along with others, she too laughs at his decision (Palakeel 1994: 179).

The elements that do not translate well into the Indian context are edited out. The repentance speech, which the Lucan younger son prepared when he found himself impoverished, is effortlessly left out, whereas it is an essential component in the Christian story. In Achrekar's narration there is no pang of conscience: since personal guilt and sinning against God does not have the same theological valence in the Hindu way of thinking. The Hindu concept of sin ranges from the simple belief that associates sin with disease, to the most sophisticated one that holds that sin is a denial and betrayal of the soul and self. In between these two, according to Dandekar, there are other perceptions that describe 'sin as a debt, or a breach of caste rules, or a defiance of god, or absence of harmony with the spiritual environment, or lack of spiritual power' (Dandekar 1987: 152). Sin as personal guilt in the Christian sense does not have the same theological weight in Hindu thought, and thus the son's speech that exemplifies this is absent from the Indian text.

Out also goes any reference to feasting on a fatted calf, which forms part of the Lucan celebration. In Nagarkar's version, the father orders 'a feast such as the town, nay, that part of the world had never seen' (Nagarkar 1995: 32), and omits any reference to feasting on meat. In a culture that shares a symbolic belief in the sacredness of cows, killing and eating calf is viewed with repugnance. In a culture where dietary regulations are informed by caste norms and where strict vegetarianism is privileged and required as a way of maintaining the sense of purity, those who consume meat – Christians, Muslims and dalits – are deemed and categorized as impure. Translating the term *fatted calf* caused considerable hermeneutical concern for missionaries. Newly converted, high-caste Christians were scandalized to read that their religion was being associated with lower-caste customs, and even urged the offending reference to a fatted calf be removed from the text.

Abbé Dubois, a Roman Catholic missionary, narrates an experience that he had in 1815. After he had preached on the parable of the Prodigal Son, about how the father had killed the fatted calf to entertain his friends in a welcoming-home party for his son, some Christians afterward told him that his mention of 'fatted calf' was very improper. Their worry was that Hindus, who were often present at such services, on hearing of the fatted calf would have their worst fears confirmed, namely that of 'the Christian religion being a low or pariah religion'. The caste Christians' practical advice to Dubois was that if he should ever give an 'explanation of the same parable, to substitute a lamb instead of the *fatted calf'*.[3]

It is not unusual for Indian Christians to resuscitate local referents from Hindu myths and *Puranas* in order to bolster their theological enterprise. They incorporate them into Christianity by Christianizing them. Indian Christian literature is replete with such examples.[4] Based on the methodological presupposition of synthesization, these retellings employ local nuances to serve different agendas. They use the very same method, but this time to Hinduize the Christian story.

Textual Gestures

Playing on the Lucan parable, both these retellings illustrate their own postmodern and postcolonial status. Nagarkar's version takes into account the text's missionary and colonial linkages and parodies them. By ironic repetition of a colonial textuality, it sets itself in opposition to the interpellative power of colonial homiletics. Nagarkar imitates the biblical parable but distances it critically by subverting the missionary ideology, which for centuries branded Indians and those outside the Christian framework as prodigals. Achrekar retells the Lucan parable from the perspective of those who have been at the receiving end of missionary propaganda, and he reverts and inverts the original text. His retelling provides an example of the ways in which the missionized turn the tables by simultaneously using and abusing the very material employed by the colonizers to mould and incorporate them. Ironically, the poignant moment in Nagarkar's retelling is when Eddie receives, as a conversion gift, a set of Hindu sacred texts – *Stories from the Mahabharata and Shri Krishna's Life* – thus overturning the age-old custom of Christian converts' receiving the King James Version as their proud possession. What these two retellings do is to dislodge Christian interpretation, otherwise regarded as uncontestable. Palakeel's story fictionalizes, exposes and, more importantly, mediates the tensions and pressures felt in extended families. The critical moment in Palakeel's story is when the son returns and observes the father's reaction. It provides a hermeneutical

---

[3] Dubois 1823: 18 (italics in original). In a recent article in a Tamil literary journal, A. Sivasubramaniyan has shown how Roman Catholic literature produced in the 1920s often changed 'fatted calf' to 'lamb' to appease caste Christians and to make Christianity appear untainted with low-caste associations (2000: 53–5).

[4] For examples of an earlier generation see Baago 1969; and for recent attempts, see Aleaz 1994 and Amaladoss 1998.

clue as to the inner workings and mindsets of both, the observer and the observed: 'I detested the frantic joy in my father's face. Fathers always rejoice when their prodigal sons return home, defeated. A father waits for the son's fall' (Palakeel 1994: 182).

What we see at work here is the postmodern use of irony – irony not as a counter-discourse, but sadly siding with normative constraints and reactionary values. These retellings are deconstructive in the postmodern sense of not relying too much on Christian polemics. They reframe the parable from the evangelized point of view. But they are not liberatory in the postcolonial sense of offering counter-models to prevailing hegemonic trends. The trope of irony is evoked, not to destabilize but to shore up the foundations of patriarchy, family values and stability of home life. These retellings work to make the Lucan parable ambiguous and thereby subvert it from outside, whilst defending the establishment views from within. As Linda Hutcheon points out, irony is 'transideologic' and malleable in the hands of those who use it. Irony, according to her, 'can obviously be both political *and* apolitical, both conservative *and* radical, both repressive *and* democratizing'.[5] These retellings engage in double-talk. While they assume a speaking position from within the colonial discourse, they simultaneously undermine the received reading and allow in ingredients that perpetuate oppressive and worn-out values.

The Indian retellings, though they appear to be dismantling the Lucan parable, in no way eradicate or erase the basic religious and theological tenets of the biblical story. They do open up the story and deviate from it, but in the end they reinstall the hierarchical tendencies of the Christian story. The fatherhood of God is restored and reconfigured as natural, given and universal. The moral of the Lucan parable and Palakeel's story is that patriarchy should never be questioned. The narratives argue for a type of father (for 'father' read 'God') who is in a position to know what is right for all and act in a nurturing way so that his children either anticipate his wishes or accept them without question. The father effectively demands not only love but also obedience and unquestioning recognition of his authority. When we see Appu eventually returning home and accepting the father, we can see that the son, to use the Indian psychologist Sudhir Kakar's diagnosis, has internalized from childhood the authority of his father:

[Y]ounger professionals have from childhood internalized the 'hierarchical tradition,' so any discrepancy between the criteria of

---

[5] Hutcheon 1994b: 35 (italics in original).

professional performance and the prevailing mores of the organization does not produce either a confrontation with the older men or the persistent, critical questioning necessary to effect change. The aggression . . . in the younger generation is blocked from expression in outright anger; instead, the conflict between intellectual conviction and developmental 'fate' manifests itself in a vague sense of helpless and impotent rage. The anxiety triggered by the mere possibility of losing the nurturing patronage of powerful figures usually prevents any deviation from the safer compliant stance. (Kakar 1992 (1981): 120)

A digression. Interestingly, the bleak version of the reunion and uneasiness of the younger son's coming home comes through in a poem written by that colonial sage Rudyard Kipling. The poem brings to the fore the son's isolation, the expression of his personal interests, and the assertion of his individuality. Essentially, it is about sons and daughters wanting to be free from paternal pressures. Listen to the words of Kipling's 'The Prodigal Son':

> Here come I to my own again,
> Fed, forgiven and known again,
> Claimed by bone of my bone again
> And cheered by flesh of my flesh.
> The fatted calf is dressed for me,
> But the husks have greater zest for me.
> I think my pigs will be best for me,
> So I'm off to the styes afresh.
>
> My father glooms and advises me,
> My brother sulks and despises me,
> and Mother catechises me
> Till I want to go out and swear.

Unnerved, the prodigal son sets off again.

> I'm leaving, Pater. Good-bye to you!
> God bless you, Mater, I will write to you . . .
> I wouldn't be impolite to you,
> But, Brother, you *are* a hound!

(Kipling 1994: 579–80, italics original)

Now, reverting to these retellings: They are reluctant to shake loose from the strict demands of orthodoxy. Family (= patriarchy) and home are seen as valuable and secure sites. Family/home provides the stabilizing influence in a world disrupted by sweeping changes occurring all around. What one is looking for is not a modernist understanding of the family, in which the self-interest and desires of the individual run counter to the collective interests of the family, as Kipling's Prodigal Son desires and advocates. Rather, what is hoped for is the promotion of the family as an imaginative and egalitarian changed space. Kakar's observation comes closer to a postcolonial notion of family. In his view, a family should be 'a more flexible, egalitarian structure in which the capacity for initiative as well as seniority governs role relationships, in which competence rather than age legitimates authority, and in which the organizational mode is non-coercive and fraternal' (Kakar 1992 (1981): 120).

Central to these retellings is the idea of home or returning to home. It is conceptualized as a private place and as a public arena. In Palakeel's story, the home is presented as a stable, comfortable, settled, and familiar place to which everyone should eventually return. Bolshevik Kuttan, one of the characters in the story, advises Appu against undertaking such a rigorous journey to find the obvious truth and tells him a story from Hindu myths to extol the virtues of home. In this Puranic story, the Lord Shiva and his consort Parvathi offered a fruit as a prize to two of their sons, whoever first circumambulated the universe. Subramanya, the exuberant one, anxious to cover the earth, took off on his divine peacock, whereas Vinayaka, whose vehicle was a little mouse, circled around his parents and claimed the reward. When his parents told him that he hadn't even begun his journey, Vinayaka's reply was: 'Yes, I've completed my journey around my universe. You're my universe' (Palakeel 1994: 181). In Palakeel's retelling, home is not the place one escapes from; it is renarrated and framed as a rightful, natural, and real space for all, including sons, to dwell.

In Nagarkar's story, the home stands for public arena, thus serving as a metaphor for nation. The 'fold' to which Eddie returns is not the tolerant, inclusive home that India encouraged for so long. When Lele Guruji invites all to come back to the fold, 'all' in his lexicon does not include Muslims. What he and his *sabha* imagine is a reinvigorated ethno-nationalist Hindu home. And if one takes the metaphor of Lele Guruji seriously – 'But faith is a torch. Unless you light torches in the hearts and souls of others, our flame will waste and die' (Nagarkar 1995: 19) – it is a home that produces arsonists for Hinduism. It is a home that stigmatizes all the minorities in India by promoting a hate-filled Hinduism that is intolerant. The home that is metonymic for India is not a shared space for different and diverse communities, nor is it accommodating enough to hold porous identities. Rather, it is a home of extreme religious nationalism. Home is presented as a seductive place of belonging and of living in community, but it is governed by the principle of inclusion and exclusion based on religious, caste and communal identities.

As a way of concluding this section, let me reiterate what I said earlier in this chapter. These retellings ironize the Lucan parable and, in the process, undoubtedly unsettle the Christian story and its received interpretation. The transideological nature of the trope allows a rerendering of value systems and cultural conventions. The retellings retain and reauthorize benevolent paternalism and the idealization of home, obedience and family values in the biblical narrative, though not necessarily in their explicit Christian form. They do not actually displace the biblical story, but they replace some of its inherent features – responsibility, guilt, forgiveness – with those of patriotism and religious bigotry, and they legitimize them as local, traditional and internal to the culture.

Appropriations, Reinscriptions

These two readings benefit from the current widespread sympathy for communities and their interpretive concerns. These concerns have to do with determining meaning as something not inherent in the texts but confected by and for the community to suit its hermeneutical aims.

Narratives will take on a life of their own outside their respective natural theological habitats. In their diasporic existence, they will be mined for different, even contrary, ideological purposes than those for which they were originally intended. Unlooped from the binds of Christian interpretative traditions, biblical narratives will keep on offering new complexities and dimensions to the story. It is safer to assume that interpretations propounded in the original contexts will not be consistent with the interpretations that emerge from the new exilic state. What these retellings do is to prevent any reemergence of one, single reading as the valid one. The proper hermeneutical response is to read them contrapuntally with the concurrent awareness of both Christian and non-Christian discourses. Such a contrapuntal reading will demystify the received and established framework and read against the grain. This means, in their attempts to understand not only the text but also its interpretation, Christian interpreters have to look beyond the traditional hermeneutical arenas, such as in the Christian West. What these new readings in foreign contexts do is to relativize the Christian text and invite and force Christian interpreters to keep their eyes open to disruptive, even uncomfortable, readings. This means constantly rethinking Christian hermeneutical conclusions, accepting them as only provisional, and acknowledging their methods as tentative. Anything other than this will be a return to the exegetical imperialism that has often marked and marred Christian scholarship.

In a way, these two retellings are postmodern, for they take liberties with the narrative. There is a sense of postmodern playfulness about them, especially in Nagarkar's retelling. They emphasize the problem of textualized truth and the impossibility of retrieving one single meaning.

The old scholarly quest for the original meaning is now replaced by the search for a 'good misreading'. Paul de Man explains a misreading as 'A text that produces another text which can itself be shown to be an interesting misreading, a text which engenders additional texts'.[6] Misreading, in Paul de Man's sense, habitually manages to turn a narrative inside out, as it were. The wilful/playful misreading of the writings of the colonized is a way of overcoming inferiority and regaining the voices and cultures that had been muted and denigrated.

These retellings do not deny the theological capital of the Prodigal Son within the Christian tradition, nor do they replace the Lucan narrative. The biblical parable retains its character and will continue to be mined for its polemical potency and for missionary preaching and propaganda. Indian reinscriptions function as hermeneutical palimpsests, where new readings, meanings and texts are written, rewritten and reworked. The idea of palimpsest is explained thus in *Key Concepts in Post-Colonial Studies*:

> The concept of the palimpsest is a useful way of understanding the developing complexity of a culture, as previous 'inscriptions' are erased and overwritten, yet remain as traces within present consciousness. This confirms the dynamic, contestory and dialogic nature of linguistic, geographic and cultural spaces as it emerges in post-colonial experience. (Ashcroft, Griffiths and Tiffin 1998: 176)

Nagarkar and Palakeel's reinscriptions do not attempt to dislodge

---

[6] I owe this quote to Ruthven 1990: 91.

or denigrate the Lucan version. It is a palimpsestic attempt to prevent a monopolistic reading of Christian homiletics. It teases out the vestigial features that surround the text and its interpretation, as a part of understanding the present.

Finally, I would like to end with the question every interpreter who deals with sacred stories wrestles with. Why are we so attracted to stories, especially religious stories, we often know? What prompts us to read and reread, tell and retell, hear and rehear, when we already know the end? What is so alluring about them? Arundhati Roy, the author of the award-winning novel *The God of Small Things*, may have a clue. What one of her characters says about the great Hindu sacred stories may well be true for other religious narratives as well:

> [T]he secret of the Great Stories is that they *have* no secrets. The Great Stories are the ones you have heard and want to hear again. The ones you can enter anywhere and inhabit comfortably. They don't deceive you with thrills and trick endings. They don't surprise you with unforeseen. They are familiar as the house you live in. Or the smell of your lover's skin. You know how they end, yet you listen as though you don't . . . In the Great Stories you know who lives, who dies, who finds love, who doesn't. And yet you want to know again. *That* is their mystery and their magic. (Roy 1997: 229, italics original)

This chapter was originally published in A. K. M. Adam (ed.), *Postmodern Interpretations of the Bible: A Reader*, St Louis: Chalice Press, 2001, pp. 195–206. Used by permission of Chalice Press.

References

Adam, Ian, and Helen Tiffin, 1993. *Past the Last Post: Theorizing Post-Colonialism and Post-Modernism*, Hemel Hempstead: Harvester Wheatsheaf.

Aleaz, Kalarikkal Poulose, 1994. *The Gospel of Indian Culture*, Calcutta: Punti Pustak.

Amaladoss, Michael, 1998. *Beyond Inculturation: Can the Many be One?*, Delhi: ISPCK.

Ashcroft, Bill, Gareth Griffiths and Helen Tiffin, 1998. *Key Concepts in Post-Colonial Studies*, London: Routledge.

Baago, Kaj, 1969. *Pioneers of Indigenous Christianity*, Confessing the Faith in India Series, 4, Bangalore: Christian Institute for the Study of Religion and Society.

Dandekar, Ramchandra Narayan, 1987. 'The Role of Man in Hinduism', in Kenneth William Morgan (ed.), *The Religion of the Hindus*, Delhi: Motilal Banarsidass.

Dubois, Abbé Jean Antoine, 1823 (1982). *Letters on the State of Christianity in India*, New Delhi: Associated Publishing House.

Edgar, Andrew, 1999. 'Irony', in Andrew Edgar and Peter Sedgwick (eds), *Key Concepts in Cultural Theory*, London: Routledge.

Gass, William H., 2000. 'Sacred Texts', in William H. Gass and Lorin Cuoco (eds), *The Writer and Religion*, Carbondale and Edwardsville: Southern Illinois University Press.

Hutcheon, Linda, 1994a. 'The Post Always Rings Twice: The Postmodern and Postcolonial', *Textual Practice* 8.2.

Hutcheon, Linda, 1994b. *Irony's Edge: The Theory and Politics of Irony*, London: Routledge.

Kakar, Sudhir, 1992 (1981). *The Inner World: A Psycho-Analytic Study of Childhood and Society in India*, Delhi: Oxford University Press.

Kipling, Rudyard, 1994. 'The Prodigal Son', in *The Works of Rudyard Kipling*, Ware: Wordsworth Editions.

Nagarkar, Kiran, 1995. *Ravan and Eddie*, New Delhi: Viking Penguin India.

Palakeel, Thomas, 1994. 'The Serpent and the Master', *Yatra: Writings from the Indian Subcontinent* 4: 171–82.

Quayson, Ato, 2000. *Postcolonialism: Theory, Practice and Process*, Cambridge: Polity Press.

Roy, Arundhati, 1997. *The God of Small Things*, New Delhi: IndiaInk.

Ruthven, K. K., 1990. *Feminist Studies: An Introduction*, Cambridge: Cambridge University Press.

Sivasubramaniyan, A., 2000. 'Fatted Calf and Fatted Lamb', *Kanaiyazhi* (January).

Woods, Tim, 1999. *Beginning Postmodernism*, Manchester: Manchester University Press.

3

Marketing the Testaments

Canongate and their Pocket-Sized Bibles

Think what would have happened to the English if they had not an authorized version of the Bible.

Gandhi 1977: 177

Without it [i.e. the Authorized Version] we can scarcely imagine English constitutionalism or English imperial expansion.

Dickens 1964: 193

A good Bible should ideally fit into the pocket of a cassock or a pair of combat trousers, or a small-tooled leather carrying case.

Sansom 2001: 10

Recently the Edinburgh-based publishing firm Canongate has brought out the Bible in the form of single books in the King James Version. Each of these volumes is introduced by a writer, not necessarily associated with the Christian tradition, who encourages the readers to approach them as literary works in their own right. The KJV, when published first, deliberately carried no marginal notes (though it did break the text up into chapter and verse). In the present day it seems that this cultural totem of Western civilization, now widely neglected, needs a preamble by novelists, pop artists, scientists, and even non-Christians to make the once familiar text come alive again. The essayists include prominent novelists: Doris Lessing (Ecclesiastes), Ruth Rendell (Romans), P. D. James (Acts), Joanna Trollope (Ruth and Esther), Will Self (Revelation), pop artist U2's Bono (The Psalms), scientist and atheist Steven Rose (Genesis), and people from other faith traditions. Jewish writers look at Exodus (David Grossman) and the books of Samuel (Meir Shalev). Among the non-biblical faiths, only Buddhism is represented. Charles Johnson, raised in the African Methodist Episcopal Church and now turned Buddhist, introduces Proverbs, and the exiled Tibetan Dalai Lama deals with the Epistle of James. Incidently, the Dalai Lama is the only non-Westerner to join the disparate, and at times contradictory, group of prologue writers. Most of them are lay people (the exception being Richard Holloway), thus investing the text with literary rather than religious legitimacy.

Although the Christian bookstores in the UK refused to stock these single volumes, they have become a publishing sensation, and have sold more than a million copies. The cover design by Angus Hyland of Pentagram of London won the silver award in the book category of the Design and Art Direct Awards. Suddenly this chic, taut, practical and portable Bible has become something that one wouldn't look embarrassed reading on the Tube. The publication also generated a fair amount of theological storm. The disagreements ranged from David Grossman's remark about Moses' life as a 'fairy tale' (Grossman 1998: vii) to Steven Rose's claim, echoing the current biblical scholarship, that Genesis stories are 'accretions of early Mesopotamian and Egyptian myths and sagas' (Rose 1998: ix). When Alasdair Gray, in his preface to the books of Jonah, Micah and Nahum, described Abraham and Isaac as 'polygamous nomads who get cattle or revenge by prostituting a wife or cheating foreigners and relatives' (Gray 1999: viii), it caused offence to Jews and Muslims, and the Board of Deputies of British Jews and the Muslim Council urged that the book be withdrawn (Millar 1999: 7).

The purpose of this chapter is to look at the following: the positive potential of this Pocket Canon; the role of the interpreter's personal voice within the process of discovering meaning in a narrative; the marketing of the Bible and appropriation of religious themes by secular marketeers; the re-iconization of the Bible through the King James Version; the colonial parallels in the investment, promotion and dissemination of the Bible; and the challenge of personal-voice criticism to biblical studies. Put at its simplest, can this disparate group of essayists rescue the Bible, which is fast losing its grip and importance in the West, and discover fresh significance in it?

Take, Read and Wait for Revelation

The introductions by various authors throw light on the texts to which they are appended. They do not burden the readers with complicated textual, historical or theoretical discussion nor baffle them with unnecessary erudition such as one finds in a standard biblical commentary. They repeatedly point to the beauty, narrative power and idealism of biblical texts. Doris Lessing waxes lyrical about Ecclesiastes containing some of the 'most wonderful English prose ever written' (Lessing 1998: ix). Louis de Bernières of *Captain Corelli's*

Mandolin applauds the 'fair share of poetry' in the text in spite of
the translators of the King James Version not having the benefit of
modern scholarship and getting their renditions 'confused and in-
accurate' (De Bernières 1998: viii). Bono rhapsodizes over the 'poetic'
truth found in the Scriptures. Peter Ackroyd locates Isaiah within the
tradition of oral poetry and hails it as 'a river made out of many
streams . . . fluent and harmonious' (Ackroyd 1999: vii). Blake
Morrison declares that John is the most poetic of all the Gospels and
'opens with one of the greatest passages of poetic prose in the
language, philosophically dense, metaphorically rich, and rhythmi-
cally lucid at the same time' (Morrison 1998: xi). For him the writer of
the Fourth Gospel is 'a poet through and through' (Morrison 1998:
xvi).

Although the idea was to present the Bible as a literary text, the
introduction is both spiritual and personal. The biblical books elicit a
testimonial mode among the introducers. What these authors seek to
do is to make the text their own. Therefore they are not particularly
interested in the different layers or deep levels of the text, but want to
have a personal engagement with it. With the exception of two, none
of these writers is a trained biblical scholar. Most opt for a personal
response, frequently drawing on memories of their first encounter
with the Bible. The Canongate publishers state that for the Pocket
Canon series an impressive range of writers was commissioned
specifically to 'provide a personal interpretation of the text and
explore its contemporary relevance'. Their biblical exegesis may be
weak, suspect and even cynical (Self sees it as a 'perverse' activity like
squeezing toothpaste out of a tube), but they are totally in command
of their personal preoccupation, personal histories. The prefaces are
replete with anecdotes, re-evaluations and even private grouses. It is
no surprise that many of these introductions come from men and
women who grew up at a time when the Bible was an unavoidable
part of their childhood experience, but who then either lived their
adult life in a declining state of faith or had an ambivalent attitude
towards the Bible and lost touch with it. Some of them fondly recall
their childhood encounter with the Bible. Blake Morrison, who spent
every Sunday morning in the choir stalls of an English village church
and at fifteen 'swapped the Apostles for another Fab Four, the
Beatles', tells the readers that re-reading the Fourth Gospel carried
him back to the place where he first heard it. In his journey back to the
text, he finds the rhythms of John's Gospel 'inspiring and sensuous'
(Morrison 1998: xvi). Bono reveals that he was a fan of David at the
age of twelve and that he found comfort in the Scriptures, despite

growing up in a divided Ireland where the organized religion came through to him as the 'perversion of faith'. He also reveals how, as part of a white rock group, 'plundering of the scriptures was taboo'. He chose Psalm 40 to end one of his albums, *War*, because of its suggestion that there will be a time when 'grace will replace karma, and love replace the very strict law of Moses' (Bono 1999: xii). Read goes on to say that as a child he was greatly impressed by how King Solomon came to acquire great riches and wealth. Byatt casts her mind back to the first bewildered reading as a Western child with the compulsory Bible in her desk (Byatt 1998: xv). Nick Cave, the Australian song writer and musician, one of the non-believing contributors, in his introduction to Mark remembers how in his early twenties the Old Testament spoke to that part of him which 'railed and hissed and spat at the world' (Cave 1998: vii). He goes on to recall how the Gospel has informed his spiritual maturity: 'The Gospel according to Mark had continued to inform my life as the root source of my spirituality, my religiousness' (Cave 1998: xi).

Interwoven with personal anecdotes are the personal complaints of the introducers. These essayists particularly bemoan the marked bloodthirstiness of the God of the Hebrew Scriptures and such perceptions precariously border on anti-Semitism. Steven Rose contends that Genesis is full of 'seemingly motiveless and often unjust Godly acts' (Rose 1998: xii). The novelist Louis de Bernières is equally unimpressed. In his preface to Job, he points out that the implicit God who emerges from the Hebrew text is one that is 'an unpleasantly sarcastic megalomaniac' (De Bernières 1998: xiii), and a 'mad, bloodthirsty and capricious despot' (De Bernières 1998: xiv). Nick Cave sees him as a 'maniacal, punitive God, that dealt out to His long-suffering humanity punishments' (Cave 1998: vii). P. D. James, too, observes that the punishment meted out to Ananias and Sapphira was typical of 'a vengeful Jehovah' (James 1999: xii). Will Self finds Revelation a 'sick text', 'a guignol of tedium, a portentous horror film' (Self 1998: xiii, xi). The Church's presentation of Jesus also gets some stick. Nick Cave writes: 'The Christ that the Church offers us, the bloodless, placid "Saviour" – the man smiling benignly at a group of children, or calmly, serenely hanging from the cross – denies Christ His potent, creative sorrow or His boiling anger that confronts us so forcefully in Mark' (Cave 1998: xi). In his introduction to the Fourth Gospel, Blake Morrison describes Jesus as self-assured, pushy and somewhat dislikeable and finds him 'wan, frozen and passive, too passive for his own good – someone who'd change wine to water, and not the other way about' (Morrison 1998: viii). Paul, too, is not spared. Fay Weldon sees him as 'a very Mandelson' of the time demanding a united front (Weldon 1998: viii).

The introducers often unhinge the narrative from its original environment, and make it speak for universal human conditions, thus perpetuating the notion of the Bible as a timeless and contextless text. Richard Holloway notes,

> We do not know who Luke was, and it does not matter, because it is the very anonymity of this text that confirms its power . . . We do not need to know anything about its provenance for it to affect us. We do not really know who wrote *Genesis* or many of the other ancient writings and we need not care, because these great texts communicate truth to us at a level that goes beyond the artistry of any particular individual. They create archetypes that express the general condition of humanity, and its sorrow and loss, heroism and betrayal. This is also why the gospels go on touching us long after we have abandoned the orthodoxies that have been built upon them. We do not know who wrote them or when, but they still have power to connect with our lives today. (Holloway 1998: x)

Joanna Trollope, introducing the widely contrasting stories of Ruth and Esther, locates them on two levels. At one level they are simple narratives, one romantic and the other dramatic, but at another level,

> they are illustrations, or images, of human behaviour, human attitudes, human arbitrariness, human trial and error, human failing, human (with divine assistance) triumph. We may not be able to identify with the time and place, but in some way, however small, we can identify with some aspect of the human condition. (Trollope 1999: ix)

Will Self, who wrote an extraordinary introduction which hardly refers to the text he was supposed to introduce – Revelation – thinks 'that this ancient text has survived to be the very stuff of modern, psychotic nightmare' (Self 1998: xiv). Fay Weldon comments thus on the magnificence of the Corinthian passage: 'The timeless truth remains. Two millennia are just the twinkling of an eye in the sight of God and/or the writer' (Weldon 1998: xii). In Louis de Bernières's view, chapter 14 of Job stands out as a moving lament for the human condition: 'Man that is born of a woman is of few days, and full of trouble. He cometh forth like a flower, and is cut down' (De Bernières 1998: viii).

Though for most of the introducers the narrative world of the Bible may seem strange, they see scriptural narratives as the defining story of humanity to which one can connect in spite of living in a different time and a different cultural space. Holloway claims, 'Luke connects with us again and again by the immediacy of his art' (Holloway 1998: x). Charles Johnson goes on to state: 'In fact, I realized that Proverbs not only speaks powerfully to our morally adrift era, but describes rather well my own often benighted rebellious-on-principle genera- tion (the Baby-Boomers) when it says "There is a generation that curseth their father and does not bless their mother. There is a gener- ation that are pure in their own eyes, and yet is not washed from their filthiness" 30:11–12' (Johnson 1998: ix).

The introductory preambles make the Bible appear as an optimistic and generous document, unapologetically holding on to the simpli- city of Christian truth. They create a cultural space in which the Bible can be popularized and still retain its place, dignity and valency. A literary presentation of the Bible may be more than an attempt to bring fresh readers to the Bible. The outcome is more evangelical than literary, and more spiritual than narrative.

These introductions simultaneously free readers from the authority and mediation of critics and entrap them in the essayists' over- simplistic and often sceptical views, capitalizing on the introducer's popularity and status as novelists, pop-icons and serious scientists. What these introductions make clear is that theory and methods are not enough to help us recognize our role and place as interpreters, nor are they enough to make us aware of our impressions and expecta- tions. Throughout these introductions, the hallmark of Protestantism is in evidence – the primacy of the individual reader responding to a sacred text in a manner quite unmediated by the authority of institu- tional readings. The aim is to rescue the text from the various ways it has been manacled. Lessing notes: 'thus do the living springs of knowledge, of wisdom, become captured by institutions, by churches of various kinds' (Lessing 1998: xii). The essayists' reading re- emphasizes and even increases the power attributed to the reader.

Interestingly, the by-line of each author is reduced to lower-case. Whether this has to do with the authors' act of humility before the holy writ, or the imaginative work of the designer is difficult to fathom. But the reverential attitude accorded to the text is copious. Here are a few examples of the essayists venerable sentiments:

> We must approach this sacred text with great respect, doubting the ability of our mind to comprehend it and of our tongue to describe it. (Ackroyd 1999: vii)

> We will go away sorrowful, deeply conscious of our inability either

to understand the Gospel, or to live up to its precepts or to have the humility to accept Divine Grace. Yet, though we are sorrowful, and though we go away, we shall never read this text without being, in some small degree, changed. (Wilson 1998: xiv, xv)

Believers and non-believers alike cannot help but be stricken with awe by its [Romans] temerity and Paul's genius. (Rendell 1999: xvii)

Undoubtedly, the whole enterprise is aimed at Western Christians. But whether the focus is on the lapsed or potential believer is not clear. The aim is to present the Bible as a classic of literature in order to attract a generation which has lost the sense of the Holy Writ. Lessing laments the loss of biblical literacy among the present generation. She recalls the day when everyone in 'Britain and for that matter everyone in the Christian world' would have heard every Sunday 'the thundering magnificence of this prose' and would have been able to identify the origin of phrases and sayings which are as much a part of our language as Shakespeare. These days, if someone hears, "There is a time to be born and a time to die . . . " they probably do think it is Shakespeare, since the Bible these days is the experience of so few' (Lessing 1998: vii). She goes on to say that 'we are very much the poorer because the Bible is no longer a book to be found in every home, and heard every week' (Lessing 1998: ix, x).

We live in a time in which secular literature is gradually gaining sacred status; the sacred literature is now being read as a secular fiction. Morrison calls the Hebrew Scriptures 'a schoolboy's adventure story' (Morrison 1998: viii). In its pages one encounters a variety of characters varying from 'hustlers, murderers, cowards, adulterers, mercenaries' to classic existentialist 'heroes', like Job. Its narratives, in Holloway's view, contain a 'catalogue of improbabilities'. Such perceptions sow doubt in the reader's mind, and do not impel them to believe. By treating the Bible as literature, sometimes going against its main tenets and often puncturing its pomposity, the introducers invite the readers to judge the Bible's credibility, thus overturning the long-held view of the sacred text's assertion of its believability. This is to be welcomed insofar as it dispels fanatical claims which often made on texts' behalf have resulted in frenzy within religious communities.

The introducers extol the intensity of the text's vision, compliment its power and beauty, admire its once powerful hold on Western culture, but not all of them believe in its theological efficacy. Their purpose in reading the Bible was not to learn the theology of Paul nor to listen to the universalism of the Second Isaiah, even if such was concealed in its pages. Rather, theirs was an attempt to get at the religious experiences and convictions that generated this literature and gave it shape. In effect, they admire its aesthetic beauty but do not accept nor are convinced by its religious potency. They marvel at its literary brilliance but are reluctant to seek guidance from its teaching or invest power in its message. Steven Rose is the most unambiguous in discarding the truth claims of the text and questions its serious claim to be a guide to morality. Rose writes: 'If believers find useful ethical values to be drawn from these stories, I must leave to those who read the Bible as allegory to make their own case' (Rose 1998: xii, xiii). As these introductions illustrate, some of the Canongate essayists participate in the project only to puncture the Bible's authority.

Sacred Text as Literature: Perils and Potentials

The current interest in the Bible for its narrative and literary quality is not a new hermeneutical phenomenon. At the end of the nineteenth century, Matthew Arnold, Richard Green Moulton, Ernest Sutherland Bates and James George Frazer (of *Golden Bough* fame) among others had been arguing for and advocated the notion of the Bible as literature and began to treat biblical narratives as novels. It was no longer possible to believe in the biblical accounts as divine oracles nor in the supernatural qualities that surrounded the life and work of Jesus. Instead, biblical accounts became narratives or literary treatises, and biblical personalities like Jesus and David became characters or heroes. Some of the earlier advocates of this view went on to produce their own edited versions of the Bible. Unlike in the present project, where the biblical books are left as they are to make their own impression on the readers, literary or religious, earlier advocates were daring enough to produce their own edited versions, and were even emboldened to excise passages that did not make any literary sense. Contrary to the current enterprise, they were radical enough to re-organize biblical narratives and select passages which did not, in their view, mar the aesthetic qualities of the Bible. Bates maintained that not all parts of the Bible were literary marvels. Bates argued that, from a literary point of view, the Bible was replete with 'irredundant repetitions' and cumbersome punctuations, and he was courageous enough to suggest an edition which required 'not the whole Bible but a coherent arrangement of the greater part' (Bates 1937: xvii). Even the printing of Canongate Bibles militates against reading them as literature. Sir Arthur Quiller-Couch, who was keen to promote the Bible as literature, questioned the traditional mode of presentation, which had verses and arbitrary chapter divisions that flattened the various literary forms contained in the Bible. He suggested in the 1920s that the printed version should reflect and retain the original narrative style of biblical writers.

> Will you still go on to imagine that all the poetry is printed as prose; while all the long paragraphs of prose are broken up into short verses, so that they resemble the little passages set out for parsing or analysis in an examination paper? (Quiller-Couch 1944: 72)

The Bates version, *The Bible Designed to be Read as Literature*, ran into a thousand pages dispensing with traditional chapter–verse format. The Canongate publishers were not that venturesome. One does not see a comparable subversiveness in Canongate's attempt to present text as literature. Although the introducers make it abundantly clear that the Bible was designed to be read as literature, Canongate publishers indulge in little editorial interference in the presentation of texts and retain the traditional verse and chapter divisions.

Endorsing the Bible as literature and endowing it with literary qualities is problematic. Among the introducers only the Dalai Lama tried to place the Epistle of James within the Buddhist genre of *lojong* (literally 'training the mind'). As a result of the overemphasis on the literary aspects of the text, coupled with the comfortable and affluent background of the essayists, the concerns of the poor and the disadvantaged go unnoticed and their plight does not occupy a central place in these introductions. These introducers are sympathetic to and respect the needs of the disadvantaged, but their solution seems to be politics of the transcendental kind which simultaneously respects the state of mind of the poor and acknowledges the goodness of the oppressors too. The Dalai Lama, who finds explicit advocacy of the poor in the James Epistle, cautions the reader that James's severe criticism of the oppressors must be seen within the historical context of the Epistle and that one should not overlook

> an important spiritual principle, which is never to forget the fundamental equality of all human beings. A true spiritual practitioner appreciates what I often describe as our 'basic spirituality'. By this I am referring to the fundamental qualities of goodness, which exists naturally in all of us irrespective of our gender, race, social and religious background. (Dalai Lama 2000: xiv–xv)

The poor are not offered uplift from their misery but are admired for their detached and dispossessed status which enables them to hear the gospel. Their state of poverty is seen as a virtue to be emulated if one wants to hear the gospel. Wilson declares that 'only those who live as though there is no tomorrow, and who do not store up treasure, can enter the kingdom' (Wilson 1998: xii).

The other outcome of the eulogization of the Bible as literature is its colonization as a Western book. The narrative features in the Bible are seen as belonging rightfully to the Western literary tradition. Peter Ackroyd observes,

> Certainly the narrative devices are clear, with affiliations to western poetry and fiction. There is, for example, satire approaching an almost Swiftian vision of disgust at the flesh, in the description of women of Zion 'with stretched forth necks and wanton eyes, walking and mincing as they go, and making a tinkling with their feet' (3:16), or in the depiction of the priests of Ephraim so drunk that 'all tables are full of vomit and filthiness (28:8). (Ackroyd 1999: xi)

The Bible, essentially an 'Eastern Book' according to Adolf Deissmann, migrated from its Mediterranean context, settled on English soil, and is now being claimed as belonging to the Western civilization and literary tradition. The Bible is now being freed from Hebraic and Hellenistic discourse practices and seen as the bearer and marker of English literary tradition. The observation of Prickett is worth pursuing.

> [A]stonishingly little critical attention has been paid to the way in which western Europe, with its cool temperate climate and abundant rainfall, was able to assimilate and successfully make use of the everyday imagery of a semi-nomadic Near-Eastern desert people as part of its own cultural and poetic heritage. (Prickett 1996: 68, 69)

One uneasy thought keeps cropping up. Is a literary approach really an important hermeneutical device or has it become a counterpart of the heritage industry, an escapist activity which replaces an historical and praxilogical engagement with nostalgia? It may serve as a stimulus not for critical engagement but for luring the readers into dreaming for a long lost imaginary idyllic past.

Authorized Bible: The Version on Which the Sun Never Sets

The publisher's textual choice of the King James Version is an interesting and intriguing one. James, by all accounts, was not particularly an attractive personality nor a progressive monarch, yet it was during his rule that the two most significant books in the English language emerged – the authorized version of the Holy Bible in 1611, and the first folio of the collected works of William Shakespeare in 1623. The former was initiated by King James's authority, and the latter had royal backing. The objective of Canongate was to present the Authorized King James Bible not as a religious text but as a work of literature that has had a profound and long-lasting impact on English literature and life. P. D. James, herself a contributor and reviewer of the first series of the Pocket Canon, wrote, 'No single book has had more influence on our national identity, our literature and the development of the English language than has the Authorised King James Version of the Bible' (James 1998: 21).

The preeminent place of the Authorized Version as the supreme literary production needs demythizing. The King James Bible is often portrayed as a definitive version, without any rivals since the date of its publication. English translations were undertaken at a time when English as a language had no literary status. It was only much later that the Authorized Version came to be praised for its literary quality. In seventeenth-century England it was the Geneva Bible which was seen as the people's Bible. It had the advantage of being printed attractively and produced in a convenient size for private use. Its version of the New Testament was the first pocket edition in English, published in 1557, beating the Canongate at least by four hundred years. David Norton, in charting the eventual triumph of the King James Version, points out that it was the commercial considerations and political influences which played a crucial role in its elevation rather than its literary merits. His contention was that the ascendancy of the King James Version owed nothing to its scholarly or literary rendering of the original texts. The King's printer and the Cambridge University Press, who had the monopoly of the Authorized Version, secured the suppression of the Geneva Bible in spite of the latter's superior printing and rendition. More significantly, the anti-monarchial notes in the Geneva Bible didn't find favour in the court of James I (Norton 1993: 1–2).

In their introduction to the Oxford World Classic Bible, Carroll and Prickett note that

[T]he Authorised Version was not, as is sometimes argued, simply the product of the English language at a peculiarly rich stage of its evolution, but of a deliberate piece of social and linguistic engineering . . . [I]t was designed to control the language of salvation, and to occupy the linguistic high ground in such a way as to allow its rivals whether the puritan Geneva or the Catholic Rheims and

Douai Bibles, less verbal space, less legitimacy, less power. (Carroll
and Prickett 1998: xxviii, xxix)

It was a political as well as a religious undertaking. As Peter Levi
aptly put it, 'If ever successful establishment prose existed, this is it'
(Levi 1974: 35).

For many in countries with a history of colonialism, the King James
Version was not 'the noblest monument of English prose', as claimed
by John Livingstone Lowes (Lowes 1938: 16), but an intruding text
that was deeply implicated in the colonizing enterprise. Christopher
Anderson, who wrote a two-volume history of the English Bible,
surveying the territorial spread of the British Empire from Hobart to
Ottawa, claimed that the Authorized Bible was 'at present in the act of
being pursued from the *rising to the setting sun*', and he went on to
claim that it was 'the *only* version in existence on which *the sun never
sets*' (Anderson 1845: xi; italics original). The Authorized Version
was first encountered in the colonies, particularly in India, as part of
colonial education. It was part of the civilizing process that concerned
itself with the moral improvement of the natives.

Two uncomfortable questions keep emerging. At a time of what
J. R. Watson calls a 'seemingly endless series of piddling translations'
(Watson 1993: 15), one wonders whether the Authorized Version has
been offered as a work of literature so much as a holy writ, which has
stood magisterially holding its own in the face of numerous upstart
versions such as New English, Jerusalem, Revised Standard, Good
News, New International, Revised English. Is the use of the King
James Version for the Canongate series some kind of nostalgia, throwing the clock back to a time when the English had one main version?
The concluding paragraph of P. D. James's review of the first series of
the Pocket Canon Bibles is indicative of such a wish.

Is it too much to hope that the day may actually come when, even if
the Church of England continues to neglect the Authorized Version
in its worship, the King James Bible will at least be part of the reading syllabus of students of English Language and Literature? Or, in
this timid, media-obsessed age of all faiths and none, would that be
regarded as politically incorrect? (James 1998: 21)

Reclamation of the Authorized Version could be seen as a ploy to
placate the traditionalist. Or it could be a ruse to woo impressionable
youth who would not dream of buying a copy of the Psalms written in
an unfamiliar prose, were it not introduced by Bono, who professes an

affinity with David as a fellow pop-star, and whom he calls 'Elvis of the Bible'.

The other uncomfortable question arises from the fact that Britain and most of the Western world are becoming more multicultural, and a new version of national belonging is emerging, due to immigration and unprecedented social and geographical mobility. Might the reintroduction of the King James Version encourage a pining for an imaginary single culture and an old homogeneous glory? The Authorized Version was seen as a common bond holding together a divergent group of people who were part of the British Empire. The popular report of the British and Foreign Bible Society recorded that a large number of copies of the Authorized Version were being sent to the colonies to keep together the disparate nations of the British Commonwealth, and it claimed that 'devotion to the ideals of the Holy Scriptures is at once the sign and instrument of that unity' (British and Foreign Bible Society 1930: 42). Now that the Empire is gone, is it the Canongate's way of recovering a singular sense of English identity?

Colonial Parallels

One notices certain parallels between the Canongate's marketing of the Bible in the West at the end of the twentieth century, and the Bible's journeys into non-Western cultures with the missionaries a hundred years ago. Unlike the missionaries of the colonial period who wanted to bring culture and morality to primitive proletariat, Canongate and its introducers appear to humanize the Western population, which is seen as decadent, secular, individualistic, materialistic and theologically illiterate. As a way of introducing the Bible, most missionaries painted the colonies as morally and spiritually degenerate and in need of salvation. Hence the Bible was made to participate in the colonial project of 'improving' the natives, in the process destabilizing people and their cultures. The Authorized Version has become the quintessence of Englishness and the measurement of humanity. Now, however, with an ironic twist, the West is seen as needing salvation. These introductions emerged from a context which is naturally Western and it is variously described as 'secular age' (Morrison 1998: xvi), 'post-Christian' age (Wilson 1998: vii), 'a time of religious transition' (Armstrong 1999: vii), and the world of investigative journalism and science (Wilson 1998: vii). Karen Armstrong in her introduction to Hebrews writes: 'In many of the countries of Western Europe, atheism is on the increase, and the churches are emptying, being converted into art galleries, restaurants, and warehouses' (Armstrong 1999: vii). She could have also said that they have been turned into Hindu temples and Sikh Gurdwaras, as has happened to some of the churches in England. In such a context, the Bible, the sacred text, is advocated primarily as a literary text and is to be read like any other book.

But the opposite was at work in colonial India. In the colonies, the Bible as literature became a pretext for the moral improvement of the natives and a source for biblicizing activities. Colonial educators envisaged a double project for the Bible – to act simultaneously as literature and as a religious text. Having pronounced that the literary or scientific or historical information contained in vernacular literature was no patch on Western learning and literature, and that the indigenous writings lacked the moral and mental power to equip the Indians (the famous/notorious 1835 Minute of Lord Macaulay: 'a single shelf of a good European library was worth the whole of native literature'), colonial administrators and educators decided that carefully selected English texts infused with biblical references could shape the minds of the Indians to appreciate and recognize the authority of the British rule, but, more specifically, to lead them to read the Bible without any compulsion from missionaries. With this view in mind, English writings, which were suffused with biblical and Christian references, were introduced into the Indian university curriculum. Shakespeare, Locke and Bacon were seen as texts that could supply and uphold Christian faith and inculcate morality and civility. Lengthy extracts from the Bible were also incorporated into text-books prescribed for the Bachelor's degree course at Calcutta University. The literary techniques employed in the Bible – narrative, plots, events and characters – were seen as more effective in attracting the attention of the students than preaching or doctrinal teachings. The Bible may be the word of God but the religious truth was conveyed through literary images and analogies. The power of the Bible was seen as lying in its powerful imagery. The objective was the personal awakening and conversion through an appeal to imagery. Gauri Viswanathan, who studied the inextricable link between English literature and the politics of the Empire, observes,

The horrors of sin and damnation were not to be understood through reason but through images that give the reader a 'shocking spectre of his own deformity and haunt him, even in his sleep' . . . To read the Bible well, to be moved by its imagery, to be instructed by its 'dark and ambiguous style, figurative and hyperbolical manner,' the imagination first had to be fully trained and equipped. (Viswanathan 1989: 55)

The concern was not immediate conversion but rather to enable them to realize their degenerate spiritual state. However, colonial educators were very particular about not subjecting the Bible to 'parsing or syntactical and other grammatical exercises of linguistic acquisition – practices that necessarily reduced the Bible from its deserved status as "the Book of Books" to merely one among many books' (Viswanathan 1989: 53). Whereas currently the Bible as literature is viewed sceptically with regard to its religious potency, in the colonies the secular use of the Bible in the university syllabus was seen as a source of religious belief and moral improvement.

In the marketing of the books, too, there are similarities. The chief instrument of evangelistic distribution during the height of missionary activity was the single Gospel or books of the Bible. The British and Foreign Bible Society used to publish and circulate scriptural portions, and their annual reports often boasted the amount of literature disseminated. The distribution figures for the so-called portions were very much greater than those for the full New Testament.[1] These portions were mainly Gospels and were sold chiefly to non-Christians at a cheaper rate. In changed circumstances, single biblical books are now aimed at a generation whose attention span may not extend more than fifteen minutes (as the TV schedulers have discovered) and who may find the tome in its entirety too demanding to handle. The hermeneutical aim remains the same. Just as in the case of the colonized, the prospective Western reader is emotionally, aesthetically, intellectually, spiritually to be liberated (Morrison 1998: xvi).

Secular Advertising and Religious Values

At a time when Christian churches are in decline and struggling to reconfigure their message, identity and role in the West, ironically it is the secular advertising agencies which have more effectively appropriated and given a wider exposure to the religious images which traditionally belonged to Christian churches. Commercial and marketing people are quick to recognize the potency of such motifs. For example, Benetton, the clothes manufacturers, have for some time successfully run controversial advertisements that have wittingly

---

[1] For instance, 1930 circulation figures were: Bibles 24,078; New Testaments 58,640, and biblical portions 5,306,027. See *In the Mother Tongue*, London: British and Foreign Bible Society, 1930, p. 50.

invoked religious ideas and themes to convey their firm's mission statement, 'united colours of Benetton'. The pictures in their commercials are noticeably simple: they explore subjects that are the common concern of all people – peace, reconciliation, life and death. The message they convey is a moral one, attracting the attention of consumers and inviting them to reflect, and eventually buy their products. Whereas Benetton uses no text, Canongate depends entirely on the written word for their marketing purposes.

Christian churches may frown upon the misappropriation of such images and texts. The very fact that secular commercial advertisers and publishers have been able to recoup and utilize these religious images and texts is a pointer that religion is still a powerful form of currency in a world which has almost wholly become secular and dominated by consumer values. Secular advertisers like Benetton who rely on the visual have been willing to exploit religious images and utilize them to sell their products. Secular publishers like Canongate have been able to exploit a reading public which is unlimited, heterogeneous, and whose reading tastes vary from secular to specialist to spiritual.

Biblical books are presented in a new format, as self-contained, separate booklets clearly disengaged from other books of the Bible, thus dislodging the Bible's unitary status. In their new form, the biblical books are able to reach wider audiences far removed from the initiated circle – the Christian faithful, the readers for whom it was originally intended. By giving them a different, portable, physical guise, the publishers put the texts within the reach of new readers who do not read them in the same way as did the original readers. These are seen as handy books that one could take to read while lazing on a deckchair in the summer, and which could act as a portable means of escape from problems of all sorts. As McKenzie has put it, 'new readers of course make new texts, and their meanings are a function of their new forms' (McKenzie 1986: 20). The traditional prerequisites for reading the Bible – an unwavering faith, seeking for the most original text, the wholeness of the Scripture – have now given way to literary pleasure, contending with the translated text in an old prose, and being satisfied with single books and separate volumes.

Personal Testimonies as Reading Practices

The most illuminating attitude towards the Bible is to be found not in a direct exegesis but in coupling the narratives with people's lives. Most of the biblical commentaries under the influence of biblical criticism have made the Bible nothing more than a subject for linguistic, historical and theological analysis, quite divorced from issues related to life. In contrast, these introducers have appropriated the Bible for what it is – a story, or stories, resonating and in some cases not resonating with their own. In a climate obsessed with theories, it is tempting to slot these subjective reflections into the newly emerging and theoretically underdeveloped category of autobiographical or personal voice criticism (Staley 1995; Kitzberger 1999). This reading practice is an undertaking in which interpreters write self-consciously out of their social and cultural location. There is a kind of a confessional and liberal feel about these readings – 'I felt it, therefore it was true.' Personal voice criticism may give an impression that it is an interpretation without texts, and its interpretative ventures may not have any bearing on the biblical books. The whole enterprise may sound like the end of the Bible and critical biblical scholarship. But what it further reinforces is how complex is our appropriation of the Bible.

The Canongate project is reflective of both modern and postmodern tendencies. The introductions are symptomatic of the modernist thinking which has polarized and housed simultaneously two conflicting but correlative Protestant attitudes to the Bible. One is the pietistic and subjective instinct, which turns inward and wallows in the text, unconcerned with the affairs of the world, and which encourages personal reading and a personal response to the Bible. The other is a rationalistic and objective instinct, which wants to seize the text and subject it to severe historical and critical scrutiny. Both instincts have one common assumption – that the real meaning lurks within the texts, and the text is the bearer of meanings. The project is postmodern in its underscoring of the fractured, the fragmented and disjunctured nature of our reality. The Bible, which was a collection of books that came to be seen as 'a book' with a sense of unity, is now reduced to a miscellany of books. The very printing mechanism which brought order, compactness and integrity to the Bible has, with an ironic twist, fractured the Bible's manufactured coherence.

The reading of the individual essayist reinforces the idea of closeted reading as opposed to communitarian forms of reading. The principal location of the reading continues to be the urban and private domain. Thus, reading has come to be seen as a solitary and private occupation rather than a social activity. It offers a moment in which one can be free from the pressures of everyday life and yet be in receipt of wisdom, consolation and, in some cases, discomfort. The reader remains the master or mistress, free to interact with and manage the text without being overpowered by it. Such private readings risk encouraging readers to internalize their spiritual and political vision and withdraw into the realm of imagination.

What we are witnessing is not only the emergence of a plurality of reading practices but also the recognition that no one mode of reading is privileged. The once supreme reign of historical criticism, which made 'disinterested', 'objective', 'scientific' and 'apolitical' reading the main virtues for engaging with the text, is now being severely challenged by context-based and ideologically committed readings of various subaltern groups – women, indigenous people, dalits and burakumin. We need to treat these different approaches – the established and the emerging voices – not as competing practices, assigning some as superior and virtuous and others as exotic and marginal. Rather we need to recognize that in different ways the practitioners of these reading modes are active participants of a shared textual and critical tradition, and in their usage of methods and application of theories they are interrelated. The art of reading then is to see connection between these reading practices. In this way one can overcome the dangers of proof-texting, obtuse academic reductionism, and ideologically closed reading. The explosion of methods for investigation of the Bible has made it imperative that biblical study be a cooperative enterprise between professionally trained scholars and those who read the Bible as dictated by experience and culture. What these introductions indicate is the need for what Edward Said advocated in another kindred discipline – literary studies – namely, secular criticism. For Said, it is an activity which frees criticism from the 'priestly caste of acolytes and dogmatic metaphysicians' (Said 1991: 5) and academic specialization. Furthermore, it alerts the critics to see connection with social and political realities in which they operate and practise their discipline. These introductions acknowledge the Bible's emotional and spiritual place in the individual's life. What is needed is a connection between academic criticism, private feeling and critical politics, so that hermeneutics can engage in radical work, thereby overcoming the distance and working for a collective desire for change.

Two examples from the introduction make it clear how vital this hermeneutical exchange is. For instance, the Israeli novelist and commentator David Grossman sees Exodus as a redemptive autobiographical story of the Jews and rightly so. He refers to it as a 'grand story of the childhood of the Jewish people, sketches the primordial face of that people as it is being formed and, as we now know, describes what will be its fate throughout the thousands of years of history' (Grossman 1998: xvi). While generations of Jews have derived both legitimation and identity from the retelling of the Exodus, indigenous people whose lands have been plundered, such as the Palestinians, native Americans, Aborigines and Tribals, find the Exodus paradigm troublesome and are less likely to be optimistic about its hermeneutical purchase.

The other case in point is the claim of A. N. Wilson, novelist and biographer. In his opening paragraph, he makes the following claim for Matthew's Gospel:

> You are holding in your hands a tiny book which has changed more human lives than *The Communist Manifesto* or Freud's *Interpretation of Dreams*: a book which has shaped whole civilizations: a book which, for many people, has been not a gospel but The Gospel. (Wilson 1998: vii)

True, a host of people including Gandhi were enthused by Matthew's Sermon on the Mount, but the Gospel also contains a crucial verse – Matthew 28:19 – the reactivation of which provided scriptural sanction for and legitimization of colonial enterprises resulting in despoiling other people's cultures (Sugirtharajah 1998: 95–100). What is increasingly clear is how important it is not to finalize the meaning and restrict its interpretation to one context. It may be profitable to think of narratives as exiles and always on the move and be appropriated in manifold forms. What this act of exchange does is to enable people not to domesticate the text and overpower it but to recognize that they have the ability to transfer it from context to context, thus shattering any attempt to finalize their meaning. Texts throw up new meanings as they meet up with new readers and contexts, and that is a good enough reason to consult all players concerned in the task of interpretation.

Reading practices are ultimately an ongoing struggle for control over texts and the monitoring of meanings. Biblical reading has been largely controlled by the producers of texts, and latterly by various Christian church authorities or professional interpreters whose readings are not only compromised by their denominational and institutional agendas but also by their authority to regulate the production and distribution of meanings. These Canongate essayists are like poachers who move across the hermeneutical territory belonging to someone else, and abduct the texts and meanings and then deliver them to ordinary readers.

New reading practices are not necessarily creating anew, but are always exploiting those already existing. Reading practices do not stand alone but are built up upon previous attempts. In the end, it has to do with the choosing of an appropriate paradigm, either within the Bible itself or outside its framework. The important thing for those who choose to work within the biblical vision is to expose the reader to a range of textual paradigms embedded within the biblical texts. Biblical writers themselves adopted this method. In the time of Paul, when it was the question of the Maccabean-style armed struggle against Rome or the subversive submission *à la* Jeremiah, Paul chose the latter. The history of interpretation is littered with such hermeneutical recycling.

Biblical hermeneutics alone cannot provide answers for life's pressing questions, or effect changes that people look for. Nonetheless, people turn to sacred texts not so much for the answers to hypothetical questions, as for the narratives that recreate a sense of living in a different time and place and which remind them about the tremendous diversity of human beliefs and experiences. Perhaps it is through these narratives that they try to reconfigure who they are and where they are going. There is a danger though that the Bible as literature may end up as an idol which Piers Paul Read rightfully identifies as the God that failed (Read 1999: xiv). Holloway himself provides a timely and apt warning. To paraphrase him, often we treat words about God as though they were equivalent to God. This can trap us in the language *about* mysteries rather than opening us to the mysteries themselves (Wilson 1998: vii).

I conclude with a few observations. The underlying theme that runs through these introductions is that we can't just read the Bible for pleasure. Perhaps it would have been possible in the pre-Saidian state of innocence? Ever since Said introduced Orientalism as a handy descriptor for managing texts, echoing the Foucaultian notion of the link between knowledge and power, both texts and readers have lost their innocence (Said 1985). To paraphrase Fanon, reading is not a pleasurable act but a political one. No reading of the text can neglect its contextuality, form, structure, intentions, however imperfectly these may be constructed and discerned. Pointing at a text's historical and political provenance and ideological bias may not increase the pleasure of reading. The most it can do is to give a clue as to who is managing the text and against whom are these texts used.

Finally, in reading these introductions, it is difficult to say whether one has come closer to grasping better the biblical truth, or whether one has come to learn a great deal about the Bible, or even whether one has been introduced to a new mode of reading practice. What we hear loudly and clearly is the authors and their often complicated lives and well-worn concerns. This does not make these introducers as inherently appealing as the texts themselves, nor does it relieve us of our obligation to read and to continue to draw pleasure out of texts. Those who are in the business of interpretation have long realized that the act of interpretation often reveals more about the interpreter than the texts which he or she tries to unravel. The 'philosopher' Madonna was spot-on, and articulated for many, when asked, 'What do people see when they look at you?' She replied simply, 'They see themselves' (Madonna 1999: 5).

This chapter was originally published in *Biblical Interpretation: A Journal of Contemporary Approaches* 10.3 (2002): 221–44. Reprinted with permission. © Brill Academic Publishers, Leiden, The Netherlands 2002.

References

Ackroyd, Peter, 1999. *The Book of Isaiah with an Introduction*, Edinburgh: Canongate Books.

Anderson, Christopher, 1845. *The Annals of the English Bible*, vol. 1, London: William Pickering.

Armstrong, Karen, 1999. *Epistle of Paul the Apostle to the Hebrews with an Introduction*, Edinburgh: Canongate Books.

Bates, Sutherland Ernest, 1937. *The Bible Designed to Be Read as Literature*, London: William Heinemann.

Bono, 1999. *The Book of Psalms with an Introduction*, Edinburgh: Canongate Books.

British and Foreign Bible Society, 1930. *In the Mother Tongue*.

Byatt, A. S., 1998. *The Song of Solomon with an Introduction*, Edinburgh: Canongate Books.

Byng, Jamie, 1998. 'God, Give Me Strength', *The Observer*, 4 October.

Carroll, Robert, and Stephen Prickett, 1998. 'Introduction', in Robert Carroll and Stephen Prickett (eds), *The Bible: Authorized King James Version*, Oxford: Oxford University Press, pp. xi–xlvi.

Cave, Nick, 1998. *The Gospel According to Mark with an Introduction*, Edinburgh: Canongate Books.

Dalai Lama, 2000. *The Epistle of James with an Introduction*, Edinburgh: Canongate Books.

De Bernières, Louis, 1998. *The Book of Job with an Introduction*, Edinburgh: Canongate Books.

Dickens, A. G., 1964. *The English Reformation*, Glasgow: Fontana Paperbacks.

Gandhi, M. K., 1977. *India of My Dreams*, compiled by R. K. Prabhu, Ahmedabad: Navgivan Publishing House.

Gray, Alasdair, 1999. *Jonah, Micah and Nahum with an Introduction*, Edinburgh: Canongate Books.

Grossman, David, 1998. *The Second book of Moses called Exodus with an Introduction*, Edinburgh: Canongate Books.

Holloway, Richard, 1998. *The Gospel According to Luke with an Introduction*, Edinburgh: Canongate Books.

James, P. D., 1998. 'Canons of Authorship', *The Times Literary Supplement*, 25 December.

James, P. D., 1999. *The Acts of the Apostles with an Introduction*, Edinburgh: Canongate Books.

Johnson, Charles, 1998. *Proverbs with an Introduction*, Edinburgh: Canongate Books.

Kitzberger, Ingrid Rosa (ed.), 1999. *The Personal Voice in Biblical Interpretation*, London: Routledge.

Lessing, Doris, 1998. *Ecclesiastes or, the Preacher, with an Introduction*, Edinburgh: Canongate Books.

Levi, Peter, 1974. *The English Bible 1534 to 1859*, Grand Rapids, Mich.: Eerdmans.

Lowes, John Livingstone, 1938. 'The Noblest Monument of English Prose', in Vernon F. Storr (ed.), *The English Bible: Essays by Various Writers*, London: Methuen, pp. 16–42.

Madonna, 1999. 'Life', *The Observer Magazine*, 26 September.

McKenzie, D. F., 1986. *Bibliography and the Sociology of Texts: The Panizzi Lectures 1985*, London: The British Library.

Millar, Stuart, 1999. 'Bono Sings the Bible Blues', *The Guardian*, 30 October.

Morrison, Blake, 1998. *The Gospel According to John with an Introduction*, Edinburgh: Canongate Books.

Norton, David, 1993. *A History of the Bible as Literature, vol. II: From 1700 to the Present Day*, Cambridge: Cambridge University Press.

Prickett, Stephen, 1996. *Origins of Narrative: The Romantic Appropriation of the Bible*, Cambridge: Cambridge University Press.

Quiller-Couch, Arthur, 1944. *Cambridge Lectures*, London: J. M. Dent and Sons.

Read, Piers Paul, 1999. *The Wisdom of Solomon, with an Introduction*, Edinburgh: Canongate Books.

Rendell, Ruth, 1999. *The Epistle of Paul the Apostle to the Romans with an Introduction*, Edinburgh: Canongate Books.

Rose, Steven, 1998. *The First Book of Moses called Genesis with an Introduction*, Edinburgh: Canongate Books.

Said, Edward W., 1985. *Orientalism*, Harmondsworth: Penguin Books.

Said, Edward W., 1991. *The World, The Text, and the Critic*, London: Vintage.

Sansom, Ian, 2001. 'Brief Encounters', *The Guardian Saturday Review*, 28 April.

Self, Will, 1998. *Revelation with an Introduction*. Edinburgh: Canongate Books.

Staley, Jeffrey L., 1995. *Reading with a Passion: Rhetoric, Autobiography and the American West in the Gospel of John*, New York: Continuum.

Sugirtharajah, R. S., 1998. 'A Postçolonial Exploration of Collusion and Construction in Biblical Interpretation', in R. S. Sugirtharajah (ed.), *The Postcolonial Bible*, Sheffield: Sheffield Academic Press, pp. 91–116.

Trollope, Joanna, 1999. *Ruth and Esther with an Introduction*, Edinburgh: Canongate Books.

Viswanathan, Gauri, 1989. *Masks of Conquest: Literary Study and British Rule in India*, New York: Columbia University Press).

Watson, J. R., 1993. 'The Bible in English Literature: Review Article', *The Expository Times* 105: 15–16.

Weldon, Fay, 1998. *The Epistles of Paul the Apostle to the Corinthians with an Introduction*, Edinburgh: Canongate Books.

Wilson, A. N., 1998. *The Gospel According to Matthew with an Introduction*, Edinburgh: Canongate Books.

4

Loitering with Intent

Biblical Texts in Public Places

> The Bible is useful for doing the Alexander Technique. I always use it in hotels.
>
> Boy George 2002: 18

> My old man was a farmer. The only books we had in the house were the Sears catalog and the Bible, and all he ever used the Bible for was to hit me on the head.
>
> Hynes 2001: 18

Let me begin by citing two new items reported in the English daily, *The Guardian*, where there were references to the Bible. The first one had to do with the Rwandan crisis. It was a letter written by Tutsi pastors to their church president, a Hutu. It was written on 15 April 1994 – the day before they were to be massacred. It went like this:

> Our dear leader, Pastor Elizaphan Ntakirutimana, How are you! We wish you to be strong in all these problems we are facing. We wish to inform you that we have heard that tomorrow we will be killed with our families. We therefore request you to intervene on our behalf and talk with the mayor. We believe that, with the help of God, who entrusted you the leadership of this flock, which is going to be destroyed, your intervention will be highly appreciated, the same way as the Jews were saved by Esther. We give honour to you. (Gourevitch 1999: 3)

The second item was about the fateful United Airlines flight 93 from Newark to San Francisco on September 11. Todd Beamer, from New Jersey, was one of the doomed passengers on board. He was a religious man and had a Lord's Prayer bookmark in the Tom Clancy novel which he was carrying with him. Now the flight was being rerouted to Washington by the hijackers, and, not wanting unnecessarily to upset his pregnant wife, Beamer called the GTE phone company, the company which provided telephone services for United

Airlines, and had an unusual talk with a telephone switchboard operator called Lisa Jefferson who was on the ground in one of the suburbs of Chicago. He and Lisa conversed for 13 minutes and during this time they recited together Psalm 23: 'Though I walk through the valley of the shadow of death I will fear no evil; for Thou art with me; thy rod and thy staff they comfort me' (Vulliamy 2001: 15).

I cite these dramatic incidents as a starting point to exploring how biblical texts are employed in the popular press. In this exploratory piece my intention is very simple – to use this reportage to raise hermeneutical issues such as how biblical texts are used in popular newspapers, the nature of texts, the interface between popular and professional reading, the role of the common reader as postillator. In looking at these issues, I draw chiefly upon *The Guardian* but occasionally bring in citations from other popular newspapers as well.

The Text Tells Them So

In looking at these textual appearances, one gets the impression that the biblical text can be used to justify virtually any extra-biblical cause. The texts are activated to perform functions which are not even remotely connected with the authorial intention. For instance, house arrest as imposed by the Afrikaner regime during the apartheid days in South Africa was supported by biblical claims. Brigadier Neels Du Plooy explained that a lot of security legislation during that oppressive period was based on biblical teaching. For example, house arrest was justified by 1 Kings 2.36: 'The king sent and called for Shimei and said unto him, Build thee an house in Jerusalem, and dwell their, and go not forth thence any whither' (Erasmus 1996: 5). In another case, the owner of the confectionery Logia Foods claimed that his firm marketed only foods prescribed by the Bible. He professed that his product, Bible Bar, was made according to the nutritional guidance provided in Holy Writ: 'A land of wheat and barley, of vines and fig trees and pomegranates; a land of olives, oil and honey' (Deuteronomy 8.8).[1] Even cloning a human embryo has a direct biblical source. Severino Antinori, who was in the thick of controversy over human cloning and human reproduction, remarked that it was his 'fascination with the Old Testament story of Abraham's aged wife Sara which led to his world-wide fame and notoriety'.[2] These textual

---

[1] Boxed item: 'Is nothing Sacred?' *New York Times*, Week in Review, 15.4.01, p. 2.

[2] *The Guardian*, 8.8.01, p. 3.

citations illustrate that there is no way biblical writers could have anticipated all these contexts in which their texts have been put to use.

Secondly, biblical texts play a part in a new kind of celebrity activism. At a time when celebrities champion worthy causes, they marshal the Bible if it is profitable to promote their case. One such occasion was when the pop idol Bono met the fearsomely right-wing evangelical Christian Jesse Helms, the US senator whose election campaign routinely exploited racial and sexual prejudices. The singer-turned-political-activist told this supposedly religious person that nearly 2,103 verses of the Bible were concerned with the status of the poor and that Jesus spoke of judgement only once and then it was not about being gay or about sexual behaviour but about social morality. When Bono quoted the verse in Matthew 25: 'I was naked and you clothed me', the senator was really moved and in tears (Bunting and Burkeman 2002: 3). Another celebrity example is provided by anti-globalization activists. One of the organizers, Kevin Danaher, in justifying the protest against the financial houses of the world, cited the temple incident where Jesus for the one and only time ever used violence. Danaher went on to claim that the violence was aimed not at the Roman soldiers, or the tax collectors, but at a specific target – the bankers (Danaher 2001: 25).

Thirdly, biblical texts are also employed to expose the insincerity of politicians and their feigned piety and in the process to puncture their sanctimonious postures. During the Iraq crisis, when President Bush talked about his vision for Iraq after the successful overthrow of Saddam Hussein, a letter writer to *The Guardian* reminded Bush, a devout and Bible-reading Christian: Let not him that girdeth on his armour boast himself as he that putteth it off (1 Kings 20.11).[3] When the British government introduced a fine of £2,000 per person for carriers which fly illegal immigrants into the country, the Immigration Advisory Service cited Matthew 2.13–15 as a way of exposing the un-Christian nature of the rule, a rule which would have put the Holy Family's case in jeopardy as they did not have proper papers. In the Matthean verse, Joseph was warned by an angel in a dream to fly to Egypt because King Herod was intending to kill children under the age of two. In a clever use of the text during the Christmas season, the Immigration Advisory Service pointed out that, though Joseph, Mary and Jesus would have had a case under 1951 Geneva Convention rules to claim refugee status had they flown into Britain, they would have been detained at Orpington detention centre because their

---

[3] *The Guardian*, 8.2.03, p. 23.

claims would have been treated as baseless and fabricated. Israel under Herod would not have been deemed to be a country under persecution. The angel would have found itself in serious trouble for aiding and abetting Joseph and his family's entry into Britain. What is more, the angel could have been fined £2,000 for bringing in each economic migrant from Bethlehem.[4] Still on asylum, when the Arch-bishop of Canterbury waded into controversy by suggesting that asylum seekers should be put in secure accommodation while their cases were being heard, Joe Philips, a professing atheist, wrote: 'The guy Dr Williams claims to follow said: I was hungry and you gave me meat, I was thirsty and you gave me drink, I was a stranger and you took me in.'[5] When President Bush challenged the world after September 11 with the words, 'Are you for us or for our enemies?', a *Guardian* columnist placed this verse in its narrative context. He reminded the American president that these words were first uttered by Joshua (5.13–15) when he was confronted by the commander of the Lord's army holding a sword. The latter replied 'neither'. On hearing this unexpected reply, Joshua knelt in humility (Geraint ap Iorwerth 2001: 21). Similarly, in mocking vein, David Ward from Cumbria, in a letter to *The Guardian*, reminded the hawkish world leaders, President Bush and Prime Minister Blair, apparently eager to attack Iraq what-ever the outcome of the UN inspectors' investigations, to return to their well-thumbed Bibles and turn to the Book of Jonah. Ward wrote: 'Jonah was sent against his will to inform the people of Nineveh (in what is now northern Iraq) that unless they repented, they would be destroyed. To his annoyance they repented. He was furious with God because God asked: "And should not I have pity on Nineveh, that great city wherein are more than six score thousand persons – and also much cattle?"'[6] This was a telling reminder by an ordinary reader to a Bible-lover such as Bush of the danger of uncontextualized use of texts.

Fourthly, the serious tone of the Bible is punctuated with humour and playfulness. During the height of football hooliganism in England, Vincent Hanna in his column referred to a Bible-quoting football fanatic, Greg, a Scot, who had taken to reciting Deuteronomy 28.35, claiming that it was relevant to a forthcoming game: 'The Lord shall smite you in the knees and in the legs with a sore botch that cannot be healed.' When Paul Gascoigne had a poor game for Rangers

---

    [4] 'Christmas without Christ', *India Today International*, 15.1.01, 24h.
    [5] *The Guardian*, 4.2.03, p. 17.
    [6] David Ward, letter to *The Guardian*, 19.9.02, p. 23.

(associated with Scottish Protestant tribalism) in a Scottish league match, the same Greg, obviously a Protestant, told Hanna that 'He (Gascoigne) should remember what God said to the other St Paul, "It is hard for thee to kick against the pricks" (Acts 9.5)' (Hanna 1996: 26). Even the ritualized form of football results aired after the matches was traced to the Hebrew Bible. Matthew Engel, an erstwhile cricket correspondent to *The Guardian*, cites one:

> And these are the kings of the land whom Joshua and the children of Israel smote beyond Jordan westwards . . .
> The king of Jericho, one; the king of Ai, which is beside Beth-el, one;
> The king of Jerusalem, one, the king of Hebron, one;
> The king of Jarmuth, one; the king of Lachish, one;
> The king of Eglon, one; the king of Gezer one.
> The king of Debir, one; the king of Geder, one.
> (Joshua 12.9ff.)[7]

This kind of playfulness is not confined to football. The motor industry also has its share of scriptural teasing. For example: 'God drove Adam and Eve from the garden of Eden in a Fury.' Biblical precedents are also found for the British motorbike: 'Joshua's Triumph was heard throughout the land, and the roar of Moses' Triumph is heard in the hills.' Jesus' embarrassment at the Honda Accord was deduced from his saying, 'For I did not speak of my own Accord' but this did not prevent the same Gospel recording that, 'the apostles were in one Accord'. Such a statement is also seen for its additional significance – the earliest historical evidence for car pooling.[8]

In keeping with this tongue-in-cheek textual burlesque, one could say that such textual usage was akin to Imelda Marcos's method of shoe selection – looking for something that fits.

Finally, disputes are sometimes conducted by brandishing biblical texts one against the other. Using irony and parody, these disputes can reveal real confidence in handling texts. Sometimes this is done with wit and charm. Two examples stand out. One is related to the gay and lesbian issue, and the other is about corporal punishment. Simon Hoggart reported a delicious example in his Saturday Diary column of how to unsettle bigotry with humour. When the daytime TV host Laura Schlessinger, who is known for her blatant bigotry

---

[7] Matthew Engel, 'Dark Escort', *The Guardian*. I am unable to provide the date and page number. My guess is circa middle-1990s.

[8] All these examples come from Giles Smith, 'And the Lord said, let there be space', *The Guardian*, G2, 4.3.03, p. 17.

towards homosexuals, cited the notorious verse Leviticus 18.22, which states that homosexuality is an abomination, a Steve Turner culled texts from the very same Leviticus in order to poke fun at her and expose the ineffectualness of using texts in too literal a way. In a reply which took the form of an epistle, Turner wrote:

> Dear Laura, when I burn a bull on the altar as a sacrifice I know it creates a pleasing odour for the Lord (Lev. 1:9). The problem is that my neighbours complain that the odour is not pleasing to them. Should I smite them? . . . Lev. 25:44 states that I may indeed possess slaves, both male and female, provided they are purchased from neighbouring nations. A friend of mine says this applies to Mexicans but not Canadians. Can you clarify? Why can't I own Canadians? . . . Lev. 21:20 states that I may not approach the altar of God if I have a defect in my sight. I admit that I wear reading glasses. Does my vision have to be 20/20 or is there some wiggle room here? My uncle has a farm. He violates Lev. 19:19 by planting two different crops in the same field, as does his wife by wearing garments made of two different kinds of thread (cotton/polyester blend). He also tends to blaspheme a lot. Is it really necessary that we go to all the trouble of getting the whole town together to stone them? (Lev. 24:10–16) Couldn't we just burn them to death at a private family affair like we do with people who sleep with our in-laws? Thanks again for reminding us that God's word is eternal and unchanging. Your devoted disciple and adoring fan. (Hoggart 2000: 12)

Another textually disputed area is the question of caning children. Those who support corporal punishment often invoke passages from Proverbs which extol the value of smacking children. When principals, teachers and parents of Christian Independent Schools challenged the banning on the grounds that it breached both biblical teaching and human rights, their lawyer, John Friel, in his petition to the courts, quoted from the Book of Proverbs 23.13 and 14: 'The rod of correction imparts wisdom, but the child left to itself disgraces its mother. Do not withhold discipline from a child; if you punish him with the rod, he will not die. Punish him with a rod and save his soul from death.' In a letter to the editor, a reader wrote: 'I was surprised that the schools' representatives did not touch on Matthew 5:39, 'but whosoever shall smite thee on thy right cheek, turn to him the other also'. In a somewhat related case in Southern California when the parents cited the text from Proverbs, the judge in passing his sentence, with his legal tongue firmly in his cheek, complimented the parents for not meting out the more rigorous form of punishment prescribed for an unruly child in Deuteronomy 23:12: 'Stone him with stones, that he die.' It is fortunate that the parents of these children were Protestants and they were unaware of the Catholic canon which contains a deutero-canonical book – Ecclesiasticus. There, chapter 30 decrees a severe form of chastisement as a good way of bringing up young children.

Speaking of caning, Phil Williamson, the headteacher of the Christian Fellowship School in Liverpool who campaigned for a judicial review of the outright government ban on parents' right to exercise physical discipline, declared that his school would not cane children but 'would smack them on the hand or leg using the teacher's hand'. Stressing his long experience in administering physical punishment, Williamson went on to say: 'With the older pupils, girls would be strapped on the hand by a lady teacher, and boys would be smacked on the backside with something akin to a ruler, but wider' (Branigan 2001: 2). Alan Halden from Hemel Hempstead, poking fun at Williamson's medieval brutality, pointed out that he failed to pass the Bible's literal test: 'The Bible distinctly says "rod", and not paddle or strap. A cane narrows and accentuates the area of pain, thus improving the beneficial effect upon the recipient. Any attempt to alleviate this undermines the fundamentalist Christian reliance on the Word.'[9] Those who support physical punishment do not confine themselves to that overused passage from Proverbs. They draw profitably on the New Testament too. When the twelve-year-old of Larry and Constance Slack failed to find her mother's coat quickly enough for them to go out on time, Laree was beaten to death with an electric rod five feet long and one inch thick. They claimed that they had beaten her in accordance with Deuteronomy 25.1–3 prescribing 40 lashes – minus one as authorized by the Jewish tradition. They were zealously reproducing St Paul's punishment by multiplying it by three times (Bates 2002: 22).

Going Public

At a time when biblical texts, biblical allusions and imagery are disappearing from the cultural consciousness of the West, the occasional appearance of biblical texts in the popular press is an indication that they still have hermeneutical purchase, especially when one tries to make sense of international conflict, sexual orientation, law and order

---

[9] Letter to *The Guardian*, 5.11.01, p. 19.

and bringing up children. Obviously newspapers are not littered with biblical quotations, but what do we make of the modicum of biblical quotations and allusions we find in them? These textual citations disclose an ambivalent attitude to the Bible. From the use of these quotations it is sometimes difficult to assess whether the sacred text of Christians is held in veneration or being mocked. For those who believe that every word of the Bible is true, the Bible is not an object consisting of printed paper and ink but a venerable and awesome artefact. Like the sightseers at the Taj Mahal, such readers come to discover and marvel, not to dissent. The text's meaning for them has been determined once and for all by the will of the author, God. In such cases, the reader is looking for enlightenment in the text. But others see texts used as forms of sacred parody. For them, it furnishes resources to ridicule and puncture the smugness of those in power.

Not all letter-writers to the press and journalists are Christians. Nonetheless, Christian texts creep into their writings. Their appropriation of texts and use of quotations could be likened to the way some medieval writers used texts from the Christian tradition as, in Bakhtin's words, a kind of 'parodic-travestying' (Bakhtin 2000: 69). In this process of parodying 'the entire Bible, the entire gospel was as it were cut up into little scraps, and these scraps were then arranged . . . In this work a correspondence of all details to the Sacred Writ is strictly and precisely observed but at the same time the entire Sacred Writ is transformed into carnival' (Bakhtin 2000: 70). It is a complex and complicated act in which the other's word is simultaneously respected and ridiculed, accepted and teased. In such usages, one is often baffled as to whether the Sacred Word is held in reverence or taken for its comic value.

In looking at the usage of texts, there are two things obvious at the outset. I shall mention one now and come back to other at the end of the chapter. What is apparent is that texts here function at a micro level – the narratives are broken into neat, pithy texts, and re-assembled, activated and invoked to elucidate a point. It is not the Bible in toto or even individual books which go to constitute the Bible but sliced-up textual pieces. It is the fragmented text which makes its way into the public arena. Those raised with the notion of a grand narrative of the Bible holding together the various parts will find the citing of isolated, split and individual texts forced out of their immediate contexts unattractive, and in some cases even detestable. For the users of these texts, the question of the wholeness of Scripture unified by a biblical theme may be not only foreign but also puzzling. They are unlikely to look for such an integrated purposive whole. They may not see a need for this. Moreover, the question about the whole-ness of the Bible is not easily settled, as ecclesiastical history over the centuries has shown.

This kind of plucking-out of texts could be termed, to use Michel de Certeau's suggestion, 'poaching'. He describes readers as travellers moving 'across land belonging to someone else, like nomads poach-ing their way across the fields they did not write, despoiling the wealth of Egypt to enjoy it themselves' (Certeau 1988: 174). Poaching is thus a hermeneutical device employed by common readers who shred texts into small, simplified and specific forms, to make sense of their existential needs, piecing them together in the way that best suits their practical needs. In a sense, common people's reading is about 'tactics and games played with the texts' (Certeau 1988: 175).

Before I expand on reading as poaching, a brief note on the history of breaking of the biblical narrative into numbered verses. This goes back to the Puritans and their Geneva Bible, which paved the way for text-twisting as an art form. The early English Bibles were in para-graph form without any numbering of individual verses or chapter divisions. The first English edition to introduce verse and chapter divisions was Whittingham's New Testament published in 1557. He followed Stephanus's Latin Bible which was the first to use divisions in both testaments. In his preface, Whittingham states: 'Furthermore, that the reader might by all means be profited, I have divided the text into verses and sections, according to the best editions in the other languages' (Pollard 1911: 276). This new literary device made it possible for preachers to point out the specific location of a particular passage, instead of introducing a hermeneutical point with prefatory statements such as 'Mark said' or 'Paul wrote it in his epistle.' This enabled a congregation to follow a text more closely. Besides making the texts easier on the eye, easily identifiable verses from the various parts of the Bible could be summoned not only to clinch a theological argument but also to authenticate it as authoritative. The truth which was once believed to reside in revelation, vision, sacraments, sacred sites was now understood to reside exclusively in texts or documents. It was something independently verifiable.

Reading as Poaching

Reading as poaching is a solitary activity which becomes a natural and easy act to an individual. The interaction with the text becomes a private and a Protestant and capitalist affair in which each individual has an encounter alone with the text. The mood seems to be that the

Bible is all I need. I do not want notes or criticisms or explanations about the authorship or origin, or the mediation of clerics and academics. Solitary reading of texts is often controlled by practical interests. More than doctrinal speculation, interpretation is application-oriented. Private readings convey personal and idiosyncratic insights, and often simplify and remythicize the biblical texts. In such readings, Scripture is taken in its plain, natural and obvious meaning. There is a desire to dispense with complicated textual nuances and find unambiguous and simple meanings of texts.

Readers as poachers continue to highlight the ongoing struggle between manufacturers of meaning and consumers. Poaching is the common reader's self-assertion through the text. It is the overturning of the control exercised by the managers of the texts, namely church and academy, who determine what parts should be read, and who employ interpreters who determine, monitor and dispense the correct meanings of a given text. More significantly, reading as poaching does not mean just disconnecting texts from their immediate habitat. Poachers can also build connections between texts, as Steve Turner has made playful use of the Leviticus texts in his amusing riposte to Laura Schlessinger.

Readers as poachers open up a great gap between popular and professional modes of interpretation. Reading as poaching further weakens the authority of the text and the meaning imposed by clerics and academics, and becomes a personal choice based on personal beliefs and contextual needs. In such cases, readers freely pick and mix the content and meaning of the text, and operate on a private 'canon within the canon' which suits them, rather than be restricted by church diktats, commentarial tradition or credal statements. It liberates the text from the control of ecclesiastical and scholastic authority. Those raised in the Enlightenment mode of interpretation will find such reading overtly literalistic, legalistic and totally careless with historical details. Scholarly practitioners have been cautioning that texts set certain limits to the way one reads them and that readers are not free to produce any meanings they like from texts, and that the possession of an interpretative history prevents any indulgence of subjective readings. However much academics tend to protect the text and guard against 'wayward readings', readers and texts are nimble and agile enough to undermine such protectiveness and are capable of producing totally unforeseen readings. The incidents I quoted at the beginning of this article are striking cases in point – the Tutsis' invoking of Esther, and Todd Beamer and Lisa Jackson reciting Psalm 13. Academics may be appalled at these easy identifications. But for the Tutsis and Beamer and Jackson, texts become a mirror in which they read their hope and despair. For them and countless people, the impetus to interpret stems from the need to make sense of their lives, and in this respect the hermeneutics of poaching is an existential impulse. Hence, there is the attempt by people to invoke clearly identifiable typological models located within the Bible and apply them directly to their current psychological, political and spiritual quagmires. In such circumstances, texts settle the readers' current existential dilemma and offer them succour.

Finally, reading as poaching raises the question: Who has the power? – The reader, or the text? If readers wield power, the text becomes an empty slate on which the readers can write any meaning. On the other hand, if power is invested in the text, then readers would have to surrender and comply with whatever the text says. The trouble with such a polarized position is that it is extremely reductionist, and views readers and texts as separate entities having lives of their own and continuing separate during the act of reading. In reality, the formation of meaning is achieved through a mutual interaction between a number of ingredients – text, context of the text, reader and his or her context.

What poaching indicates is that texts and their meanings are not final but that the texts derive their meaning in their encounter with context and reader. They are like sojourners who hardly ever go back to the habitat they left behind. Texts in essence are moulded by the context in which they are located. Because they are malleable and accommodative, they are vulnerable. Ultimately, what reading as poaching indicates is that it is not possible to finalize a text, or restrict it to one context, or predetermine its meaning.

Postcolonial Postscript

During the Middle Ages under the influence of ecclesiastical authorities the Bible was installed with intrinsic power and had a recognizable identity. Access to it was limited. In the current context, the Bible is marketed as a consumable commodity and made available to all. As a religious package, in an open market, it has to vie for attention with countless other texts. Its authority, identity and meaning are clarified in connection with other texts which arise out of different theological and secular needs. In a sense, texts are always in transit between contexts, and like nomads they do not have a fixed abode or a steady identity. Their transitory attachment to contexts, their indeterminate nature, and their potential to generate meanings in manifold ways, are all well exploited by readers. In such a hermeneutical scenario, to chutnify what Ecclesiastes said: 'Of producing meaning there will be no end.'

Let me come back to the second striking feature of the usage of texts, which I promised to do in the middle of the chapter. What is conspicuous is that almost all the citations in the popular press come from the King James Version. At the height of the British empire, Anderson cockily proclaimed that this was 'the only version in existence on which the Sun never sets' (Anderson 1845: xi). Now, to use Homi Bhabha's words, 'the holiest of books – the Bible – bearing both the standard of the cross and the standard of empire, finds itself dismembered' (Bhabha 1994: 92). The founding totem of the Western world has now ended up in the popular press as 'an erratic' and 'an eccentric' cultural artefact sans religious authority or theological clout.

References

Anderson, Christopher, 1845. *The Annals of the English Bible*, vol. I, London: William Pickering.

Bakhtin, M. M., 2000 (1981). *The Dialogic Imagination: Four Essays*, trans. Caryl Emerson and Michael Holquist, ed. Michael Holquist, Austin: University of Texas Press.

Bates, Stephen, 2002. 'Witness on the Watchtower', *The Guardian*, 26 January.

Bhabha, Homi K., 1994. *The Location of Culture*, London: Routledge.

Boy George, 2002. 'This Much I know', *The Observer Magazine*, 18 August.

Branigan, Tania, 2001. 'Christian Schools Ask for Right to Hit Pupils', *The Guardian*, 3 November.

Bunting, Madeline, and Oliver Burkeman, 2002. 'Pro Bono', *The Guardian*, G2, 18 March.

Certeau, Michel de, 1988. *The Practice of Everyday Life*, trans. Steven Rendall, Berkeley: University of California Press.

Danaher, Kevin, 2001. 'Power to the People', *The Observer*, 4 October.

Erasmus, Paul, 1996. 'Confessions of an Apartheid Killer', *The Tiddler: The Observer's Little Bit Extra*, 6 October.

Geraint ap Iorwerth, 2001. 'In Search of a Gentle God', *The Guardian*, 7 December.

Gourevitch, Philip, 1999. 'The Beautiful Land of Death', *The Guardian Saturday Review*, 6 March: 1–3.

Hanna, Vincent, 1996. 'And Over to Deuteronomy', *The Guardian*, 6 June.

Hoggart, Simon, 2000. 'Simon Hoggart's Diary', *The Guardian Saturday Review*, 16 September.

Hynes, James, 2001. *The Lecturer's Tale*, New York: Picador.

Pollard, Alfred W. (ed.), 1911. *Records of the English Bible: The Documents Relating to the Translation and Publication of the Bible in English, 1525–1611*, London: Oxford University Press.

Vulliamy, Ed, 2001. 'Let's Roll', *The Observer*, 2 December: 15–16.

5

A Modern Tool-Shed for a Global Village

Academic Critics have largely abandoned the broadly civilizing function of criticism.

Robert Weimann[1]

Don't be fooled by the whitewashed apparent objectivity of the ivory tower. Until the ivory turns to a rainbow with all countries represented, you would do well to be suspicious of the so-called 'facts'.

Nozipo Maraire[2]

In this chapter, I would like to concentrate on two hermeneutical issues. One is related to the role and function of historical critical tools, and the other to the place and representation of a Third World biblical critic in a global village.

Historical Criticism and Its Role

Interestingly, the quest for the historical Jesus, the application of historical methods, and the conquest of the lands and texts and artefacts of other people, emerged in Europe more or less at the same time. I would like to make it clear that my attitude towards historical criticism is one of an ambivalence. On the one hand, I would like to affirm the historical method, and I can see its benefits, but on the other, I can see its damaging effects when it is transferred to other parts of the world and especially when it is used as a tool to conquer and subjugate other peoples' texts and stories and cultures. I need not remind biblical scholars of the liberative nature of historical criticism when it first emerged in Europe. The method freed and relativized the absolutist theological and ecclesiastical readings of the time and made Christianity and its origins and traditions earthy, questionable and

---

[1] Quoted in Terry Eagleton, *The Function of Criticism: From the Spectator to Post-Structuralism*, London: Verso, 1994, p. 107.

[2] Nozipo Maraire, *Zenzele: A Letter to my daughter*, London: Weidenfeld & Nicolson, 1996.

humane. Those of us who are currently engaged in postcolonial criticism find the historical method helpful in decoding texts both sacred and secular, until now seen simply as innocent and symbolic but manifestly embodying values of high imperialism.

Recently, the Asian American cultural critic Amy Ling has reminded us that the 'tools possess neither memory nor loyalty; they are as effective as the hands wielding them' (1993: 741). Biblical interpretation brims with such instances. To take an example from the colonial archives, look at the exegetical practices of William Robertson Smith and John William Colenso. The former, a Scotsman who never ventured out of the British Isles, used the then emerging high criticism to relegate the primal religions in order to vindicate the uniqueness and divine origins of the biblical religion. Critical tools enabled him to associate indigenous religions with primitive stages which were seen as being on their way to progress and civilization. The latter, an English Anglican who worked among the Zulus in South Africa, used the same tools, and what is more, used concepts from the very primal religion which Smith saw as primitive, in order to open the texts for the Zulus. Critical methods informed Colenso, not only in coming up with a name for the Zulu God, but also in seeing parallels with Jews of old. What is more, for Colenso, the same Zulus provided cultural clues for reconstructing the religious practices of Israelites. More importantly, Zulu religiosity helped him to imagine God's love as a universal one, found in the sublime passages of other textual traditions such as those of the Hindu, Sikh and so forth. Colenso's commentary on Romans combines both Western critical methods and Zulu cultural insights, to illuminate the Pauline text for the indigenous people. I am sure there are plenty of examples in current interpretative practices as well.[3]

I also see the historical method as an ally in protecting the text. A critic's role is not only to subvert and to destabilize the text, but also to protect the text against wayward readings. The text has to be protected not because of its divine propensities but because of the danger of its being read out of its historical and cultural contexts. In this task, the use of historical critical method may not be totally disadvantageous.

Historical critical methods are invaluable for what I call creating a hermeneutics of distance. At a time when Western biblical interpretation is relentlessly seeking to bridge the so-called hermeneutical gap between the text and the reader, it may come as a surprise to some that

---

[3] See Chidester 1996: 129–40, and Draper 1999: 13–32.

I advocate a hermeneutical distance between the text and the reader. This original sin, as I call it, is worth committing. The reason being that there is already a hermeneutics of proximity in operation in many reading communities. In an effort to interpret their lives with the help of the Bible, the tendency is to flatten the difference between the biblical world and the current situation. The fusion already exists in the ordinary reader's mind. Whenever there is a personal tragedy, it is immediately likened to that of Job; or when faced with life-threatening situations, it is assumed that they are comparable to Daniel's situation, and God's intervention is expected as in the case of the Jewish hero. The ordinary reader easily identifies with Bible, biblical events and biblical characters. Though existentially we may have no difficulty in seeing the relevance of the Exodus and the Exile, we must admit that these events are not about us. There is no attempt to separate biblical times and the current situation. What the historical critical method provides is a hermeneutics of distance. Any hermeneutics based on the quest for easy biblical identity is bound to produce self-righteousness. The trouble with easy identification with the biblical event, people and motifs, is that one tends to see oneself and one's enemy in biblical stereotype: two good examples being the Zionist movement and the Afrikaners in South Africa. Such a parallelism does not give much scope for fresh dialogue and understanding. One tends to overlook the enormous political, cultural and historical differences between the present and the biblical period.

Though historical criticism was liberative, particularly to the Western, white and middle-class, it had a shackling and enslaving impact on women, blacks and people of other cultures, as the recent exegetical works of these groups have manifestly demonstrated.

To some of us the historical critical method is colonial, because of its insistence that a right reading is mediated through the proper use of historical-critical tools alone. For example, look at the opening lines of George Strecker's *The Sermon on the Mount: An Exegetical Commentary*: 'No proper exegesis of the Sermon on the Mount can ignore the results of more than two hundred years of historical research into the New Testament.'[4] Such a claim rules out, at the outset, the right of a reader or an interpreter to use any other means to understand the text, and those who do not practise the methods nor engage with them are seen as outside the circle and as outcasts. Moreover, such readings are seen as emotional and sentimental. The inference is that any culturally informed reading by an Asian or an African, or any politically

---

[4] I owe this point to Daniel Patte.

inspired reading of a Solentiname peasant, is ruled out. The peasants in Solentiname under the oppressive rule of Somoza intuitively recognized the class identity of Nicodemus, whereas David Rensberger had to plough through lexicons and commentaries to come up with the same exegetical conclusions. People with no theological training or exegetical expertise can arrive at meaning because they connect with the experience of struggle. That is to say that untrained readers arrive by intuition at a meaning which the modern scholars only reach by hard slog. In other words, because of the totalizing tendencies of the historical critical method, culturally diversified and politically informed reading will not get a look-in.

Historical tools became useful to missionary educators in their relentless aim to propagate biblical faith as historical, and as opposed to Hinduism which was seen as ahistorical and mythical. For establishing such a claim, historical-critical tools were seen as an appropriate pedagogical instrument and an ally. These missionary educators were passionately evangelical in introducing the intricacies of this wonderful instrument. Stanley Thoburn, a contributor to the Indian Christian Students' Library series, hailed it as a divine boon: 'The scientific method is one of the greatest gifts that God has given to man, and none can deny the marvellous achievements that have come through its use' (1961: 34). The pedagogical use of historical analysis as a method of reading the Bible was the hermeneutical strategy used by the commentators in this series, in order to expose their students to the errors of their own shastras and the defects of their own philosophical systems, while simultaneously enabling them to internalize the modernist virtues of objective certitude and determinacy. A historical consciousness was seen as a necessary virtue for sifting fact from legend and as a way of establishing the factual basis of the biblical faith. Listen to the words of Anthony Hanson, the British New Testament scholar who started his teaching career in India and who wrote in the same series:

> We must be willing to have our Bible examined by any reasonable standard of historical criticism, because it is then that the character of Christianity founded on real historical events will stand out clearly . . . On the other hand, events related in the Hindu Scriptures are found to be for the most part legend. (1961: 34)

Historical tools have been used to verify the truth or falsehood of the scriptures. Different cultures have different attitudes towards their sacred writings. In certain cultures, especially in India, written texts are not accorded a high status in matters of faith, and dependence upon them is viewed dimly. It may make sense to those raised in the historical critical method to ask, Did God create the world in seven days, or did Jesus multiply the loaves, or did he rise on the third day? But it does not make sense to a Hindu, to subject his or her texts to such historical questions as whether stories about Rama are true or who is the author of the *Bhagavad Gita*. It may be perfectly all right for Christians, whose belief is rooted in history and historical accounts, to ask whether New Testament references to the historical Jesus are true or not. To ask a comparable question about, say, Rama is to exhibit ignorance of other people's stories, texts and their attitude to history.

Listen to a dialogue that went on between a German writer Bichsel and an unnamed Hindu from Bali. One day the German asked the Balinese whether he believed the history of Prince Rama – one of the holy books of the Hindus – is true.

Without hesitation the Balinese answered 'Yes.'

'So you believe that the Prince Rama lived somewhere and some when?'

'I do not know if he lived,' he said.

'Then it is a story.'

'Yes, it is a story.'

'Then someone wrote this story – I mean: a human being wrote it?'

'Certainly some human being wrote it,' he said.

'Then some human being could have also invented it.' The German felt that he had triumphed, and thought that he had convinced the Indonesian.

But the Balinese said: 'It is quite possible that somebody invented this story. But true it is in any case.'

'Then it is the case that Prince Rama did not live on this earth.'

'What is it that you want to know?' the Balinese asked. '*Do you want to know whether the story is true, or merely whether it occurred?*'

'The Christians believe that their God Jesus Christ was also on Earth,' the German said. 'In the New Testament, it has been described by human beings. But the Christians believe that this is the description of the reality. Their God was really also on Earth.'

The Balinese friend thought it over and said: 'I had been already so informed. I do not understand why it is important that your God was on Earth, but it does strike me that the Europeans are not pious. Is that correct?'

'Yes it is,' said the German.

What is clear from this conversation is that the German and the Hindu had different concepts of truth and what is history. For the young Balinese his holy book remains true even though the narrative contents and events could have been fabricated and scripted by a human being. He does not know, and is not even interested in knowing whether Rama actually lived, for it does not really affect the truth of the *Ramayana*. Historical criticism would not dream of taking a stance that would make the existence of Jesus on earth irrelevant to the truth of the Bible. The Balinese is not only drawing a distinction between a story and history but also suggesting that the historicity of the *Ramayana* is irrelevant to the story being true. But to those who are raised in Indian thought patterns, the Indian epics are not fictions, nor are they facts. Interestingly, for the Balinese, to know that the Bible is true is what makes the European impious. 'Impiety is to believe that one's religion is true.' To ask, which the historical critical method tends to do, whether the stories in the Indian epics are true or false is to exhibit a profound ignorance of the culture whose stories they are. To question their truth status is to assume they are knowledge items, which they are not.[5]

Secondly, those who engage in historical criticism still believe in the authority of the text. The text is paramount and it becomes an object of scrutiny and investigation. Only through texts, it appears that the Bible could provide knowledge. In the West, knowledge is believed to reside in documents, and it is principally mediated through texts, and truth's content is textual in nature. What is vital for us is not the legitimacy of a form of Christianity embedded in the text, nor a sieved-out record of the early Christian text's relationship with the original meaning of Christianity. Instead, the text has to be judged by its ability to provide avenues of resistance, emancipation and empowerment which undermine the hegemonic discourses and establishment.

Thirdly, historical criticism was seen as a transferable pedagogic strategy to illuminate the mental darkness of Indian minds with their superstitious ways. Professor Hollenweger tells the story of John Mbiti, the first African to get a doctorate in Germany. When he went home, a great ceremony was organized to welcome him and honour his rare achievement. During the celebration a woman got possessed by a spirit. The elder said to Mbiti, 'You say that you have studied the Bible in Germany. Now cast out the evil spirit in this woman.' Mbiti said: 'Well, you all know that I studied with Bultmann, and according to him there are no evil spirits. He has demythologized all.' When the crowd heard this, they said, 'What is the use of studying in Europe? Before, you could heal. Now you can't.'

---

[5] Most of the materials in these two paragraphs are based on S. N. Balagangadhara's work. I have used freely not only his concepts but also some of his phrases and vocabularies. See Balagangadhara 1994: 408–13.

Biblical criticism as it is practised today lends support to the hypothesis that, if a reader is not conversant with the latest critical scholarship, it is his or her fault. With its exotic methods, constant shifting of scholarly opinions, and continual revision of the period-ization of biblical history, the critical enterprise has become living proof of Bernard Shaw's dictum that every profession is a conspiracy against the laity. What Joseph Parker wrote in the early days, about what then was known as the higher criticism, still rings true:

> I am jealous lest the Bible should in any sense be made a priest's book. Even Baur or Colenso may contrary to his own wishes, be almost unconsciously elevated into a literary deity under whose approving nod alone we can read the Bible with edification. It is no secret that when Baur rejected the Epistle to the Philippines as un-Pauline, Christian Europe became partially paralysed, and that when Hilgenfeld pronounced it Pauline Christian Europe resumed its prayers. Have we to wait for a communication from Tübingen, or a telegram from Oxford, before we can read the Bible?[6]

The speed with which scholarship is moving these days can make one feel miserably outdated. In a culture which instantly prostrates before the cult of the latest, biblical scholarship is responsible for those numbers swelling. Whether the latest scholarly theory has any relevance to the context is seldom addressed.

Added to this is over-specialization in the field, which has resulted in, what Said calls, the 'cult of professional expertise'. The relentless engagement in fruitless historical pursuits and theories has made biblical scholars marginal to what is going on in their own societies. Said's solution is fully applicable to biblical scholars as well. He calls for an amateurism of approach which does away with 'priestly' and abstruse speculations, and advocates engagement in worldly causes:

> However much intellectuals pretend that their representations are of higher things or ultimate values, morality begins with their activity in this secular world of ours – where it takes place, whose interests it serves, how it jibes with a consistent and universalistic ethic, how it discriminates between power and justice, what it reveals of one's choices and priorities. (Said 1994: 89)

What is needed is a type of critical practice that will not only go beyond literary-historical activity, but will place scholarship well within the grasp of the reading public, and will significantly place

---

[6] Cited in Neil 1963: 286.

scholarship at the service of the people and their day-to-day social and political concerns.

Global Village and Third World Biblical Critics

The problem for us in the global village is not what we do with historical criticism, its usefulness or its non-usefulness. What concerns Third World hermeneuts is the systematic editing-out of their work. Mainstream scholarship often acted repressively and prohibitively towards Third World biblical discourse. What I see here is the hermeneutical strategy of negation at work. David Spurr, who has mapped out the different rhetorical strategies of Western thinking to deal with other cultures, defines negation as a strategy

[b]y which Western writing conceives of the Other as absence, emptiness, nothingness, or death. This exploration leads to the formulation of two principles; first, the negation serves to reject the ambiguous object for which language and experience provide no adequate framework of interpretation; second, . . . negation acts as a kind of provincial erasure, clearing a space for the expansion of the colonial imagination and the pursuit of desire. (Spurr 1993: 93)

The efforts of Asian and African and Latin American thinkers during the colonial period and later are either ignored or seen as not worthy of any serious attention by Western biblical scholars. There is a tendency to overlook the long tradition of biblical interpretation. I have in mind some of the efforts of the Indians during the Empire days. There are comparable examples in other countries as well. For instance, even long before Albert Schweitzer embarked on the modern search for the historical Jesus, Raja Rammohun Roy was engaged in such a task, although he did not identify his investigation in those terms. In his *Precepts of Jesus: The Guide to Peace and Happiness* (1820), employing his own version of the reader-response criticism which is currently in vogue in biblical scholarship, he was indeed searching for a historical Jesus who was a moral guide. Hong Xiuquan's reworking of Mark's Gospel during the Taiping revolution; Matsumura Kaiseki's editing-out of canonical material and the production of his own version known as the Dokkai Bible; the appropriation of the Bible by the Harrist and Aladura movements, and the hermeneutical presuppositions of such attempts, were overlooked or sidelined. Unfortunately, the efforts of these people were not seen as sophisticated enough to be studied within biblical disciplines, but were relegated to church history, mission studies or practical theology and not offered their

proper place in biblical studies. My intention is not to be triumphalis-
tic and say that we in the Third World attempted all these hermeneutical pursuits, but to serve as a reminder that there is a long
tradition of biblical discourse which has been eclipsed not only by the
dominant biblical scholarship in the West but sadly also by our Third
World theological institutions.

The current changing scenario at the global level has serious implications for Third World hermeneutics. First, there is a slow but per-
ceptible fragmentation of Western theologies. The Western theologies
which invaded our space, and took upon themselves the mantle to
speak for all, have lost their nerve. This has occurred either through
postmodern fragmentation or through vigorous internal critiquing.
Western theologies have become more regional, autobiographical
and confessional. A typical example is the recent issue of *Semeia* on
autobiographical criticism, wherein every contributor started by
stating his or her social location, sexuality and the constituency which
she or he was aiming at or addressing. If hermeneutics is seen as
something personal and an isolated enterprise, where then is the
room for dialogue and mutual critiquing? Third World hermeneutics,
especially the liberation variety, arose as a way of critiquing the
universalistic and eurocentric, individualistic, patriarchal and anti-
environmental tendencies of these Western theologies. Now we have
been pushed further to the periphery in the name of postmodern
celebration of the local and the different.

The second implication for Third World hermeneutics is the postmodern prohibition against subject-centred enquiry. Postmodernism,
among other things, is suspicious of representation, agency and self-
identity. Why is it that, at a time when previously silenced people
have begun to script their own stories and speak for themselves, the
West celebrates the death of the author and proclaims that the mega-
stories are over. The West is currently experiencing the loss of grand
discourse and is frowning at the idea of the power of agency, at a time
when the subalterns are trying to make their stories heard. The
Postmodern Bible, produced by the cultural collective, with its under-
estimation of grand stories and unsigned articles, is an example of the
current trend in the West. At a time when postcolonial theorists are
trying to recover subaltern histories and stories, we are informed that
there is no history to be narrated or stories to be told.

Finally, there is a passionate call for ethical interpretation and the
involvement of the biblical critic in the ongoingness of life. I have no
problem with that and I warmly support it, but at the same time, I
would like to acknowledge that we as biblical critics have only a

limited role. Sometimes we become grandiose about our function and aims. Theologians often assume the role of legislators, and expect that their hermeneutical treaties will change the world. The task of the hermeneut is not to change the world but to understand it. Hermeneutics does not create revolution; it changes people's perceptions and makes them aware of the need for revolution. Its function is to make people see more, feel more, rekindle the fire of resistance.

References

Balagangadhara, S. N., 1994. *'The Heathen in His Blindness . . .': Asia, the West and the Dynamic of Religion*, Leiden: Brill.

Chidester, David, 1996. *Savage Systems: Colonialism and Comparative Religion in Southern Africa*, Charlottesville: University Press of Virginia.

Draper, Jonathan A., 1999. 'Hermeneutical Drama on the Colonial Stage: Liminal Space and Creativity in Colenso's Commentary on Romans', *Journal of Theology for Southern Africa* 103 (March 1999): 13–32.

Hanson, Anthony T., 1961. *Jonah and Daniel: Introduction and Commentary*, The Christian Students' Library, 9, Madras: The Christian Literature Society.

Ling, Amy, 1993. ' "I" am Here', in Robyn R. Warhol and Diane Price Hernd (eds), *Feminisms: Anthology of Literary Theory*, New Brunswick: Rutgers University Press.

Neil, W., 1963. 'The Criticism and Theological Use of the Bible, 1700–1950', in S. L. Greenslade (ed.), *The Cambridge History of the Bible: The West from the Reformation to the Present Day*, Cambridge: Cambridge University Press.

Said, Edward W., 1994. *Representations of the Intellectual*, London: Vintage.

Spurr, David, 1993. *The Rhetoric of Empire: Colonial Discourse in Journalism, Travel Writing, and Imperial Administration*, Durham, N.C.: Duke University Press.

Thoburn, S. 1961. *Old Testament Introduction*, The Christian Students' Library, 24, Madras: The Christian Literature Society.

6

Getting the Mixture Right

Promises and Perils of Postcolonial Criticism and Biblical Interpretation

We need the theories. They may be false, but they focus inquiry.

Ninian Smart[1]

I am not a theorist – I follow my nose.

Harold Pinter[2]

This chapter will fall into four parts. First, I will try to establish a case for the relevance of postcolonialism in the twenty-first century when colonies have largely disappeared. Secondly, I will try to address the issue as to why there is a reluctance among biblical scholars to employ postcolonialism as a critical tool. Thirdly, I will highlight the areas where postcolonialism and biblical studies can productively engage with each other. Fourthly, I will highlight some of the areas post-colonialism still has to address, and will end not with a summary but with a hermeneutical issue which has been vexing some of us who are in the business of reading and interpreting.

Neo-Imperial Urge

Recently, the notion of empire has been making an entry into public discourse through public pronouncements. Some politicians, civil servants and public intellectuals have been plainly advocating the usefulness and advantages of recolonization. There is a proposal to resurrect colonialism as a possible remedy for global ills. The much-maligned word 'empire' is being replaced with a new lexicon of 'reordering'. At the October 2001 party conference, the British Prime

---

[1] Ninian Smart, 'Intellectual Crisis of British Christianity', *Theology* 68 (535) (1965): 37.
[2] *The Guardian Review*, 12.10.02, p. 17.

Minister Tony Blair came out with his own version of moral imperialism in the face of global terror through a reordering of disastrous,
unsuccessful and wretched parts of the world by force if necessary.[3]
But a much more sinister idea was advocated by one of his former
foreign-policy makers, Robert Cooper. Cooper's contention is that
there is a greater need for colonialism now than there was in the nineteenth century. In his reckoning, in the pre-modern states, often the
former colonies, where the state has failed, and which pose a threat to
the postmodern nations, 'all the conditions for imperialism are there'
(Cooper 2002: 17).[4] What is needed in the face of these threats is a new
kind of imperialism – a postmodern imperialism which accommo-
dates human-rights issues and cosmopolitan values, and which 'like
all imperialism aims to bring order and organization but which rests
today on the voluntary principle' (Cooper 2002: 18). What Cooper
calls 'voluntary imperialism' (2002: 18), or 'co-operative empire'
(2002: 19) is in fact an uncompelled scheme under which nations get
together with their neighbours, the strong with the weaker. This is a
world in which 'the weak still need the strong and the strong still need
an orderly world' (Cooper 2002: 19) which is efficient, stable, well-
governed and, most significantly, open for Western investment and
economic growth. Such a commonwealth, according to Cooper, will,
like Rome, provide 'its citizens with some of its laws, some coins, and
the occasional road' (2002: 19).

Since September 11, there has been a concerted call to revive
imperial practice by the US and its allies. They have been asked to
make a transition from the informal imperial agreement of the post-
war era to an enforcement of direct 'international colonial' supremacy
over villainous nations which threaten the Western way of life. One
person who is at the forefront of such an argument is the conservative
Oxford historian Niall Ferguson. In an article in *The Guardian* in the
aftermath of September 11, Ferguson counselled America that 'transition to formal empire from informal empire is an affordable one'.[5] In
his recent book, Ferguson has urged the USA to follow the example of
the Victorian imperialists who had no compunction in overthrowing
rogue states from Oudh to Abyssinia, and introducing commerce and

---

[3] See *The Guardian*, headline dated 3.10.01, 'Let us reorder this world'. For
Tony Blair's full speech, see pp. 4, 5.
[4] See also his article, 'Why We Still Need Empires', in *The Observer*, 7.4.02,
p. 27.
[5] Niall Ferguson, 'Welcome the New Imperialism', *The Guardian*, 31.10.01,
p. 20.

Christianity. It is now the turn of the USA to do the same by sorting out bad regimes and terrorism, and spreading the gospel of democracy and free trade. He exhorts the Americans by reminding them of Kipling's poem 'The White Man's Burden', which the sainted colonialist wrote in 1899 to persuade them to accept their imperial responsibilities (Ferguson 2003: 366). In the USA, the right-wing commentator Charles Krauthammer has spoken about the 'US' uniquely benign imperium', and proclaimed America as the new Rome: 'The fact is, no country has been as dominant culturally, economically, technologically and militarily in the history of the world since the Roman empire.'[6]

In this call for the renewal of empire, other public intellectuals have also entered the scene with enthusiasm. Recently, there has been a spate of books and TV series to 'set the record straight'.[7] Charles Allen's *The Buddha and the Sahibs: The Men who discovered India's Lost Religion*, William Dalrymple's *White Mughals: Love and Betrayal in Eighteenth-Century India*, and Niall Ferguson's TV series and book *Empire: How Britain Made the Modern World*, are notable examples of the current revisionist exercise. In this revisionist history, the rise of the British empire has nothing to do with the Protestant work ethic or Western individualism but is all to do with the 'British sweet tooth' (Ferguson 2003: 14). Even in Australia there is a public debate going on as to how to view colonial history.[8] Serious historians, too, have joined the fray. Nicholas Dirks has shown in his recent analysis how a colonial historiography produced by erudite scholars of the Cambridge school of Indian historians and the celebrated volumes of the *Oxford History of the British Empire*, work on the premise that 'colonial conquest and rule were fragile at best' and 'that neither colonial power nor knowledge was really so bad' (Dirks 2002: 311).

This is not the place to evaluate their work, nor am I the right person to do it, but I think a few comments are in order.

This gentler form of imperialism is an old call to bring order and organization to states which are seen as barbarous and semi-anarchic in the interests of capitalism and corporate interests. This is a concerted attempt by politically correct right-wing pundits to rewrite history and make empire an acceptable beast, a lovable rogue. These

---

[6] Quoted in Jonathan Freedland, 'Rome, AD . . . Rome, DC?', *The Guardian*, G2, 18.9.02, p. 2. Freedland's article draws striking similarities between the old Roman imperium and the current imperialistic tendencies of the USA.

[7] See Allen 2002: 7.

[8] David Fickling, 'One Country, Two Histories', *The Guardian*, 17.1.03, p. 19.

conservative interpreters are offering a counter-narrative to those unsporting critics who keep on emphasizing the cruder aspects of empire – land-seizures, genocides, economic exploitation and racial and sexual violence. They claim that the benefits the empire bestowed on its subjects outweigh its nasty side, which was merely a matter of flaws and mistakes. They project education, democracy, transport, fostering of globalization, overseas investment, free trade, many examples of social alliances and cultural cooperation between different peoples, and above all the raising of levels of prosperity all around, as the great boons of the empire. Possibly there is some truth in all this. What makes these efforts basically erroneous is their failure to acknowledge the basic presupposition of all empires, whether Roman or British, of a superior race ruling over inferior ones. To recall the atrocities of empire is not to stand in judgement on the earlier generations but to remind ourselves that even well-run empires are brutal and murderous. 'Let's not forget', as the historian Maria Misra jogged our memory recently, 'that Leopold's central African empire was originally called the International Association for Philanthropy in Congo.'[9] Interestingly, only those from the former colonial nations are saying the empire was attractive, efficient and exemplary, barring a few aberrations. They refuse to understand how the formerly colonized themselves perceive the European 'discovery' of their lands and peoples. Orientalists were not involved in a neutral, scientific enterprise in the 'European Age of discovery'. Discourses which celebrate the contributions of Orientalists without taking into account the colonial violence against which their narrative unfolds are dubious. Moreover, more recently, the much-hyped globalization and free market fail to acknowledge the devastating impact these have on local indigenous industries which have neither the political nor the economic clout to compete with giant corporations. The result is the destruction of communities and their sources of income and way of life.

In the face of this new imperial renaissance, postcolonial critique has become necessary and indeed paramount to resist any selective reading of history or romanticization of the past. To quote Nicholas Dirks:

> Postcoloniality might then remind us of the fact that history, culture, and modernity have always been corrupt, invariably predicated on violence and domination, the terms of conquest for colonization itself . . . Postcolonial history is the epic story of seduc-

⁹ Maria Misra, 'Heart of Smugness', *The Guardian*, 23.7.02, p. 15.

tion and betrayal, destined to repeat itself again and again, even as it seeks to put the colonial past behind, for all time. But it also teaches us there is no going back, to a time when tradition, or identity or civilization might be recuperated whole. To think otherwise would be to open history to other forms of seduction and betrayal. And that would leave us all without any of the lessons history might still be able to teach. (Dirks 2002: 315)

When neo-colonial relations are being forged increasingly between Western nations and their former colonies, postcolonialism continues to be an effective and a necessary analytical and discursive tool.

Failing to Catch the 'Post': Postcolonialism and Biblical Interpretation

Although postcolonialism has made a considerable impact on a number of disciplines it has not penetrated deeply into mainstream biblical scholarship. There, it still remains a minority exercise. There may be a number of reasons for this marginalization. One could be the conservativism of the discipline. The discipline is still governed by the historical-critical method. Its supposed neutrality and objectivity are seen as venerable virtues. Any political and ideological reading is seen as an unhealthy intrusion into the discipline.

Second could be diffidence among biblical scholars to make their work relevant to the contemporary situation. A typical example is the construals of Jesus by the current Jesus Seminar. The significance of Jesus that they come up with lies in portraying him as an odd, discomforting and politically disinterested figure who is an embarrassment both to conservatives and to radicals. What Robert Grant said long ago, that biblical scholars did not 'sell their birthright as critics and historians for what has been called a "pot of message"', is still true for today. He identified two seductions which biblical scholars should avoid – 'the craving for instant relevance', and 'the academic temptation to contribute mere sound to "the current discussion"' (Grant 1968: 50).

The third and perhaps most pertinent reason for the failure of postcolonialism to make any impact on biblical scholarship could be that postcolonialism as a critical category emerged at a time when there was a general fatigue among scholars with regard to theory. There is a sense of exhaustion about too much theory-chasing and a suspicion that these theories will add nothing to what is already in the texts. Theories are seen not only as arcane but also as spoiling the act of reading for pleasure. To paraphrase Saul Bellow, theories tend to reduce masterpieces to discourse. Our task and our business is to read them and not employ theories to dissect and analyse and read ideas into them. What biblical scholarship has to realize is that the importance of critical theories increases when reading and interpreting of biblical texts becomes professionalized and the Bible is offered as a subject in secular academic institutions. An inevitable outcome of this repositioning is the added significance of critical theories and the fruitful employment of them.

The Asian theological scene is no more encouraging than the Western. Postcolonialism as a critical category has not fared well in the Third World. Except for a few scholars such as Archie Lee and Angela Wong working in Hong Kong, and a couple of articles in the *Bangalore Theological Forum*, there is total silence. At least three reasons could be attributed to this. One, most Asian theological colleges are free-standing institutions with no other academic departments and disciplines associated with them. There is no dialogue with other secular and liberal departments where theories are forged, tested and discussed.

Two, most Christians in India come from the depressed classes and are the beneficiaries of the colonial civilizing mission. They only saw the kinder side of colonialism, through schools, medical work and development projects, hence the reluctance to raise awkward questions about the colonial enterprise.

Third, and most significantly, biblical interpretation in Asia, and especially in India, is still consumed and determined by the nineteenth-century colonial debate between Orientalists and Anglicists. At the time of the introduction of colonial education in India, the Orientalists advocated vernacular languages and indigenous methods whereas the Anglicists insisted on English and Western sciences as a way of modernizing India. Thus the same debate – whether to use indigenous or imported methods, which dominated the upper strata of Indian society – continues to be replicated in multifarious ways, and continues to dominate and direct critical thought in biblical interpretation. The result is that we have advocates who want to refine biblical interpretation by employing Western methods, and others who want to revive indigenous reading practices to energize hermeneutics.

Turning to indigenous methods has not yielded any profitable reading, but has only served to spread revivalist tendencies. To begin with, the older Sanskritic texts which expound these indigenous methods, and good translations of them, are not easily accessible for interpreters. The net result is that an Indian theological student is not familiar with these methods. What G. N. Devy said in a literary context is equally applicable to biblical interpretation: '[An Indian interpreter] may show an emotional solidarity with the cause of Indian criticism, but at the same time the student may not be able to mention even one Indian text of literary criticism with any degree of familiarity, excepting those texts which are the most contemporary' (Devy 2002: xii).

Moreover, modern India has moved on from the intellectual tradition which produced such reading practices. Critical methods at best evolve out of and for specific hermeneutical and contextual needs, and as such a current interpreter cannot have a meaningful and extensive intellectual relationship with fifth- or twelfth-century Sanskritic critical tradition. The Indian literary critic Patankar's forewarning of the formidable obstacles in using vernacular methods is worth heeding:

> But nobody would analyse a modern Indian play on the basis of the Sanskrit structuring principles of *sandhis* and *sahdhyangas*. Nor do we get a detailed analysis and evaluation of a modern play in terms of *ālambana* and *vibhāvas*, *anubhāva*, *uddipana* and *vyabhicaribhavas*. Occasionally, we run into a critic who says that a particular novel is suffused with a *karuna rasa* . . . If the modern critic's responses do not spontaneously get articulated in the old Sanskrit theories, if these theories are not already there in the womb of the creative and critical process of a modern man, then theories cannot legitimately claim to be part of our today. (Patankar 2002: 392)

A few attempts made by Indian biblical interpreters to use *rasa* and *dhvani* methods of interpretation remain within a group of specialists, and there is not much awareness of their exegetical attempts outside the circle. This turning away or turning back to vernacular methods has not only resulted in being too nationalistic but has also failed to move the debate forward and has thwarted any chance of Indian hermeneutics keeping abreast with contemporary thinking.

Certainly there is nothing wrong in using Indian methods or calling oneself Indian or Sri Lankan or Chinese and being proud about it. But what one needs to realize is that Sri Lankanness or Indianness are fluid concepts and are constantly changing. Twenty-first-century Indians or Sri Lankans may have little in common with those Indians and Sri Lankans who were part of Sanskrit and Pali tradition. One doesn't have to carry three thousand years' baggage with one. In other words, as Patankar warns, one should be circumspect in drawing from an ancient heritage which one has moved on from, and in some cases outgrown. In his view, 'asking us to use theories like that of *rasa* will be a form of cultural tyranny' (Patankar 2002: 393).

Biblical interpretation which has emerged from the peoples who were once colonized has been called variously 'Third World', 'Nativist','Liberationist' and 'Contextual'. At least in four respects, a 'Postcolonial' approach has advantages over these models. First, it brings to the fore the historical and cultural reality of colonialism. Second, it draws attention to the effects of colonization and colonial ideals on interpretative works. Third, it engages in reconstructive reading from the perspective of postcolonial concerns, and fourth, it recognizes not only the dubiousness of the colonial past but also the dubiousness of the contemporary world order in the form of global-ization and its neo-colonizing tendencies.

The Current Captivity

There are at least three marks of current biblical scholarship for which postcolonialism can offer correctives. One is Europeanization, the second is racialization, and the third is the negation of 'the other'.

Europeanization

There is a Europeanization of biblical scholarship. This means putting Europe at the centre – theoretically, politically, racially, and, for our purpose, theologically. For instance, in exegetical and interpretative writings there is a tendency to make Christianity a European faith. The history of the missionary activities in Acts is of course predomi-nantly the history of the gospel leaving its original Jewish environ-ment and reaching Europe. My criticism is that the commentators make too much of this. Listen to the words of David Edwards: 'Within these years (i.e. AD 30–AD 60) Christianity ceases to be a belief held by a few Jews in Palestine. It becomes global: the world religion which is to be the chief foundation of Europe, and which is to spread across the Atlantic and wherever Europeans go' (Edwards 1975: 9).

Ernst Haenchen, whose commentary on Acts has reached canonical status, goes on to reinforce such an idea. Chapter 15 is of course a turning-point, the 'centerpiece' and 'watershed' of the book (Haenchen 1971: 461), but for Haenchen this is because it covers the crucial decision regarding the Gentile mission, 'whose goal is, of course, Europe'. He further claims that it is not without reason that

Asia Minor is dismissed in three verses (16.6–8). Paul's travelling from Troas to Macedonia is 'heavily underscored' (Haenchen 1971: 461). Haenchen's proposition is that now Paul is seen as the chosen 'instrument of Christ' and at the Apostolic Council he wins his battle against his Judaist opponents, and gets high praise in the Apostolic Decree. 'This recognition', according to Haenchen, 'legitimizes the great work to which Paul now sets his hand: the founding of the European Gentile Church' (Haenchen 1971: 462).

From now on, the focus changes, and the future of the advancement of the gospel is placed within the rubric of world mission, whose epicentre is to be Europe. Now, the focus is not Jerusalem or even her daughter congregation, Antioch, but the European cities such as 'Macedonia, Athens, Corinth, Ephesus: these will be the new landmarks in the history of the mission' (Haenchen 1971: 462). West Asian regions such as Syria and Cilicia, which Paul and Silas traversed, are seen as backward, lawless places 'heavily infected by Oriental paganism' – the type of territory not suitable for Paul to exercise his 'characteristic ministry'. What attracted Paul to Europe? Its imperial infrastructures, its law and order and its roads. Here is the conjecture of one commentator:

> His vision of a victorious gospel embraced the Roman world. He saw the great totalitarian state knit into a mighty whole from Palestine to Spain by the authority of the Emperor and the reverence for him which was later to be exalted into a religion. He saw the strong-points, the strategic bases, held by the legions. He saw the network of roads which ensured their mobility, and which passed as arteries of trade, culture, and defence through all the wide provinces from the Thames to the Nile. It fascinated him, the conscious object of his life was the capture of those strategic bases for Christ. His projected visit to Spain (Rom. 15:24, 28), and his eagerness to reach Rome itself, are related to this preoccupation. (Blaiklock 1964: 125)

European mission needs a European. The next move is to make Paul a European. F. F. Bruce asks the question: How come a faith originated in Asia became associated with Europe and European civilization? The answer is, through Paul, who had 'inherited a large measure of Hellenistic culture and the coveted privilege of Roman citizenship' (Bruce 1965: 209). Blaiklock goes even further and endows him with European manners and culture. He projects Paul as the man who has caught 'the flavour of western thought' and learned 'to appreciate the Greco-Roman outlook' (Blaiklock 1964: 84). And what is more, Paul has 'logic in his mode of argument' which was 'not the fruit of Hebrew mysticism' (Blaiklock 1964: 84). It was the motifs inherited from Hellenistic culture which made him the founder of Western Christian theology. It is not the ageing rural and illiterate Jewish apostles Peter and James who are going to play the crucial role, but the diasporic, urban and European Paul who will 'bear the weight of the world mission' (Haenchen 1971: 462).

The conversion of the Ethiopian takes place early in the Lukan narrative because its context is the mission to Judaism, with which the eunuch is identified. But the consequences and significance of this black man's conversion are not followed up, thanks to a convenient theological contention that Paul's missionary vocation is the one thing that matters. Mainstream biblical scholarship tends to seize upon Luke's missiological plan, focused on making Paul the evangelist for Europe, to the marginalization of such a figure as the Ethiopian. Incidentally, the legend has it that it was this Ethiopian who brought the gospel to Sri Lanka.

Racialization

At least two current studies have shown how racialization has entered into Western biblical scholarship by means of intellectual resources employed by those scholars who helped to shape the discipline. Shawn Kelley's main contention is that modern biblical scholarship 'has been influenced by the category of race' (Kelley 2002: 5). This influence, according to him, is sometimes sophisticated and at times scheming and deep. The reason for this racialization is due to these intellectual resources. Current biblical scholarship is constrained and directed by three intellectual movements – Hegelianism, Heideggerianism and Romanticism. As long as scholarship is rooted in these intellectual and philosophical frameworks, it will remain embedded in racial tendencies. Kelley, in his work, has paid particular attention to three influential schools: the Tübingen School, which was intensely Hegelian; Bultmann and his students, who were clearly Heideggerian existentialists; and the parable-scholarship of Funk and Crossan, who were indebted to Heideggerianism and Romanticism. Kelley is particularly critical of the 'New Hermeneutic' movement, which was very influential in the American biblical scholarship in the 1960s and which took over Bultmann's racialist ideas – his existential anthropology, his views on authenticity, temporality and 'the they' – without modifying their racial overtones. Kelley writes: 'The problem facing current scholarship, I wish to reiterate, is one of objectionable intellectual resources rather than of flawed intentions. Current scholarship remains racialized because its intellectual resources pull it in that direction, not because its practitioners necessarily want to affirm white supremacy. If the problem is one of resources rather than intention, then the solution comes by turning elsewhere for intellectual sustenance' (Kelley 2002: 225).

Similarly, Halvor Moxnes has demonstrated how colonialism, nationalism, race and ethnicity, as categories of identity, had a significant bearing on geographical studies of Galilee at the time of Jesus, in nineteenth-century biblical scholarship in Germany. The leading figures in this construction were F. Schleiermacher, D. F. Strauss and E. Renan. Moxnes has shown how these scholars, influenced by the racial ideologies of the time, came up with Galilee as a non-Jewish region and the home of a non-Jewish Jesus. This ideological paradigm was unintentionally carried on in the twentieth century by New Testament scholarship which did not show any interest in the geographic regions of Palestine. A typical representative of this position is E. P. Sanders, for whom Galilee was not unique religiously, socially or politically.[10]

Negation of 'the other'

Another mark one notes in current biblical scholarship is that of negation of 'the other'. Negation as a discursive device 'serves to reject the ambiguous object for which language and experience provide no adequate framework of interpretation' and acts as 'a clearing space for the expansion of the colonial imagination and for the pursuit of desire' (Spurr 1994: 92–3). There is a tendency among biblical scholars to either discard or diminish the African and Asian presence in the biblical texts. They are inclined to declare geographical areas which cover biblical accounts as culturally and theologically sealed-off areas, and are reluctant to accept that biblical writers could have been influenced by non-Jewish or non-Hellenistic ideas. Randall Bailey has observed that when looking at the geography of the biblical period, 'one gets the impression that other than Syria-Palestine, the Arabian Peninsula, and Mesopotamia, there is no other part of the ancient world to be considered in relation to the history of ancient Israel' (Bailey 1991: 166). The vigorous efforts of recent African-American scholarship have been able to rectify this distortion and make main-

---

[10] See Moxnes 2001a; 2001b.

stream scholarship recognize and acknowledge the existence and contribution of Africans to the biblical canon.[11]

Although there is evidence of Buddhist and Hindu presences in the Mediterranean world during the formative years of Christianity, this presence is hardly recognized. Whereas Indologists have long argued and provided evidence for intercultural exchanges between these two regions, biblical scholars behave as if nothing worthwhile could have come from outside Hebraic and Hellenistic thinking. One notable case in point is the current 'Jesus Seminar', which has conveniently and persistently avoided the questions related to the possibility of Eastern presence and its influence on the development of early Christianity. An exception among the 'Jesus Seminar' participants is Marcus Borg. He has published a volume of parallel sayings of the Buddha and Jesus. This sayings collection is the result of Borg's spiritual journey, which went through various stages from an exclusive Christianity, to scepticism, to religious pluralism. Borg makes it clear that his enterprise was 'not to make a scholarly case for similarity' (1997: xvi). This was based on his instincts rather than on any academic reasoning. For him, one Enlightened Master borrowing from the other is 'unlikely and unnecessary' (1997: xiii). His newly found open stance does not prevent Borg from taking a pot shot at the Buddha. Admitting that he is not a scholar of Buddhism, he engages in an old-fashioned Christian-biased comparative hermeneutics and finds that the Buddha lacked the 'political and social passion' (1997: xi) which Jesus possessed. What Borg fails to note is that the young Gotama began his career in criticizing the caste-based Brahminical social structure of his day. After his Enlightenment, the Buddha did not 'stay back to enjoy his solitudinal bliss, but returned to the society he once repudiated, and began to preach a dhamma which opened up a new vision and a new path invariably in conflict with the existing order. The new system of social values that the Dhamma contained came alive not only in the verbal formulation of the Master but also in the personal style of his social involvement' (Pieris 1984: 7). The Buddha's teachings on social questions, varying from the immorality of the caste system to the duties of the state, are found in his didactic and mythical discourses (Pieris 1984: 11). The social and political dimension of the Buddhism known as 'Engaged Buddhism', which sought to combine theory and praxis, had a great impact on countries like Sri Lanka,

---

[11] The literature is too vast to be recalled here. A useful entry to the discussion is Cain Hope Felder, *Stony the Road We Trod: African American Biblical Interpretation*, Minneapolis: Fortress Press, 1991.

Vietnam, Japan, Tibet and Taiwan even before Latin American liberation theology emerged on the scene (Queen and King 1996).[12]

Borg's explanation of the Buddha's lack of social conscience was
that, unlike Jesus, he was not from the peasant class. The passion for
justice, in Borg's view, 'comes from the experience of injustice' (Borg
1997: xii). This view advances the case of the now discredited identity-
politics which resorts to personal experience as a special access to
truth.

R. C. Amore has established that both masters – the Buddha and
Jesus – share a common message, that they urge their disciples to
strive for purity of mind free from anger, greed, lust and anxiety. In
Amore's view, after Jesus' death, it was the Indian notion of *avatar*
which helped the early Christian communities to interpret the event:

> The doctrines of the preexistence of Jesus, the stories about his birth
> and infancy, and the belief in his return to heaven followed the
> Buddhist model. This avatar pattern was combined with other
> interpretations of Jesus derived from Jewish expectations: Messiah,
> Son of Man, Descendant of David, and so forth. I suggest that the
> Buddhist avatar model helped Christianity transform the Jewish
> messiah concept into a saviour figure that was understandable to
> the gentiles. Among the non-Jews of the West it enabled Christian-
> ity to compete successfully with the old Hellenistic and Roman
> cults as well as with the new Mithra religion of the Roman empire.
> (Amore 1978: 185)

The Buddhist influence is not confined to the Gospels alone. Its
presence is evident in other parts of the New Testament. A conspicuous instance is James 3.6. A phrase in this verse – 'wheel of nature' or
its alternative, 'wheel of birth' – has caused considerable difficulties to
exegetes. The phrase does not have any Jewish association. It is clear
that if there is any influence of Eastern ideas, it is here that it is visibly
prominent. The phrase, the 'wheel of birth' has deep associations with
Hindu–Buddhist tradition, and suggests birth and rebirth.

Postcolonialism has been good at disrupting discourses which are
racialized, nationalistic and identity-bound. Current postcolonial
theorizing about racism, and its analytical concept, hybridity, can
release biblical scholarship from its misguided notion of euro-

---

[12] For parallels between Latin American liberation theology and Engaged
Buddhism, John D'Arcy May, 'What do Socially Engaged Buddhists and
Christian Liberation Theologians Have to Say to One Another?', *Dialogue* 21
(1994): 1–18.

centrism, its erroneous concept of race, and its deluded state of insularity. Postcolonial racial theories have dealt most significantly with the contradictions and ambivalence of racial purity. It can help biblical scholarship to jettison its unsavoury allegiances to Romanticism, Hegelianism and the existentialism espoused by Heidegger.

The postcolonial analytical category, hybridity, with its accent on mixed cultural legacies and fruitful cross-pollination of cultures, can offer a compelling case for having a re-look at the biblical geography. It will enable those biblical scholars who have painted an insular, monocultural and culturally wholesome character for biblical lands to situate them within a multiplicity of cultural possibilities and perspectives, and view them as a complex landscape of many cultures. The postcolonial concept of hybridity as an analytical vehicle will challenge and resist fictitious notions of cultural purity and authenticity claimed for biblical cultures by speaking of texts, culture, race and history as fluid and amalgamated. It will liberate Christian discourse from its habitual binary division of us and them. It will help to free biblical discourse from its Orientalistic tendencies and prevent colonial clichés from creeping into it. Postcolonialism will prove to be a vigorous and egalitarian ally for biblical scholarship, which otherwise positively reeks with conservative tendencies and racial flair.

Future Concerns

I have, among other things, two concerns about postcolonialism. One is about its accessibility, and the other is its relation to religions. Postcolonial criticism has so far functioned at two levels: at the high level of theorizations, critical studies in books and journal articles and presentations at academic guilds; and at the middle level in the form of pedagogical sessions in classrooms, graduate seminars and term papers. It has yet to reach the level it ought to reach – the people. Gwen Fielding, an English nurse, a character in Sanjay Nigam's diasporic novel *Transplanted Man* who gave up studying English literature and took up nursing, sums up the frustration: '"When I was in grad school, I went to a seminar where two professors got into a fierce debate over whether a new term *post-somethingism*, ought to be hyphenated. The argument went on and on – to the point of absurdity. That was when I realized how much I *needed* the opposite of all abstraction. I wanted to use my hands, touch people, care for them"' (Nigam 2002: 53). Readers, even graduate students, are unable to plough through the convoluted language and the impenetrable prose in which the discourse is written. The result is not so much the death of the author but the death of reading itself. It was Sivanandan, the Sri Lankan Marxist, who said that 'the people we were fighting for should be the people we were writing for' (Sivanandan 1994: vi). If postcolonialism is to reach a broader audience, and if it is to be interesting and stimulating to non-specialists, then it ought to listen to the words of the Palestinian poet, Rashid Husayn:

> No one taught you to read Mother!
> But all taught you not to read,
> That is why
> I always try
> to set my poems
> in simple words.[13]

My other concern is the reluctance of postcolonial critics to discuss the question of religion. Postcolonialism, as we have seen earlier, is good at dealing with race and gender, but less so with faith. In a multi-cultural society, people are being classified in terms of these religious affiliations. In the Huntingtonian vision of civilizational clash, the clash is going to be between Western civilization and Islamic, Buddhist and Hindu civilizations. The old liberal progressive view that with industrialization, education and wealth, a secular world will emerge, has proved to be false. In fact, the opposite is happening. Far from a withering away of religions, what we are witnessing is a vibrant emergence of religions which at times is virulent. We have presidents who have Bible studies before cabinet meetings, couch their public speeches with biblical allusions and, more alarmingly, are keen to promote a 'biblical world view'. President Bush's favourite book is 'the Bible – a good political handbook'.[14]

The pioneers of postcolonial discourse come from the Islamic world – Albert Memmi from Tunisia, Frantz Fanon from Algeria and Edward Said from Palestine – but rarely do their writings reflect the potency of religions in these regions. Said's own preference for secular criticism over theological has a different provenance, rooted in his wariness of religious fundamentalism in general and Zionist exclusivism in particular. In his scathing attack on Michael Walzer's *Exodus and Revolution*, Said is baffled by Walzer's 'astonishing reliance upon God'. For Said, there is no way to distinguish between the

---

[13] Quoted in Amitav Kumar, *Passport Photos*, Berkeley: University of California Press, 2000, p. 226.

[14] Ed Vulliamy, 'The President Rides out', *The Observer Review*, 26.1.03, p. 2.

claims put forward by competing monotheistic clergies – Ayatollah Khomeini, Ayatollah Begin, Ayatollah Gemayel and the Falwells, the Swaggerts, and the Farrakhans (Said 2001: 177). While conceding that religions provide certitude and solidarity, Said's view is that religion 'furnishes us with systems of authority and with canons of order' (Said 1983: 290) whose effect is to coerce submission or agressive conversion of others. In such a situation, Said advocates 'a secular and human vision, one based on the idea of human history not being the result of divine intervention but a much slower process than the politics of identity usually allow'.[15] In Western discourse secular values espoused by the Enlightenment have become the benchmark to evaluate religions. In this comparative exercise, Christianity scores very positively and Islam is seen as lagging behind. Its moribund state is attributed to a lack of individual and intellectual growth and its failure to go through a Christian-style Reformation. After September 11, Western commentators have been habitually pointing out that Islam as a faith is locked in a medieval mindset. The subtext here is that with the Reformation and Enlightenment savagery and tolerance have been banished from Western Christendom. Those who are familiar with history will know that the real instigators of great evils in the nineteenth and twentieth centuries – fascism, Nazism, communism and colonialism – all came from the Christianized West. Postcolonial criticism has its roots in non-religious ideologies and frameworks – Marxism, post-structuralism and psychoanalysis. Postcolonial criticism now occupies a crucial position in academia which is mainly secular and liberal. Up until now, postcolonial criticism has been impervious to the significance of religions and the theological and religious beliefs of peoples.[16] The non-religious focus

---

[15] See his interview with Jennifer Wicke and Michael Sprinker, in *Edward Said: A Critical Reader*, ed. Michael Sprinker, Oxford: Blackwell, 1992, p. 232. Interestingly, Said's *The World, the Text and the Critic* starts with 'Secular Criticism' and ends with 'Religious Criticism' (Said 1983: 1–30, 290–2).

[16] There are a few scholars who have looked at Hinduism, Islam, Buddhism and Confucianism from a postcolonial perspective, chiefly addressing orientalist tendencies represented in construction of these religions both by Western interpreters and by nationalists. These books do not evolve a postcolonial theory or strategy to deal with or appreciate these religions. See Anouar Majid, *Unveiling Traditions: Postcolonial Islam in a Polycentric World*, Durham, N.C.: Duke University Press, 2000; Richard King, *Orientalism and Religion: Postcolonial Theory, India and 'The Mystic East'*, London: Routledge, 1999; and J. J. Clarke, *Oriental Enlightenment: The Encounter Between Asian and Western Thought*, London: Routledge, 1997.

of postcolonial discourse has not only widened the gap between theory and the religions, but has also failed to assess the sociological, political and communal functions these religions have in postcolonial societies. Religious ideas and symbols have been employed profitably in the colonial period as means of resisting, overthrowing and holding out against Christian supremacism and colonial atrocities. There is a noticeable gap between the theoretical investments of post-colonialism and the hermeneutical interests of postcolonial societies. The credibility of postcolonial criticism will depend on its ability to provide a theoretical framework for understanding religions in the post-Enlightenment and postmodern era.

A Hermeneutical Conundrum

Finally, to bring this to a close, instead of summing up, let me leave you with a conundrum which we as interpreters and readers of texts constantly face. Do we hand over the responsibility to ancient sacred books to deal with the problems we face today, or do we stop reading them and seek for alternatives? Two characters, one in a novel and the other in a film, typify the choices one faces today.

Gwen, the English nurse whom I have already referred to, the character from Sanjay Nigam's *Transplanted Man*, believes in the life-changing, healing powers of literature. She cultivates a motherly relationship with one of the patients – a dying Indian politician whose every body part was transplanted – because of their shared interest in literature, and passes on books to him in the hope that one of the books will somehow heal him and make him active again. She gives him first some outstanding works in Western literature – Austen, Eliot, Dickens, Trollope and every Brontë. When these books fail to have any impact, she changes to Eastern literature – *Sakuntala*, the haiku of Basho, Kabir's devotional poems and the *Tale of Genji*. When this, too, proves unsuccessful, she tries her own form of contrapuntal reading. Then she tries 'pairing a nineteenth century English classic with the work of a living Asian writer, hoping that some combination of West and East, colonial and postcolonial, dead and alive, might do the trick' (Nigam 2002: 215).

While Gwen was desperately 'searching for just the right passage – the perfect sequence of words that would forestall the death of the Transplanted Man' (Nigam 2002: 215), Amsterdam Vallon in the film *Gangs of New York* finds it fruitless to depend on the text. In this recent film, as he is leaving the reform school, the character played by Leonardo DiCaprio is given a copy of the Bible. The first thing he does after coming out of the premises is to throw the Bible into the nearby river. He knows that to face the nineteenth-century gangster world of New York, full of murderous villains and xenophobic thugs, the good book might not be the ideal one.

This is the choice we have – either to embrace the book or discard it. Or, is there a third, in-between way? A viable way out of this dilemma might be to rely on the postcolonial in-between position. In-between-ness will resist any clear domination of either of these positions and enable us to work through them and forge a new hermeneutic and a postcolonial theology.

References

Allen, Charles, 2002. *The Buddha and the Sahibs: The Men who discovered India's Lost Religion*, London: John Murray.

Amore, Roy C., 1978. *Two Masters, One Message: The Lives and Teachings of Gautama and Jesus*, Nashville: Abingdon.

Bailey, Randall C., 1991. 'Beyond Identification: The Use of Africans in Old Testament Poetry and Narratives', in Cain Hope Felder (ed.), *Stony the Road We Trod: African American Biblical Interpretation*, Minneapolis: Fortress Press, pp. 165–84.

Blaiklock, E. M., 1964. *The Acts of the Apostles: An Historical Commentary*, London: Tyndale Press.

Borg, Marcus, 1997. *Jesus and Buddha: The Parallel Sayings*, Berkeley: Ulysses Press.

Bruce, F. F., 1965. *The Book of the Acts: The English Text with Introduction, Exposition and Notes*, London: Marshall, Morgan & Scott.

Cooper, Robert, 2002. 'The Post-Modern State', in Mark Leonard (ed.), *Re-Ordering the World: The Long-Term Implications of 11 September*, London: The Foreign Policy Centre, pp. 11–20.

Devy, G. N., 2002. 'Preface', in G. N. Devy (ed.), *Indian Literary Criticism: Theory and Practice*, Hyderabad: Orient Longman, pp. xi–xvi.

Dirks, Nicholas B., 2002. *Castes of Mind: Colonialism and the Making of Modern Knowledge*. Delhi: Permanent Black.

Edwards, David, 1975. *Good News in Acts: The Acts of the Apostles in Today's English Version*, London: Fontana Books.

Ferguson, Niall, 2003. *Empire: How Britain Made the Modern World*, London: Allen Lane.

Grant, Robert M., 1968. 'American New Testament Study, 1926–1956', *Journal of Biblical Literature* 87(1): 42–50.

Haenchen, Ernst, 1971. *The Acts of the Apostles: A Commentary*, Oxford: Basil Blackwell.

Kelley, Shawn, 2002. *Racializing Jesus: Race, Ideology and the Formation of Modern Biblical Scholarship*, London: Routledge.

Moxnes, Halvor, 2001a. 'The Construction of Galilee as a Place for the Historical Jesus – Part I', *Biblical Theology Bulletin* 31(1): 26–37.

Moxnes, Halvor, 2001b. 'The Construction of Galilee as a Place for the Historical Jesus – Part II', *Biblical Theology Bulletin* 31(2): 64–77.

Nigam, Sanjay, 2002. *Transplanted Man*, New York: HarperCollins.

Patankar, R. B., 2002. 'Aesthetics: Some Important Problems', in G. N. Devy (ed.), *Indian Literary Criticism: Theory and Practice*, Hyderabad: Orient Longman, pp. 389–416.

Pieris, Aloysius, 1984. 'The Political Vision of the Buddhists', *Dialogue* 11(1–3): 6–14.

Queen, Christopher S., and Sallie B. King, 1996. *Engaged Buddhism: Buddhist Liberation Movements in Asia*, Albany: State University of New York Press.

Sivanandan, A., 1994. 'Editorial', *Race and Class* 36(2).

Said, Edward W., 1983. *The World, The Text, and The Critic*, London: Vintage.

Said, Edward W., 2001. 'Michael Walzer's *Exodus and Revolution*: A Canaanite Reading' in Edward W. Said and Christopher Hitchens (eds), *Blaming the Victims: Spurious Scholarship and The Palestinian Question*, London: Verso, pp. 161–78.

Spurr, David, 1994. *The Rhetoric of Empire: Colonial Discourse in Journalism, Travel Writing, and Imperial Administration*, Durham, N.C.: Duke University Press.

Part II
Remapping Christian Theological Discourse

7

Postcolonialism and Indian
Christian Theology

> Theology at 120°F in the shade seems, after all, different from theology
> at 70°F. Theology accompanied by tough chapatis and smoky tea
> seems different from theology with roast chicken and a glass of good
> wine. Now who is really different, theós or the theologian?
>
> Klaus Klostermaier (1969: 40)

In her recent Booker Prize-winning novel, *The God of Small Things*,
Arundhati Roy described the arrival of Christianity in Kerala, in a
boat, like tea seeped from a tea-bag (Roy 1997: 33). Unfortunately,
Christianity has remained, and is still regarded as, an Englishman's
'cuppa'. The Englishness of Christianity is very well captured in
another Indian novel, *Red Earth and Pouring Rain*, when the Begam,
one of the characters, tells her sons, 'Convert; all this is useless;
become what I have become; I call myself a Christian but what I have
really become is an Englishman' (Chandra 1995: 401). I start with
these illustrations to indicate the popular perceptions of Christianity
and Christians in the minds of ordinary people. Ever since an Indian
or an Asian became a Christian, the constant question has been how to
be an Indian and a Christian at the same time.

What I would like to do in this chapter is to identify different trajec-
tories of Indian Christian theology, and provide some markers for the
future.

Looking for the Native

Like the Indian sages of old, I would like to start with a story, but
before that, as a warm-up, a few words need to be said. Up until now,
one of the interesting pursuits of Indian Christian hermeneutics has
been to search for the authentic Indian. Or to put it another way, our
quest has been about how to make Christian theology Indian. Some
scholars argue that the true Indian is to be found only in the speech of
an *adivasi*, a common person or an illiterate villager, in a few folk

forms, and to some extent in the writings of modern rural and dalit writers. I would like to use an anecdote used by Anantha Murthy, the Kanada novelist and literary critic, to exemplify a point. It concerned a painter and a peasant, and it was actually based on an incident witnessed by Anantha Murthy at an academic conference (Murthy 1982: 66–78). Incidentally, the painter in the anecdote was also at the same conference. This painter was narrating his going around villages in North India studying folk art. Near one of the villages a lonely cottage at the foot of a hill attracted him. Approaching the cottage, he saw through the window a piece of stone, which caught his attention. It was decorated with *kumkum* – the powder that Indian women wear on their foreheads as an auspicious mark. He wanted to photograph the stone that the peasant worshipped and asked the peasant if he could take it outside where the light was better. After taking the photograph, the painter felt uneasy for having removed the stone that the peasant had revered and worshipped, and expressed his regret. However, he was not prepared for the peasant's reply and was astonished to hear the man saying: 'It doesn't matter. I will get another stone and anoint it with *kumkum*.' The painter was staggered by the hermeneutical implications of the reply: any piece of stone on which the peasant smeared *kumkum* became God for him. What mattered was his faith, not the stone. Overwhelmed by the reply, the painter went on to challenge his fellow conference attendees. Did they understand the manner in which the peasant's mind worked? Could they apprehend the essentially mythical and metaphorical imagination which directed his inner life? Was it possible for them to appreciate the complex pattern of ancient Indian thought, since they were all caught up in narrow confines of Western scientific rationality? Should they not have preferred the so-called superstition of the peasant which helped him see organic connections between the human and natural world surrounding him, to the scientific rationality of Western science, which has driven the world into a mess of pollution and ecological imbalance?

The painter continued. He went on to tell his audience that Western education had alienated all of them utterly from this peasant, and from the 70-percent illiterate Indian mass who populate the villages. In his simplicity the peasant still kept alive the mode of thinking and perception which had been revealed to the sages from the dawn of time. If we didn't understand the structure and mode of this peasant's thinking, we could not become true Indian writers. Therefore we should free ourselves from the enslaving rationalistic modes of Western scientific thinking. Only then would we be able to understand the vital connection between this peasant and his world and between him and his ancestors who had ploughed the same patch of land for generations. Western modes of perception – whether scientific positivist, or even Marxist – would not enable them to understand what sustained this Indian peasant. These European-born theories, the painter concluded, would only serve to make all of them feel inferior, and thus turn their country into an imitation of the West.

Anantha Murthy reports that the instantaneous response of the conference participants was one of embarrassment and shock. They were all profoundly moved by the painter's argument. The painter's peasant stood there before them as an authentic Indian, untouched by the ideas of the grand masters of literary theories who used the peasant as a mere point of reference to define their positions. The immediate awareness among the conference attendees was that they had all been alienated from their cultural and artistic roots.

Contours of Indian Christian Theology

One of the dominant features of Indian Christianity has been the tendency to be retrospective or ironic. There is a lingering backward glance, to look again for the prime sites of ancient India, and to look to its texts, architecture, art, painting and poetry for inspiration and new directions. From K. M. Banerjea in the colonial days to Amaladoss in post-independence time, Indian theologians have profitably drawn on the Hindu religious and theological heritage. Such an exercise, the search for an untouched ancient Indian heritage, has been seen as innovative in its implicit opposition to the imported and universalizing nature of Western methodologies. We admire their insiders' view of Hindu philosophy, but now we need to be sceptical about their celebratory attitude towards Indian tradition. Indeed, they made it possible for us to mobilize the ancient Indian truths in our theological enterprise, but now we need to question the conservative 'clinging' to certain Indian aesthetic modes. Repeatedly, in the name of indigenization/inculturation, Christian themes such as Incarnation, Atonement and the Trinity were superimposed on to Hebraic and Hellenistic concepts, in an attempt to force a spurious theological validation, which does not easily emerge organically. There have been two offshoots of such an enterprise.

First, in reinvoking spiritual aspects of our heritage, we have silenced and overlooked the rational and sceptical aspects of our past. The Indian traditions were not merely spiritual and devotional. There were materialists, such as the Lokayata and the Sankhya schools, and there were 'atheistic' religions such as Jainism and Buddhism. Interestingly, some of us looked to Marx unnecessarily, when a more local variety was available. In other words, we have been reinforcing the European image of India as the eternal spiritual home, an image concocted by the European Orientalists in the eighteenth century, as the handmaiden for colonialism. In projecting the spirit of India as timeless, changeless, we fail to note the struggles and miseries of the present.

Secondly, all these attempts – indigenization/inculturation and even the more recent contextualization – are evangelistic and apologetic in tone and content. They are concerned with injecting, translating or interpreting a given text and the given gospel for a culture. The Bible and the gospel are taken for granted. Listen to the words of Shoki Coe, recalled by Kosuke Koyama: 'The gospel must be culturally contextualized, yet it must "gospelize" the cultural context itself. This means that the gospel remains a stumbling block and no contextualization can domesticate it' (Koyama 1993: 702). These modes of doing theology – be it indigenization or contextualization – are all a one-sided movement by a form of Christianity largely shaped by Western thought-patterns, in order to occupy, discredit and dislodge local cultures. The notion is that the other cultures have to be transformed. All these efforts have been superficial at best and paternalistic at worst.

Thirdly, it means that what we were doing in the name of indigenization was to employ Hindu language as a way of defining ourselves. Initially, we used it against the colonialist, and later as a way to gain recognition among the Indian nationalists who contested our authenticity. We used the Hindu heritage, its religious and philosophical concepts and language, in my view, not earnestly, but often phonily and cynically. Later, when Hindu fundamentalist groups invoked the very essence of Hinduism, and forged a Semitic version of it, we then became tongue-tied and were unable to argue against their version. We called it foul, and in our desperation branded them as reactionary. We encouraged and applauded when other minority groups in India claimed their distinctiveness. Muslims are permitted to be proud of being Muslims, Sikhs can be proud of being Sikhs, and Christians can be proud of being Christians. But when Hindus began to assert their self-consciousness and asked, 'Is it a crime to be a Hindu in our country?' we made it awkward for them to hold that self-consciousness, by lecturing them on the importance of secular values and telling them that an ideal Hindu is a secular Hindu.

As a way of ending this section, let me make now a few observations. I find that the leading trends in Asian theologies are robustly conservative. In their attempt to articulate a relevant theology, these theologians have asserted the Christian faith and defended a high value of biblical authority and a form of Christian faith formulated in pre-Enlightenment times. The defences are very often sophisticated. Mobilizing the latest tools, the theologians explain why their condition requires a re-affirmation of the basic message of the Bible, and, unapologetically, they hold on to missionary intentions.

All theologies, whether indigenist or 'subalternanist', contain uniformly positive ethnic and gender stereotypes. These theologies often depict a history of long centuries of oppression, poverty, pain and suffering. Dalit, Buraku, tribal and Asian women theologies, when they are pitched against the pollution-based, hierarchically and patriarchically influenced Indian theology, look radical and challenging. But when they are accessed by others and taken out of their context and introduced and studied in the Western academies, they reinforce all the negative aspects of Indian society.

One of the crucial problems we face today is the much-talked-about gap between theology inculcated in the seminary and the theology advocated by the institutionalized Church. Most of those who occupy key positions in the institutionalized churches in Asia have gone through a theological education which exposed them to the contextual and intertextual nature of biblical narratives and Christian doctrines. They have been introduced to the current thinking on inter-religious dialogue. But there is hardly any attempt to translate these insights into institutional practice or incorporate them into institutional theological pronouncements. Yet, in their statements and communications, the Bible is being summoned without any awareness of the complexities of using such a document. When are those who make pronouncements on behalf of the institutional churches going to come to terms with the latest scholarship, and listen to what the scholars have been telling them? Sadly, the gap between theology and church doctrine is too wide to be bridged. Obviously, the churches prefer fundamentalism to theological scholarship, since fundamentalism allows them to keep their doctrines intact, their institutions safe. Theological scrutiny would require them to revise their beliefs and reconfigure their identity.

Changed Circumstances and Emerging Factors

One of the basic assumptions of Indian theology has been to engage in theological activity as though people live settled lives, and as though those lives can be conceptualized in terms of a cultural totality of shared values and meanings. Diversity rather than homogeneity mark the continent as a whole. But now the question is: what is the value system which links umbilically the commuter in Singapore, the paddy grower in Burma, the urban dweller in Bombay flats and the countless peasants trying to eke out an existence in different Asian countries. The major part of Indian Christian theology, and for that matter most of Asian theology, carry out their task with an assumption of rooted, localized, integrated and self-contained communities, who lead settled lives. Indigenous theologies were celebrated when people led a settled life and thought in terms of cultural wholes. The connection between the vernacular and the global is now so deep that it is very difficult to determine what is native and what is non-native. At a time when there is intermixing of cultures, at both popular and elitist levels, and when local/global and vernacular/metropolitan divides are shrinking; when people's lives are being rearranged by globalization, and when there is a constant movement of people due to political conflicts and natural disasters, finding cultural-specific analogues may be an increasingly difficult task. Alternatively, of course, the new multi may throw up its own hitherto undiscovered parallels. It is important to see that global/vernacular, rural/metropolitan as relational and relative concepts. To treat vernacular and metropolitan hermeneutics as contrasting pairs – one as narrow, stable, intuitive and closed, and the other as open, progressive, rational and fluid – is to miss the point. Important frameworks of life and sources of identification should be sought in the cultural sites which have emerged in the interstices of the local and global condition. We need to direct our attention to the interrelationship of moving and dwelling in a whole world of global interconnections.

What we need to be aware of is the change of scenario in the theological firmament. The hegemonic Western theologies which took upon themselves the mantle to speak for all, and invaded our space, have lost their nerve. This has occurred either through postmodern fragmentation or through vigorous internal critiquing of gay and lesbian theologies, or because the English 'Don Cupittian' variety of dry middle-class intellectualism has become untranslatable in other contexts. These Western theologies have become more regional, autobiographical and confessional. A typical example is the recent issue of *Semeia* on autobiographical criticism, where every contributor started by declaring his or her identity, social and geographical location, sexuality, and the constituency which she or he was aiming at and addressing (*Semeia* 75 (1995)).

Third World theologies, especially the liberation variety, arose as a way of critiquing the universalistic, Eurocentric, individualistic, patriarchal and anti-environmental tendencies of these Western theologies. We have not only lost an enemy but also have been pushed further to the periphery in the name of postmodern celebration of the local and the different. We need to pay attention to the fact that over the years not only the Master himself has changed, but along with him, his language of discourse, too, has modified. The master discourse no more talks about civilizing mission. The new lexicon is not about rescuing the benighted natives but concerns the universal ethics of human rights. Whether the much-talked-about Asian values, hard work, prudence, loyalty to family and a sense of community will survive the economic progress which has brought freedom to the women and the younger generations remains to be seen.

In our discursive resistance, we tend to take a high moral ground. We employ the language of moralism and use words such as truth, responsibility, guilt, which we acquired mainly through missionary and convent school education. Hence our preoccupation with grand theorizing about how Europe underdeveloped Asia or Africa. The West we are now addressing is not familiar with such a vocabulary. Recently, through its postmodernist culture, the West has been telling us that the language of guilt, truth and responsibility is foreign to present-day multinationals and international powerbrokers and military strategists. They speak a different language, the language of success and efficiency, performance and profit. The moral agenda has moved on. The failure to note this moral shift may mean, according to Denis Ekpo, that we are barking up the wrong tree: 'We may be thinking that we are still striking at the West when in fact we may be boxing a straw West entirely of our making' (Ekpo 1996: 12).

Future Markers: Postcoloniality and the Hybridized State

The most important factor in the changed status is the state of post-coloniality. Postcoloniality is perhaps the sign of an increased realization that it is not feasible to deduce a civilization, a custom, a narrative history, a literature, from the wider transfiguring influences and trends of the increasingly shrinking globalized world. In other words, it is not always feasible to recover the authentic 'roots' or even to go back to the real 'home' again. In an ever-increasing multicultural society like ours, where traditions, histories and texts commingle, interlace, a quest for unalloyed pure native roots could prove not only to be elusive but also to be dangerous. It could cause complications for the everyday business of living with neighbours of diverse cultures, religions and languages. This means finding oneself subject to an ever wider and more complex web of cultural negotiation and interaction. What postcoloniality indicates is that we assume more-or-less fractured, hyphenated, double, or in some cases multiple, identities.

We don't need another messianic narrative to supplant the exhausted indigenization/contextualization model. All around there is a hermeneutical fatigue, and a feeling that we have heard these things before.

There is a great concern in certain circles that, unlike the West, we have not produced great theological giants. The point is not to reproduce our own native schools of Barth, Baillie or Bultmann. Indian theology, or for that matter any contextual theology, cannot afford to be imitative. What these schools do is to perpetuate, fetishize and fête the thoughts of the 'Master'. For me the theology is alive not in the writings of these masters, valuable as they are, but in the everyday activity of living in a society which is multicultural, multilingual and multiracial.

When one is exposed to others who profess a different faith, speak a different language and draw inspiration from different texts, one realizes one's own provincialism and limitations. One is faced with new realities. One such reality is that the communities we belong to and live in are no longer groups of people with shared concerns but persons with competing interests who try to accommodate each other's concern and endeavour to arrive at amity and accord. It is almost a cliché to say that we live in a world of diversity and disagreement. The words of the Indian critic Aijaz Ahmad are apt here: 'It is a field of contentions and conflicts. Every nation has at a given time not one culture but several, not as unity in diversity but also as unity of opposites' (Ahmad 1997: 2; http//www.thehindu.com. fline.fl1416/14160760.htm). It seems that God values variety and variance, and God seems to want a world where we have to work out with others the truth. The colonialist mode of interpretation offered a simple choice between truth and falsehood. If one is right, the other is invariably wrong. What postcolonialism does is to force us to choose between truth and truth. The validation of one does not depend on the negation of the other. What postcoloniality makes us realize is that the divine has made an impact on people in diverse ways, thus occasioning a variety of legitimate responses to that experience. It is here that one must strive for answers which have no precedents in the text or tradition. It is here one has to be daringly original and true to one's experiences and visions.

Theologians often assume the role of legislators, and expect that their hermeneutical treaties will change the world. The task of theologians is not to change the world but to understand it. Theology does not create revolution; it changes people's perceptions and makes them aware of the need for revolution. Its function is to make people see more, feel more and rekindle the fire of resistance.

India has celebrated the golden jubilee of her independence. As she begins the new millennium, what will be the future markers of Indian Christian theology? There seem to be three options, each of which in some way could be a temptation. One, to long for a time when Indian theology will triumph over its rivals and the subcontinent will confess the name of Christ. This was the missionary expectation, but the relatively small numerical success to date, and recent reinvigoration of major religions, makes this only a utopian dream. Second, to hold on to institutional power, but to get rid of its Western image by superficially infusing Christian doctrines and rituals with Indian ideas. In this way Indian Christianity can settle down as a subcultural sect and provide a curiosity value. Third, to undergo an enormous reassessment, give up its claim to be the sole conveyor of truth and renegotiate its role built on differences. Rather than striving to redeem India, Indian Christian theology's future would lie in its ability to evolve a hybridized style of identity. Its relevance will be measured not by its ability to invoke lost authenticates of ancient India or to superintend the purity of the gospel, but by its ability to create an allegory of theological hybridity.

Like any other theological proposition, hybridity, too, can become a powerful ideology in the current hermeneutical warfare. In the face of more coercive discourses which insist on a single truth, single worldview and single history, the postcolonial mode of hybridization can be seen as more pliable and accommodative, and more willing to incorporate dissent. This hybridization can in its turn become a demon and effectively take possession of and try to control the interpretative agenda. Given the choice between the coercive and adaptive discourses, I would go for the latter, at least for the time being. At a time of virulent nationalism and communalism, hybridization, with its insistence on critical integration, not only deflates particularisms but also facilitates redefinitions of identities.

What hybridity, as a discursive practice, does is to shift the conceptualization of identity. Rather than seeing identity as a stable reference point, it switches to a different 'epistemological paradigm in which it is liminality, instability, impurity, movement and fluidity that inform the formation of identities' (Chow 1998: 166). In one sense, the hybridized state is not new. One of those earlier theologians who took seriously the hybridized form as a mode of doing theology was the Bengali, Brahmabandhab Upadhyay (1861–1907). He brought out the essence of the hybridized state, when he wrote in *Sophia*:

> By birth we are Hindus and shall remain *Hindu* till death. But as *dvija* (twice-born) by virtue of our sacramental rebirth, we are Catholics, we are members of the indefectible communion embracing all ages and climes. In customs and manners, in observing caste and social distinctions, in eating and drinking in our life and living we are genuine Hindus, but in our faith we are neither Hindu or European, nor American nor Chinese but all-inclusive. Our faith fills the whole world and is not confined to any country or race; our faith is universal and consequently includes all truths. (Upadhyay, in Baago 1969: 36)

Upadhyay contests the notion that postcolonialism as critical practice might have started after the lowering of the flags of the empire. The writings of Upadyay and countless others during the colonial period indicate that whenever a native writer put pen to paper to reconfigure his or her identity in the face of colonial assault, the project of postcolonialism might have got under way. The postcolonial notion of hybridity is not about the dissolution of differences but about renegotiating the structure of power built on differences. It is not synonymous with assimilation. Assimilation is something that the colonialists, and later the nativists, advocated. It is a two-way process – both parties are interactive, so something new is created. Living in multiple contexts means reforming the Christian identity. In this way it will be accepted as complementary to other religious discourses in India and as a companion in the search for truth and religious harmony. The very survival of Indian Christian theology, or for that matter the Indian church, depends on its capacity to respond to a society which is at times tolerant, but often sceptical of a minority community committed to a religion with foreign origins and linked and conflated with recent colonialism.

As a way of ending, let us go back to the painter and peasant. Though Anantha Murthy was moved by the painter's remarks, on reflection he says that he had a nagging doubt:

> Isn't the authentic Indian peasant, whose imagination is mythical and who relates to nature organically, also an important cult figure of the Western radicals who are reacting against their materialist civilisation? What if these spiritual reactions in the West are their

way of keeping fit, and the 'decline of the West' theory is glibly repeated humbug? . . . As a result we keep reacting rather than creating; we advocate the absurd, or in reaction to it admire the authentic Indian peasant all of them masks to hide our own uncertainties. In the morass of poverty, disease and ugliness of India, isn't the Westernized Indian unauthentic and inconsequential, and the traditional peasant an incongruous and helpless victim of centuries of stagnation? (Murthy 1982: 72)

Third World theologies, desperately looking for a new mode of perception in the face of new forms of colonialism and threatening features of globalization, are certainly attracted by the simple peasant/aborigine/tribal who has remained through the centuries impervious to the cultures of the conquerors. It is also tempting to freeze a part of the indigene's life as if it represented the whole, and confine him or her to the local. Such an indigene may be no more than a creature of the hermeneutical imagination. Even if that imaginary indigene exists, he or she, like the peasant at the foot of the hill, may not be the least bit interested in the issues discussed here. But as Anantha Murthy says, 'It is important to know that he or she exists; our hypersensitive, highly-personal nightmares will at least be tempered with the irony of such knowledge' (Murthy 1982: 76).

This chapter was originally published in *Studies in World Christianity* 5.2 (1999): 229–40. Reprinted with permission of Edinburgh University Press.

References and Further Reading

Ahmad, Aijaz, 1992. *In Theory: Classes, Nations, Literatures*, London: Verso.

Ahmad, Aijaz, 1997. 'Cultures in Conflict', *Frontline* 14.

Ashcroft, Bill, Gareth Griffiths and Helen Tiffin, 1992. *The Empire Strikes Back: Theory and Practice in Post-Colonial Literatures*, London: Routledge & Kegan Paul.

Baago, K., 1969. *Pioneers of Indigenous Christianity*, Bangalore: CISRS.

Chambers, Iain, and Lidia Kurti, 1996. *The Postcolonial Question: Common Skies, Divided Horizons*, London: Routledge.

Chandra, Vikram, 1995. *Red Earth and Pouring Rain*, London: Faber & Faber.

Childs, Peter, and Patrick Williams, 1997. *An Introduction to Postcolonial Theory*, London: Prentice Hall.

Chow, Rey, 1998. 'The Postcolonial Difference: Lessons in Cultural Legitimation', *Postcolonial Studies* 1.2.

Ekpo, Denis, 1996. 'How Africa Misunderstood the West: The Failure of Anti-Western Radicalism and Postmodernity', *Third World Perspectives on Contemporary Art and Culture* 35.

Gandhi, Leela, 1998. *Postcolonial Theory: A Critical Introduction*, Edinburgh: Edinburgh University Press.

Klostermaier, Klaus, 1969. *Hindu and Christian in Vrindaban*, London: SCM Press.

Koyama, Kosuke, 1993. 'Christ's Homelessness', *Christian Century*, 14–21 July.

Loomba, Ania, 1998. *Colonialism/Postcolonialism*, London: Routledge.

Mongia, Padmini, 1996. *Contemporary Postcolonial Theory: A Reader*, London: Arnold.

Moore-Gilbert, Bart, Gareth Stanton and Willy Maley, 1997. *Postcolonial Criticism*, London: Longman.

Murthy, U. R. A., 1982. 'The Search for an Identity: A Kanada Writer's Viewpoint', in G. Amirthanayagam (ed.), *Western Writers in Dialogue: New Cultural Identities*, London: Macmillan.

Roy, Arundhati, 1997. *The God of Small Things*, New Delhi: IndiaInk.

Sugirtharajah, R. S., 1998. *Asian Biblical Hermeneutics and Postcolonialism: Contesting the Interpretations*, Maryknoll, N.Y.: Orbis Books.

Sugirtharajah, R. S., 1998. *The Postcolonial Bible*, The Bible and Postcolonialism, 1, Sheffield: Sheffield Academic Press.

Trivedi, Harish, and Meenakshi Mukherjee (eds), 1996. *Interrogating Post-Colonialism: Theory, Practice and Context*, Shimla: Indian Institute of Advanced Study.

Williams, Patrick, and Laura Chrisman, 1993. *Colonial Discourse and Postcolonial Theory: A Reader*, Hemel Hempstead: Harvester Wheatsheaf.

8

The Magi from Bengal and their Jesus
Indian Construals of Christ during
Colonial Times

I have tried to orientalise him [Jesus] as much as possible.

P. C. Mozoomdar (1933-38)

Recently literary scholars, historians and anthropologists have been remapping their disciplines, scouring their own fields for colonial motifs. Such investigations have given rise to what are known as post-colonial theories and discourse. What this chapter intends to do is to utilize some aspects of this postcolonial discourse in order to appraise some of the christological constructions which emerged in India during colonial days. The chapter has three interrelated objectives. First, it tracks how some Indians freed themselves from the hege-monic images of Jesus propagated by missionaries during the days of the Empire – images which denigrated their culture and history – and also tracks how some Indians came up with their own sketches of Jesus. Secondly, by reinvoking these colonial encounters, it challenges the notion that the colonialized were only ever docile, incoherent, mute and hapless consumers of imperialized interpretations. Thirdly, it uses the christological controversy as a template for providing an early example of decolonization.

Unlike perhaps other faith traditions, Indian Hindus have worked out elaborate and varied images of Jesus. The Hindus who were at the forefront of fashioning a christological discourse during the nine-teenth century were three upper-caste, urbanized Bengali Brahmins – the magi from Bengal, as I should like to call them – Raja Rammohun Roy (1772?-1833), Keshub Chunder Sen (1838-84), and P. C. Mozoomdar (1840-1905). They were, to borrow a phrase from Salman Rushdie, the original 'Macaulay's Minute men' (Rushdie 1995: 165) – the ideal colonized subject envisaged by Thomas Macaulay in his famous minute of 1835: 'a class of persons, Indian in blood and colour, but English in taste, in opinions, in morals and in intellect' (Macaulay

1935: 359). In other words, they were the products of the colonial system and its cosmopolitanism. All three belonged to the Hindu ethical and reform group called the Brahmo Samaj (Society of God). These men mapped out their understanding of Jesus in response to the missionaries' essentialist, and biased view of Hindus, but they never lost their admiration and affection for Jesus and his teachings. Compared to the then prevalent European images of Jesus worked out by H. S. Reimarus (1694–1768), D. F. Strauss (1808–74) and Ernest Renan (1832–92), which were marked by scepticism, and an anti-Christian slant, and projected Jesus as a sad, mistaken and failed reformer, the portrayals by these Indians were, by contrast, enthusiastic and positive and projected a person worthy to be followed and emulated. Keshub Chunder Sen, in one of his lectures, entitled 'India asks, "Who is Christ?"', said: 'I am thankful to say I never read anti-Christian books with delight, and never had to wage war with my Christ' (Sen 1901: 391). He went on to urge India to receive Christ as her bridegroom:

> Oh, the bridegroom is coming; there is no knowing when he cometh. Let India, beloved India, be decked out in all her jewellery – those 'sparkling oriental gems' for which the land is famous, so that at the time of the wedding we may find her a really happy and glorious bride. The bridegroom is coming. Let India be ready in due season. (Sen 1901: 392)

First let me bring out the images of Jesus these men fashioned, as a response to the dominant christologies of the missionaries.

Asiatic Jesus, Oriental Christ

Rammohun Roy: Jesus as a moral teacher

Rammohun Roy, who was himself at the forefront of reinventing his own Hindu tradition by de-centring its idolatrous and polytheistic elements, found the Jesus of the missionaries, immersed in evangelical doctrines of atonement and Trinity, unacceptable. The metaphysical and miraculous dimensions in which Jesus was presented did not appeal to Rammohun Roy, a beneficiary of the Enlightenment and its values, and he was keen to stress and elevate the moral and rational dimensions. Dissatisfied with a Jesus embedded in evangelical dogma, Rammohun Roy went on to do to Christian texts what he did with his own Hindu texts – he stripped away the doctrinal accretions which had gathered over the years. He was looking for a Jesus who was an Asiatic moral teacher, and wanted to locate him within the Eastern spiritual tradition. He textualized his quest in *The Precepts of Jesus: The Guide to Peace and Happiness. Extracted from the Books of the New Testament, Ascribed to the Four Evangelists* (1820). This was even before Strauss had started his lives of Jesus project in Europe. The *Precepts* is a compilation of synoptic materials, minus genealogies, miracles, historical incidents and doctrinal references. Roy saw his task as to 'free the originally pure, simple and practical religion of Christ from the heathenish doctrines and absurd notions' (1978 (1906): 921). In the introduction to the *Precepts of Jesus*, he reiterates his hermeneutical position. His aim was to present the essence of the gospel, which for him lay not in the doctrines, as the missionaries claimed, but in the moral teachings of Jesus. He also sought to purge the Gospel narratives of their miracles, which he called 'heathen notions', because he believed that anyone who was rational enough to reject Hindu mythologies would find them ridiculous and unhelpful. What in effect the *Precepts of Jesus* did was to wrest Jesus from his place as the focal point of the missionary preaching, and to reframe him as a moral teacher and a true guide to God. In other words, such a portrayal called in question the powerful pillars of evangelical Christianity – belief in the atonement, the doctrine of the Trinity and the divinity of Jesus, and the self-sufficiency of the Christian scriptures. His objective was to present the essence of the gospel, which he considered to be contained in the moral teachings of Jesus, not in doctrines, as the Baptist missionaries at Serampore insisted. During the height of the controversy generated by the *Precepts of Jesus*, Rammohun summed up his position in a letter to a friend:

> I regret only that the followers of Jesus, in general, should have paid much greater attention to inquiries after his nature than to the observance of his commandments, when we are well aware that no human acquirements can ever discover the nature even of the most common and visible things, and, moreover, that such inquiries are not enjoined by the divine revelation. (1978: 919)

He saw his task as rescuing Jesus from the imperial portrayals, which he regarded as a travesty. The implication was that he could do a better job in presenting Jesus than the missionaries, because they were obsessed with their evangelical theology. He went on to say, 'I hope to God these Missionaries may at length have their eyes opened to see their own errors' (1978: 922).

Keshub Chunder Sen: Jesus as an Asiatic

Before the European colonization, India had been introduced by the
persecuted Nestorians to a Jesus who showed solidarity with their
cause. Keshub Chunder Sen and his contemporaries, however, were
brought up on images of Jesus which identified him with the
European race and its sentiments. It was against this aggressive and
muscular christological landscape that Keshub Chunder Sen engaged
in his christological quest. He used oration as a mode of communicat-
ing his vision of Jesus. The four open lectures he delivered, in front of
an audience composed mainly of middle-class educated Hindus,
colonial officials and a mixed group of missionaries, encapsulated his
views of Jesus. In these lectures he set out to do three things. First, he
wanted to revalorize Indian values and traditions which, as he put it,
had been 'Europeanized' (Sen 1904: 52) and slaughtered by European
invasion:

> Alas! Before the formidable artillery of Europe's aggressive civili-
> zation, the scriptures and prophets, the language and literature of
> the East, nay her customs and manners, her social and domestic
> institutions, and her very industries have undergone a cruel
> slaughter. (Sen 1904: 51)

Secondly, he wanted to make it clear to Indians that the Jesus whom
the missionaries were parading was not an Englishman, but an Asian,
with whom Indians could easily feel at home, for he had similar
manners, instincts and sentiments. In a lecture entitled 'Asia's
Message to Europe', he asked,

> For England has sent unto us, after all, a Western Christ. This is
> indeed to be regretted. Our countrymen find that in this Christ, sent
> by England, there is something that is not quite congenial to the
> native mind, not quite acceptable to the genius of the nation. It
> seems that the Christ that has come to us is an Englishman, with
> English manners and customs about him, and with the temper and
> spirit of an Englishman in him . . . But why should you Hindus go
> to England to learn Jesus Christ? Is not his native land nearer to
> India than England? Is he not, and are not his apostles and immedi-
> ate followers more akin to Indian nationality than an Englishman?
> . . . Gentlemen, go to the rising Sun in the East, not to the setting Sun
> in the West, if you wish to see Christ in the plenitude of his glory
> and in the fullness and freshness of his divine life . . . Recall to your
> minds, gentlemen, the true Asiatic Christ, divested of all Western
> appendages, carrying on his work of redemption among his own

people. Behold he cometh to us in his loose-flowing garment, his dress and features altogether Oriental, a perfect Asiatic in everything . . . Surely Jesus is our Jesus. (Sen 1901: 363–5)

And thirdly, Keshub Chunder Sen wanted to reclaim Jesus for Asia. He saw in the coming of the missionaries an indication of their returning Christ to his rightful home:

It is not the Christ of the Baptists, nor the Christ of the Methodists, but the Christ sent by God, the Christ of love and meekness, of truth and self-sacrifice, whom the world delights to honour. If you say we must renounce our nationality, and all the purity and devotion of Eastern faith, for sectarian and western Christianity, we shall say most emphatically, No. It is *our* Christ, *Asia's* Christ, you have come to return to us. The East gratefully and lovingly welcomes back her Christ. (Slater 1884: 101, emphasis original)

Keshub Chunder Sen was relentless in telling his audience that all the great religious figures of the world were of Asian origin, and that Asia was the birthplace of the major religions. He situated Jesus as one among many ongoing, revealing instances of God, along with earlier manifestations who had come before him, such as: Sakya Muni, Confucius, Zoroaster and Moses, and those like Chaitanya and Kabir who followed him. Though he regarded Jesus as the 'Prince of Prophets', and reiterated that he deserved 'the profoundest reverence', Sen went on to say yet again that 'we must not neglect that chain, or any single link in that chain of prophets, that preceded him, and prepared the world for him; nor must we refuse honour to those who, coming after him, have carried on the blessed work of human regeneration for which he lived and died' (Slater 1884: 10).

P. C. Mozoomdar: orientalizing Christ

Mozoomdar's hermeneutical concern, as the title of his book *The Oriental Christ* indicates, is to orientalize Christ. In a lengthy introduction, where he acknowledges his theological debt to his friend and mentor Keshub Chunder Sen, Mozoomdar juxtaposes two competing figures of Jesus – the stern, exclusive, historical, doctrinal, figure of Western muscular Christianity, and the homely, poetic, loving, sweet Jesus of the Galilean lake (1933 (1833): 40). In his reckoning, the Eastern Christ is 'the incarnation of unbounded love and grace', and 'the Western Christ is the incarnation of theology, formalism, ethical and physical force' (1933: 41). Mozoomdar's construals of Jesus

resemble those of Hindu adherents in relation to their chosen deity,
where closeness to the deity is expressed not necessarily through
abstract images but through intimate ritualistic acts. His portrayals of
Jesus as the bathing, fasting, weeping, pilgrimaging, dying and reign-
ing Christ fall within this category.

In concluding this section, we need to note that these formulations
of Jesus, as a moral teacher, an Asiatic ascetic and an Oriental guru,
did not go down well with the missionaries. In fact, these Bengalis
had to battle on two fronts: on the one hand, there were the missionaries, who wanted to thrust forward their own form of evangelical
Christianity; and on the other, there were their own Hindu pundits,
who wanted to assert the superiority and sufficiency of Hindu religious texts and ritual practices in the face of the militant and jaun-
diced view of the missionaries. What in effect these portrayals did
was to invalidate one of the pillars of evangelical Christianity – the
divinity and the atoning power of Jesus. They wrested Jesus from his
place at the focal point of missionary preaching, and refrained him as
a moral teacher, a great man and a true guide to God. The missionaries were the products of an evangelical revival and piety and could
not envisage Jesus without his sacrificial death. In Rammohun Roy,
Keshub Chunder Sen and Mozoomdar, the missionaries faced an
unexpected enemy. In England, as dissenters, they faced the strong
theological arm of high-church Anglicanism, whereas in India they
came up against opponents who, from a different cultural, religious
and linguistic position, not only threatened their cherished doctrines,
but far worse, de-centred Jesus and made him look like a culturally
relative figure. The following words of Rammohun Roy typify the
position of the Bengalis:

> If the manifestation of God in the flesh is possible, such possibility
> cannot reasonably be confined to Judea or Ayodhya, for God has
> undoubtedly the power of manifesting himself in either country
> and of assuming any colour or name he pleases. (1978: 980)

It would be presumptuous on my part to say that I have done justice
to the powerful and often complex portrayals of Jesus worked out
by these men. Nor can I claim that I have attempted to situate their
christological constructions over against the philosophical and religious backdrop which influenced and informed their articulations.
There are many studies which address these issues.[1] Some of these

---

[1] See, for instance, M. M. Thomas, *The Acknowledged Christ of the Indian
Renaissance* (London: SCM Press, 1969); R. Boyd, *An Introduction to Indian*

tend to evaluate the works of these men from the perspective of Christian theology, for their failure to measure up to it. Others try to rehabilitate them within the Hindu philosophical and religious fold. As I indicated earlier, I have a different hermeneutical agenda. My main objective is to foreground colonialism as the site in which the christologies of these men were worked out, and to detect in their work marks of an early instance of postcoloniality, which the present-day postcolonial theorists speak about.

Marks of Cultural De-Colonization

Culture and the hermeneutics of power

Postcolonial theorists talk about three forms of decolonization: political, economic and cultural (Pieterse and Parekh 1995: 1–19). Political decolonization points to territorial freedom, which has been largely achieved. Various forms of development strategy are seen as a form of economic decolonization; and transition from Western hegemonic cultural control is seen as intellectual decolonization.

These Bengali christologies are early instances of cultural decolonization. They emerged as a response to an active confrontation with a dominant system of thought, and their Bengali authors were pioneers in addressing the relationship between interpretation, culture and power. Now, nearly one hundred and fifty years later, we are witnessing a similar unmasking of the dominant christologies. This time it is being done through the work of the Latin American, feminist and African theologians who are uncovering concealed biases in these christologies. The three Bengalis were the first to expose and call in question the acceptability of a Christ who was couched in European terms and arrived in India with colonial power. In their view, these were not christological formulations in the genuine sense, but assertions of power, or as Rammohun Roy himself put it, they were undertaken by 'men possessed of wealth and power' (1978: 212), and their interpretations were 'elevated by virtue of power' (1978: 201). Such an image they looked upon as oppressive and unacceptable. Being high-caste Hindus, Jesus for them was a *mlecha*, an outsider, but admitted into India along with the imperialists. To quote Mozoomdar: 'He [Jesus] is a mlecha to Hindus, a kaffir to Mohammedans . . . he is

---

Christian Theology (Madras: The Christian Literature Society, 1969); D. C. Scott, *Keshub Chunder Sen* (Madras: The Christian Literature Society, 1979); H. Staffner, *Jesus and the Hindu Community: Is a Synthesis of Hinduism and Christianity Possible?* (Anand: Gujarat Sahitya Prakash, 1987).

tolerated only because he carries with him the imperial prestige of a conquering race. Can this be the Christ that will save India?' (1933: 34). Their way of de-Europeanizing Christ is to retrieve the Jesus of the Gospels, and to place him within his own continent and situate him along with the long line of Asia's illustrious religious figures. In the words of Keshub Chunder Sen,

> Let all people in this country who bear the Christian name remember that it is not by presenting a western Christ to our countrymen that they will be able to regenerate India. If you like, present the English side of Christ's many-sided character to the English nation. If you wish, present a German Christ to Germans, and an American Christ to the American people. But if you wish to regenerate us Hindus, present Christ to us in his Hindu character. When you bring Christ to us, bring him to us, not as a civilized European, but as an Asiatic ascetic whose wealth is communion, and whose riches prayers. (1901: 390)

Colonial racialization and stereotypes also played a key role in their christological debate. The imperial discourse generated the image of the Englishman as manly, strong and brave, and the Indian/Bengali as effeminate, weak and cowardly. This racialization created stereotypical images of the other – of Asians, as an inferior race (Sinha 1995). In one of his lectures, Keshub Chunder Sen captured the mood of the colonialists at that time:

> They say, Asia is a vile woman, full of impurity and uncleanliness. Her Scriptures tell lies; her prophets are all imposters; her people – men, women and children – are unfaithful and deceitful. There is neither light nor purity in Asia. The entire continent is given to ignorance and barbarism and heathenism; and nothing good, it is said, can come out of this accursed land. (Sen 1904: 50)

Mozoomdar, too, records that Europeans often treated 'Hindus as a primitive Eastern race' (1933: 14).

The answer of these Bengalis to the missionaries' description of the degradation and decline of Asia was to reinstall Asia as the site of everything that is best in religion, science and literature. Rammohun Roy went on to claim that for science, literature or religion, the world was indebted to '*our ancestors* for the first dawn of knowledge which sprang up in the East, and thanks to the Goddess of Wisdom, we have still a philosophical and copious language of our own, which distinguishes us from other nations who cannot express scientific or abstract ideas without borrowing the language of foreigners' (1978:

906, italics original). They were reinvoking, to use the phrase of Keshub Chunder Sen, the 'glory of our Asiatic home' (1904: 55). Thus Asia became the ground for rehabilitation, and Jesus was reinstated as an Asiatic endowed with various imagined Asian qualities. They pointed out everything that was good in India: her spirituality, her religious leaders, literature, art, music were completely Asian in origin. They re-valorized Asia as the site, not only for the birth of Christianity, but also for all the major faith traditions in the world. In a letter to the editor of *Bengal Hurkaru*, Rammohun Roy wrote:

> Before 'A Christian' indulged in a tirade about persons being degraded by '*Asiatic* effeminacy', he should have recollected that almost all the ancient prophets and patriarchs venerated by Christians, nay even Christ himself, a Divine Incarnation and the *founder* of Christian Faith, were ASIATICS. So if a Christian thinks it degrading to be born or to reside in *Asia*, he directly reflects upon them. (1978: 906, italics and capitals original)

Keshub Chunder Sen was equally enthusiastic about reasserting his Asianness. He asked: 'Shall we not magnify our race by proclaiming Christ Jesus as a fellow-Asiatic? Surely, the fact that Christ and other masters all belong to our nationality, and are all of Asiatic blood, causes a thrill of pride in every Eastern heart' (Sen 1904: 55–6). He said in another lecture:

> I rejoice, yea, I am proud, that I am Asiatic. And was not Jesus Christ Asiatic? [Deafening applause] Yes, and his disciples were Asiatic, and all the agencies primarily employed for the propagation of the Gospel were Asiatic. In fact, Christianity was founded and developed by Asiatics, in Asia. When I reflect on this, my love for Jesus becomes a hundredfold intensified; I feel him nearer my heart, and deeper in my national sympathies. Why should I then feel ashamed to acknowledge that nationality which he acknowledged? (1901: 33)

As a way of legitimizing European intervention, colonizers were actively involved in producing images which reinscribed the cultural and religious differences between the imperialists and the imperialized natives. One interesting aspect of the debate generated by the *Precepts of Jesus* was the deployment of the term 'heathen', both by the colonizer and the colonized. Joshua Marshman, the Baptist missionary, in his debate with Rammohun, kept on referring to the latter as 'heathen'. By using a term which was part of the imperial vocabulary of the time, he was denying the possibility that a native was capable of intelligent articulation. His was the rhetorical strategy of debasing the 'other', and making the arguments of the native unworthy. It was insensitive and injudicious on the part of Marshman to call Rammohun Roy a heathen, for he was well aware of him as a formidable scholar and a religious reformer who was at the forefront of emancipating his own Hindu tradition. Rammohun Roy considered the use of the term 'unchristian'. He appealed to the public to judge whether the compiler of the *Precepts of Jesus* was a believer or a heathen, based on the evidence of the text. He went further and claimed that it was the missionaries' presentation of Jesus which was imbued with heathen notions. Rammohun Roy was not a passive assimilator of colonial categories. He reappropriated the word initially mobilized by the missionaries, and recast it and turned it against them. In his case, it was an ironic reversal, and a good example of what Homi Bhabha would call the mimicry and mockery of authority.

Cultural transactions: hybridity and cross-culturality

The other characteristic features of postcoloniality are hybridity and cross-culturality. One of the significant marks of colonialism is the mixing of races and cultures. Cross-culturality and hybridity occur when an invading power tries to obliterate or assimilate the native cultures. Cultural studies view the hybridized nature of postcolonial writing as a sign not of weakness but of strength:

> Such writing focuses on the fact that the transaction of the post-colonial world is not a one-way process in which oppression obliterates the oppressed, or the coloniser silences the colonised in absolute terms. In practice it rather stresses the mutuality of the process. It lays emphasis on the survival, even under the most potent oppression, of the distinctive aspects of the culture of the oppressed and shows how these become an integral part of the new formulations which arise from the clash of cultures characteristic of imperialism. (Ashcroft et al. 1995: 183)

These men saw their task as revitalizing Hinduism and modernizing Indian civilization by borrowing, infusing and mixing them with whatever was good in Western tradition and Christianity. Rammohun Roy saw a future in which the Vedanta would be amalgamated with Western scientific methods, and Indian moral values with Western political values. Similarly Keshub Chunder Sen wanted to synthesize ancient wisdom with modern Western enterprise (Parekh 1989: 60). Keshub Chunder's New Dispensation Church had all the hallmarks of harmonizing and synthesizing. Sen celebrated this 'critical synthesis' (Bikhu Parekh's phrase) thus:

> All great religions are mine. Mine too is the mountain on which Christ Jesus preached his famous sermon. Mine also the Himalayas on which Aryan devotees lost themselves in contemplation. Mine likewise is the memorable Bo tree under whose shade the great Buddha attained final Beatitude. Sinai is mine, saith Asia, and the Jordan is mine, and the great Ganges is mine. The Vedas and the Bible are mine, the cross and crescent are mine. (1904: 57)

In a lecture Keshub Chunder Sen gave in Calcutta, he put it thus:

> Thus shall we put on the new man, and say, the Lord Jesus is my will, Socrates is my head, Chaitanya my heart, the Hindu Rishi my soul, and the philanthropic Howard my right hand. And thus transformed into the new man, let each of us bear witness unto the new gospel. Let many-sided truth, incarnate in saints and prophets, come down from heaven and dwell in you, that you may have that blessed harmony of character, in which is the eternal life and salvation. (1881: 28)

Seen generally from the Christian polemical point of view, such a mixing and fusing is condemned as syncretistic, inauthentic and a watering-down of the gospel. But seen from the perspective of colonialism, it has an affirmative purpose. It is a sign of resistance and survival, and an act of validation in the face of colonial hegemony.

Some Concluding Observations

Jesus who is the centre of Christian faith was now in the hands of people who did not accept him on conventional Christian terms nor perceive him through traditional biblical categories. These men were able to incorporate Jesus into the Hindu framework without feeling any need to give up their own religious tradition. For them, the gospel of Jesus did not offer anything dramatically new or different from the teachings of their seers or their own sacred texts. In Jesus, or in his teachings, they did not see a new testament or fresh good news but the reappearance or restatement or re-localization of the eternal dharma. Jesus was, in essence, restating anew some overlooked aspects of the perennial message. Mozoomdar put it thus: 'each prophet has his personal surroundings, his peculiarities of time and circumstance. There is about him the local, the personal, the historical, as well as the universal . . . Those who leave these out of consideration can never understand the true character of the man whom they view as their exemplar' (1933: 16).

The thrust of their christological construction was that they had the innate capacity, denied to the missionaries, to refigure a Jesus appropriate to Indian context. They thought that they had a natural gift of spirituality, the power of discernment, and possessed the necessary cultural, national and spiritual ability to articulate who Jesus was better than the missionaries could. Being Brahmins, they believed that they had the inherent, divine gift of teaching others. Mozoomdar encapsulates their mood:

> It is the fact that the greatest religions of the world have sprung from Asia. It has, with some accuracy, been said, therefore, that it is an Asiatic only who can teach religion to Asia . . . But the efforts of European agencies, suggestive and helpful as they are, do not go far enough, do not go deep enough, but still float on the surface, and affect the merest externals of human life. It is a national ideal only that can touch the undercurrents of national trust and aspiration. And let us assure our European friends that, in religion at least, Hindus have a powerful national life, which remains all but utterly uninfluenced by foreign preaching. (1933: 14)

At a time when missionaries were using Jesus to expose the deficiencies of Hindus, the Bengalis took it as their task to show how the ancient Asiatic tradition can elucidate their experience of Jesus. In confronting the negative European depictions, the colonized used the language and the technique provided by the colonizer. These were the anglicized Bengali gentry, who benefited most from colonial rule. They even welcomed the British presence and never aimed for the physical removal of the British. Keshub Chunder Sen was seen among his own followers as a 'semi-Europeanized young innovator' (Dalton 1982: 4). He even went so far as to say that the British nation had been 'brought here by the hand of Providence' (1904: 436). These Bengalis accepted the paradigm of representation manufactured by the colonizer. In the nineteenth century, there were two schools of thought which were influential in shaping the colonial cultural map – the Anglicists and the Orientalists. The former saw their task as vitalizing the moribund Indian culture by injecting Western values, whereas the latter saw their task as sanctifying and elevating the ancient Hindu courtly culture as a way of preserving India. Inspired by these schools, these Bengalis sought to shape the Indian to meet the hostilities of the missionaries and their imperial demands. Though occupying distinctly different terrains, the imperialized and the imperializer were interwoven and locked together according to the parameters set by the dominant force.

It is paradoxical that for the restoration of self-confidence and pride in their national heritage, they drew on and transformed the landmark instances supplied mainly by the work of European scholars, who fabricated for them a monumentalized India. They exploited to the full the binary types generated by colonialism – Asia as spiritual, eternal, intuitive and ascetic – and transformed them to their own advantage in order to resist and survive. Negatively they were reinforcing further the image of the East as the alluring other. Positively they made use of the work of the Orientalists to make their own people realize that their culture was ancient and one of which they could be justifiably proud. They never spelt out what this 'Asianness' or 'Indianness' was that they were trying to recover. Though they reacted to the missionaries from the West, they themselves were missionaries, but missionaries with a difference, missionaries in the sense of negotiating a new sense and a new purpose for their own people whose lives were being dramatically re-shaped by colonial demands.

In reinvoking, mobilizing and directing their attention to illustrious characteristics of Vedic and Sanskritic tradition, they not only overlooked the hierarchical features of ancient Indian courtly tradition, but also in the process erased the aspirations of Muslims, Dalits, the indigenous peoples and the rural poor, from their hermeneutical considerations. As Sumanta Banerjee put it, 'For them these lower orders still remained an invisible mass, their actual problem beyond the comprehension of the educated Bengalis . . .' (1989: 640). How these subalterns have engaged in their internal decolonization and tried to recover their self-identity is another story.

One final comment. These Bengalis in a way set the trend for mobilizing ethnicity as a site for christological construction. Under colonial pressure, it was natural for them to turn inward and rebuild their wounded self-image, by emphasizing Indianness, and infusing Jesus with worthwhile and distinctive Asian racial characteristics. In perceiving him as an Asiatic, or Oriental, what in effect they did was to ethnocize Jesus. Now, in a changed post-colonial context, to reiterate ethnic, racial and nationalistic traits will sound like racist exclusivism. Currently we witness an emergence of many an ethnocized Jesus – Jesus as Black, Native Indian, Hispanic, Chinese, etc. In the Fanonian hermeneutical schedule these ethnocized christologies fall within the second phase, that of self-discovery and national pride.[2] As

---

[2] Fanon's three phases are imitation, self-discovery and resistance. See Fanon 1990: 178–9.

a way of repairing the lost dignity of the victims of imperialism, these constructions were a historical necessity. But christology should go beyond the role of simply being a defensive ideology. At a time when one operates with multiple frames of reference and the maps of what it means to be an Asian or African are being redrawn, to reinvent Jesus with cultural traits may be a way of avoiding our present reality. If we persist with such a hermeneutical approach, we will be like the man in the Buddha's story who was so excited with the raft when crossing the river that he carried it with him wherever he went and was unwilling to part with it. As the Buddha would have said, an ethnocized christology, or for that matter any christology, is like a raft – it is for crossing over and not for clutching onto forever.

This chapter was previously published in Stanley E. Porter, Michael A. Hays and David Tombs (eds), *Images of Christ: Ancient and Modern*, Sheffield: Sheffield Academic Press, 1997, pp. 144–58. Reprinted with permission of Continuum.

References

Ashcroft, Bill, Gareth Griffiths and Helen Tiffin, 1995. *The Post-Colonial Studies Reader*, London: Routledge.

Banerjee, Sumanta, 1989. *The Parlour and the Street: Elite and Popular Culture in Nineteenth Century Calcutta*, Calcutta: Seagull Books.

Dalton, D. G., 1982. *Indian Idea of Freedom*, Gurgaon: Academic Press.

Macaulay, T. B., 1935. *Speeches by Lord Macaulay with his Minute on Indian Education*, ed. G. M. Young, London: Oxford University Press.

Mozoomdar, P. C., 1933. *The Oriental Christ* (1833), Calcutta: Navavidhan Publication Committee.

Parekh, Bhiku, 1989. *Colonialism, Tradition and Reform: An Analysis of Gandhi's Political Discourse*, New Delhi: Sage.

Pieterse, J. Nederveen, and Bhiku Parekh, 1995. 'Shifting Imaginaries: Decolonization, Internal Decolonization, Postcoloniality', in *The Decolonization of Imagination: Culture, Knowledge and Power*, London: Zed Books.

Roy, Rammohun, 1978. *The English Works of Raja Rammohun Roy with an English Translation of Tuhfatul Muwahhiddin* (1906), New York: AMS Press.

Rushdie, Salman, 1995. *The Moor's Last Sigh*, London: Jonathan Cape.

Sen, Keshub Chunder, 1881. 'We Apostles of the New Dispensation' (pamphlet), Calcutta: Navavidhan Publication Society.

Sen, Keshub Chunder, 1901. *Keshub Chunder Sen's Lectures in India*, London: Cassell.

Sen, Keshub Chunder, 1904. *Keshub Chunder Sen's Lectures in India*, London: Cassell.

Sinha, Mrinalini, 1995. *Colonial Masculinity: The 'Manly Englishman' and the 'Effeminate Bengali' in the Late Nineteenth Century*, Manchester: Manchester University Press.

Slater, T. E., 1884. *Keshub Chunder Sen and the Brahma Samaj: Being a Brief Review of Indian Theism from 1830–1884 together with Selections from Mr Sen's Work*, Madras: SPCK.

9

Complacencies and Cul-de-sacs
Christian Theologies and Colonialism

> In life one must for ever choose between being one who tells the stories
> and one about whom stories are told.
>
> Shashi Tharoor, *The Great Indian Novel* (1989: 164)

One of the weighty contributions of postcolonial criticism has been to put issues relating to colonialism and imperialism at the centre of critical and intellectual enquiry, and, with some success, to alter the premises in several subject areas within the humanities and social sciences. While these disciplines are coming to terms with the reality of colonialism, what is striking about systematic theology is the reluctance of its practitioners to address the relation between European colonialism and the field. There has been a marked hesitancy to critically evaluate the impact of the empire among systematic theologians, both during and after the European expansion. Theologians in the West cannot excuse themselves by suggesting that the empire had little impact 'at home'. New studies in literature, visual culture, geography and history in the last decade have demonstrated the numerous ways in which the empire was central to English domestic life and popular consciousness.[1]

While other disciplines have grappled with the wider cultural implications of the empire, European colonialism has never been a popular subject for theological enquiry in Western discourse despite the very substantial links between the churches in Britain and the

---

[1] For the influence and impact of cultures of the colonies in British art, journals, novels, dress habits, and children's books, see Julie F. Codell and Dianne Sachko Macleod (eds), *Orientalism Transposed: The Impact of the Colonies on British Culture*, Aldershot: Ashgate, 1998; David Armitage, 'Literature and Empire', in *The Oxford History of the Empire: The Origins of the Empire: British Overseas Enterprise to the Close of the Seventeenth Century*, New York: Oxford University Press, 1988, pp. 99–123; and Kathryn Castle, *Britannia's Children: Reading Colonialism through Children's Books and Magazines*, Manchester: Manchester University Press, 1996.

missions in the colonial world. My colleague, Robert Beckford, claims that more books have been written by Western theologians about being nice to animals and the environment than about colonialism or race. For instance, the two major surveys of English theologies, Vernon F. Storr's *The Development of English Theology in the Nineteenth Century 1800–1860* (1913) and Elliott-Binns's *The Development of English Theology in the Later Nineteenth Century* (1952), which narrates the story from where Storr left off, do not mention the existence of the empire or colonialism. These volumes maintain a certain reserve when it comes to discussing the impact of colonialism. They devote a considerable amount of space to the impact of German biblical scholarship, of rationalism and of the rise of atheism, but the empire is absent from their discourse. It is not as if leading Anglican theologians of the nineteenth century such as Maurice and Westcott did not take serious theological interest in the empire, but these surveys make no reference to this aspect of their work. Or, for that matter, for the later colonial period, take a look at the two leading British theological journals, *The Expository Times* and *Theology*. During the period from 1900 to 1960 they did not carry a single article on colonialism or on the impact of the empire. The main preoccupation of theologians of the time according to Mascall, who surveyed the theological scene as it was in the closing years of British imperialism, was with the new discoveries of scientists, historians and literary scholars and how they were making Christian living extremely difficult and the Christian faith vulnerable (Mascall 1960: 1–7).

Justifying Empire

Exceptions to this were two books published in the 1950s. One was *Caesar the Beloved Enemy* by an English mission-executive, Max Warren (1955), and the other was *Nations and Empires* by a German American, Reinhold Niebuhr (1959).[2] Naturally, they came out of

---

[2] The American title was *The Structure of Nations and Empires*, New York: Charles Scribner's Sons, 1959. The original title suggested by Niebuhr was *Dominions in Nations and Empires: A Study of the Structures and Moral Dilemmas of the Political Order Relevant to the Perplexities of a Nuclear Age*. T. S. Eliot, who was at Faber & Faber, was appalled at the title and urged the American publishers to come up with something simpler. See Richard Wightman Fox, *Reinhold Niebuhr: A Biography with a New Introduction and Afterword*, Ithaca: Cornell University Press, 1996, pp. 268–9. Though Niebuhr's ethical articulations were aimed at North American and European audiences, he had a considerable influence on Asian theologians in the 1950s and 1960s. T. B.

different political, social and cultural contexts. Warren's book was written after Indian independence and about the time when African nations were agitating for independence and bursting with liberatory aspirations. More to the point, England was about to lose its colonies and relinquish its role as an imperial power. Niebuhr's book came out at a time when the Cold War was at an embryonic stage, and Western politics was concerned at communist expansion, and in the international political landscape America and Russia were emerging as the two neo-colonial superpowers.

At the risk of over-simplifying the complex ideas of these two theologians, let me paraphrase and reconstruct what they said about colonialism and empire. Warren was probably one of the few interested in working out a theology of imperialism. For him, such a task was incumbent upon anyone who was engaged in Christian mission. This theological reflection was fuelled by the idea that Asia and Africa had been associated with the political, economic and cultural aggressions of the West (Warren 1955: 12). What Warren does in the name of theologizing is to dismiss all notions of imperialism as 'minted in hell' (1955: 28) or as an 'organized vice' (1955: 20), and rehabilitate it by calling it the 'Beloved Enemy', as indicated in his subtitle. In other words, imperialism is now reconstructed as a likeable rogue. He seeks to make the whole sordid enterprise native-friendly. His aim is to make imperialism 'command respect' (1955: 31). He prettifies and sanitizes colonialism in five ways.

First, for Warren, imperialism 'has a place in the purpose and providence of God' (1955: 18). In biblical terms, imperialism has eschatological significance, being preparatory in character. It has provided law and order, it has made obscure tribes citizens of the world, and drawn them into a common cosmopolitan culture. Otherwise these backward nations of Africa would have remained 'an empty map on which cartographers would have put elephants in place of towns' (Warren 1955: 28). Secondly, empires can be 'a vehicle of great good to a subject people' (Warren 1955: 36). In Warren's view, no other method had been devised so successfully for keeping the peace and making progress possible. Under imperialism, 'love, power and

---

Simatupang acknowledges his indebtedness to Niebuhr during the Indonesian independence struggle. M. M. Thomas was another, but he distanced himself from Niebuhr's view when the latter veered away from his earlier Marxist tendencies and embraced right-wing ideas. See M. M. Thomas, 'Non-Western Dynamics and American Strategy: A Third World View of Christian Realism', *Christianity and Crisis* 45(1) (February 1986): 8–10.

justice have been seen to take shape redeeming some tragic situation'
(1955: 31). Thirdly, imperialism has a virtuous and an ethical ring
about it. The empire is about exercising 'vocational consciousness',
and 'vocational feeling'. These were the ideas Tillich considered as
hallmarks of the now emerging American superpower. Warren found
these abstract Tillichian ideas acted out in concrete examples of
colonial benevolence such as working for an unheard-of tribe in
Sudan, or creating an Indian Civil Service. Fourthly, he cites a number
of grateful 'natives' for applauding the work of the empire. These
voices support the authorial intention of emphasizing the advantages
of the empire.[3] Fifthly, he attributes the atrocities committed in the
name of colonialism to human failure – the sinful nature of human
beings. Colonialism is an exercise of power by sinful human beings,
which reaches its widest range of potential good and evil under the
form of imperialism.

For Niebuhr, too, colonialism was an inevitable stage in the development of civilizations. Countries exposed to colonialism were either
'on the primitive level of tribal life' or, as in the case of ancient cultures
like India and China, lacking in 'technical means of communication
which are important sources of cohesion in an integral community'
(Niebuhr 1959: 202). Colonialism is about strong nations relating to
weaker nations. It is God's purpose for less privileged peoples and a
temporary, passing phase. As for Warren, so for Niebuhr imperialism
was not in itself immoral. Each empire must be considered individu-
ally. He also made a distinction between older and modern empires.
The earlier empires were marked by nationalistic imperialism, where
the stronger dominate the weaker. These were morally inferior to
modern empires. The new empires are merely servants of the universal community (Niebuhr 1959: 22). Colonialism, for Niebuhr, was

---

[3] The two 'native' voices used by Warren were Rajah Rammohun Roy and
K. M. Panikkar. Though in Rammohun Roy's time, the mood was that of pro-
empire, he was not a passive applauder of colonialism. He sided with Irish
peasants against the absentee landlords, and showed solidarity with the
people of Latin America by throwing a public dinner at the Town Hall of
Calcutta when constitutional government was established in the Spanish controlled South America. See Susobhan Sarkar, *On the Bengal Renaissance*,
Calcutta: Papyrus, 1985, p. 21. More significantly, he wrote: 'Enemies to
liberty and friends of despotism have never been, and never will be ultimately successful.' See Sophia Dobson Collet, *The Life and Letters of Raja Rammohun
Roy* (1900), Calcutta: Sadharn Brahmo Samaj, 1962, p. 131. In Panikkar's view,
Warren's was a classic case of selective reading which overlooks his devastating critique of mission. See Panikkar, *Asia and Western Dominance*, London:
George Allen & Unwin, 1965, especially p. 297.

triggered off by three motivations – missionary, economic and political.

First, the missionary motive. This, for Niebuhr, should not be confused with mission in the conventional Christian sense, but is a desire to spread and advance the benefits of the religious, political and technical resources of strong nations. The missionary motive is based on the conviction that empires are 'trustees of civilization' and that they are able to 'bestow a value of universal validity' (Niebuhr 1959: 203). Secondly, he concedes that imperialism is motivated by economic factors, though Niebuhr strongly disputes the communist charge of 'capitalist aggressiveness' as the sole intention. In his view, the ethnic and cultural arrogance of European empires caused much more devastation in the colonies than did economic exploitation. Thirdly, there was the political motive, which takes into account self-defence, security, power, prestige and glory. It is worth noting that Niebuhr, before the Second World War, was a liberal Marxist and cautioned against the dangers of US imperialism, but changed his mind when America emerged as a superpower and talked about responsible use of its new-found power (Stone 1981: 183–4).

Warren and Niebuhr present empire as morally neutral, open to misuse, but with the right rulers a worthy enterprise. What Warren and Niebuhr failed to acknowledge was the fundamental premise of empires. Empires are basically about technically and militarily advantaged superior 'races' ruling over inferior and backward peoples. When imperial powers invade, the conquered are not permitted to be equal to the invaders. This was true of all empires, Roman to British and American. This basic assumption of superiority is never questioned in their writings.

The writings of Niebuhr and Warren emphasize lofty intentions of uplifting depraved but appreciative natives. There is a passionate belief in empire, but how the whole enterprise is essential to the well-being of the Western powers hardly comes into the equation. While pointing out the benefits bestowed on the colonies, no reference is made to colonies as sources of raw material, cheap labour, secure markets and potential sites of investment. India's importance for the wider mercantile interests of the British empire is rarely addressed. This apparently 'native-friendly', sympathetic and favourable face of colonialism conveniently overlooks the predatory aspect of the economy of colonialism.

In the name of theologizing, what we have here is old-fashioned imperial self-justification based on ignorance of the rich heritage of other peoples' traditions and an excessive optimism about what the

West has done and can do for Asia, Africa and Latin America. Such an attitude overlooks what those at the receiving end felt about the process. The basic imperial assumption that Western values ought to prevail throughout the world is fine from a liberal Western perspective, but it does not always follow that the rest of the world wishes to adopt them. The Welsh resistance leader spoke for all the conquered people, when he was captured and brought before the emperor in Rome, and said: 'Because you desire to conquer the world, it does not necessarily follow that the world desires to be conquered by you.'[4]

For most European theologians at the time, the empire was a matter of divine dispensation, and, as such, beyond ultimate criticism. Stephen Neill, who on the whole took a similar line, was a little more cautious when he came to his conclusion: 'The history of the Christian mission in the colonial period must in the end be left to the judgement of God, who alone knows all the facts, who alone can exercise a perfectly objective and merciful judgement' (Neill 1966: 424). What is ironic about this statement is that the people who passed indiscriminate judgements on other peoples' cultures, manners and customs, are unusually silent when it comes to scrutinizing their own. What is also ironic is that systematic theology in Britain has continued to the present day as complacently unwilling to confront the reality of empire and its postcolonial consequences.[5]

Responding to the Raj

Indian Christian responses to colonialism vary with the particular constituency one is looking at. Among the vast majority of Indian Christians from the subaltern class – a class largely rural, semi-literate, minimally if at all Westernized, and non-brahminical – who came to Christianity mainly through mass conversions, the common attitude was one of gratitude and admiration. For these converts, who were mainly outcasts and tribals, their principal encounter with the colonial power was through the mission agencies and their welfare work. They were the recipients of the beneficent effects of missionary work. These converts from the oppressed classes experienced for

---

[4] Cited in *The Guardian*, 9.6.02, p. 15.

[5] For a survey of the current status of British theology, see David Ford, 'Theological Wisdom, British Style', *Christian Century*, 5 April 2000, pp. 388–91; 'British Theology After a Trauma: Divisions and Conversations', *Christian Century*, 12 April 2000, pp. 425–31; and 'British Theology: Movements and Churches', *Christian Century*, 19 April 2000, pp. 467–73. British Black theology does not even get a mention.

themselves the schools and hospitals that the missionaries ran and personally benefited from their work. They saw their dignity being restored by the intervention of missionaries and colonial administration in cases like the Upper Cloth Movement in South Tranvancore. A community which has stigma attached to it as being the lowest of the low, is now being repeatedly told by missionaries that, contrary to the Aryan racist myth, the Bible teaches that all people are descended from one human being made in the image of God. As Christians, 'they have special prerogatives and privileges bestowed upon them by their Divine Master which places the poorest and humblest Christians above the princes and rulers, and the richest and the mightiest people of this world'. They 'were not part or a section of the Indian nation in the same way other communities are'. On the contrary, 'they were a nation, a separate nation, a holy nation separate and distinct from all other nations of the world'.[6] Such claims and bestowal of these epithets, 'holy nation', 'separate nation' and 'the new people of God', were an unimaginable boon to these culturally marginalized and economically deprived people. These converts saw only the positive side of missionary activity. Moreover, they were taught by missionaries who had no interest in criticizing a system which worked to their advantage.[7] The *Missionary Herald* reported that missionaries did more to reconcile Indians to 'the British regime than any other single Western element operating in India'.[8] The British Raj, to these disadvantaged Indians, was different from the Raj experienced by high-caste Western-educated Hindus. More to the point, they preferred British rule to the enormous oppression they suffered under their own Hindu neighbours. They feared that if the British left, the social and economic benefits and achievements they had gained under the British regime would be lost. When orthodox Hindu voices began to be heard in contradistinction to the liberal national movement, these Christians from the depressed classes feared for their place in the new India. The letter columns of missionary journals of the time were full of such fears. Here is one of them:

> Unquestionably I agree with Bishop Subhan that Christianity is in danger, and unless we rise unitedly to confront it, our position will be delicate in new India. Already cases have been brought to my

---

[6] *The Indian Witness* 77(28) (1947): 217.

[7] There were a handful of missionaries such as C. F. Andrews, Jack Winslow and his associates, including Verrier Elwin, who were exceptions to this and offered a critique of the empire.

[8] *Missionary Herald* (April 1879): 144.

notice, when poor Christians have been approached by members of other communities to change their religion. The economic condition of the Christian community is dreadful, and unemployment of its members by the government and Hindu concerns would reduce the community to poverty and destituteness, with the result that many of its members would find salvation in changing their faith.[9]

For the majority of these converts, what mattered most were their local networks of caste, family and village rather than a pan-Indian identity in a newly freed India.

Another constituency was that represented by the national Christian forum in the form of the National Council of Churches of India. The Council was formed in 1923, at the height of colonialism, and consisted mainly of Protestant churches. The leadership of the Council was initially largely in the hands of foreign missionaries. Kaj Baago, who studied the history of the NCC, points out that the Council on the whole was 'anxious to defend British policy both past and present in India' (Baago 1965: 28) and theological critique was low on its agenda. During the agitation for Home Rule, all that the Council did was to issue statements which were 'vague, woolly and cautious in their choice of words, so that they could be interpreted both ways' (Baago 1965: 28). Their only repeated gesture was to organize prayers for peace: 'We may not offer advice, but we will give ourselves to prayer, and endeavour as far as in us lies to promote the spirit of goodwill' (Baago 1965: 38). The editorial in the council's journal, dated August 1947, the very month India gained its independence, is interesting and reflects a fear of Hindu domination like that of low-caste Christians. While praising the relinquishment of power by the British as a tribute to their 'sincerity and statesmanship', it went on to question the proposed new symbols of the nation – the national flag, the national anthem, the national dress and salutation. The editorial[10] found that the national flag did not symbolize the unity of India and objected to the Asoka Wheel included in it because it represented a different philosophy of life – the transmigration of souls, which not all communities subscribed to. The editorial felt that the proposed national anthem – Bankim Chandra's celebrated hymn to the motherland, *Bande Matram* – was written in a high-flown Hindi, the tune 'most uninspiring'. Perhaps the editor was uncomfortable with a hymn that had been a potent rallying call during the mass

---

[9] *Indian Witness* 77(30) (1947): 233.
[10] The editors were all Indians – R. B. Manikam, M. T. Titus, J. W. Sadiq and E. C. Bhatty.

nationalistic struggle.[11] The editorial conceded the new national salutations such as *salam* and *namaste* as harmless, but thoroughly opposed the idea of the Gandhi cap, previously proscribed by the British authorities because of its symbolic potency, replacing the 'majestic turban'.[12] All along the attitude of the NCC had been cautious, detached and apolitical.

Among the group of high-caste, Western-educated converts in the middle of the nineteenth century, British rule was seen as an opportunity – an opportunity to reconfront their culture, reclaim it and reshape it to meet the demands of the time. These 'babus' welcomed the British presence but perceived its function in their own way. They saw in the work of Orientalists an important dimension of their cultural achievements now being elevated and acquiring recognition. This unearthing of a monumental past by the Orientalists provided an opportunity for these 'babus' to bask in an ancient glory and to shake Hindu and Aryan culture out of its theological complacency and degradation. What was important for them was the instrumentality of British rule in providing a stimulus to revitalize the now debased Aryan culture and identity and in the process advance the cause of national rebirth. K. M. Banerjea, an outstanding national figure of his time, saw, in the coming of the British, the mystery of Godliness which was revealed to the ancient seers, and which had been hitherto 'locked up, as under a seal, in musty manuscripts', now being brought into 'the light under the auspicious patronage of England's crown' (Philip 1982: 198).

As with most of their Western counterparts, there was a reluctance among the most of these Indian theologians to criticize colonialism. One could attribute two reasons for this. The early converts, especially the ones who articulated their faith in a written form, were faced with two urgent questions and spent their energies addressing these rather than engaging in a theological evaluation of the empire. One, to prove that they were true patriots, and the other to demonstrate that the Christianity they embraced was not a foreign religion but was continuous with Vedic Hinduism. The general perception of Indian converts at that time was that they were perceived as people who had given up their national customs and habits and had become deracinated. The Brahmo Samajists constantly castigated the converts for forsaking their true religion and cultural practices. Keshub Chunder

---

[11] It was Rabindranath Tagore's *Jana gana mana* which became the official national anthem for the Republic of India.

[12] 'Editorial Notes', *The National Christian Council Review* 67(8) (August 1947): 343–4.

Sen, in one of his public addresses, taunted Indian Christians for their tendency to imitate their rulers:

> I must therefore protest against that denationalization which is so general among Native converts to Christianity. (Cheers). With the religion of their heathen forefathers, they generally abandon the manners and customs of their country, and with Christianity they embrace the usages of Europeans; even in the dress and diet they assume an affected air of outlandishness, which estranges them from their own countrymen. They deliberately and voluntarily cut themselves off from Native society as soon as they are baptized, and, as an inevitable consequence, come to contract a sort of repugnance to everything Oriental, and an enthusiastic admiration for everything European. (Hear, Hear) They seemed to be ashamed of their country and their nationality. (Sen 1901: 34–5)

Brahmabandhab Upadhyay, himself a convert, noted how others looked at Christians: 'People here understand by the term "Christian", a man who drinks liquor and eats beef, who hates the scriptures of India as lies and her inspired men as imposters' (Lipner and Gispert-Sauch 1991: 2). Faced with such criticism, these early converts sought to project themselves as patriotic Indians. The way they went about this was to project Christianity not as an alien religion but as part of the Vedic tradition. Thus, they were proud to be Christians. They argued very persuasively that Christianity, far from being an imported and an alien faith, was truly the heir of the ancient Indian tradition as distinct from the decadent contemporary Hinduism. Like Indiana Jones, they raided their own textual archives to demonstrate that these Vedic texts were already Christian or modernist, so that conversion to Christianity was not in any way an act of disloyalty to India. They were able to demonstrate that Vedic Hindus and Christians in India were the true descendants of the Vedic Aryans. In *Arian Witness*, written to prove the 'patriotic honour' of Indian Christians, Banerjea told his readers that it was the Western-educated Hindus who had deviated from the faith of their forefathers, and that only Hindu Christians were the true upholders of the theory and practice of their primitive ancestors. He went on to claim that they were 'the Brahminical Arians of India, and that if the authors of the Vedas could by any possibility now return to the world, they would at once recognise the Indian Christians, "far more complacently" as their own descendants, than any other body of educated Indians' (Banerjea 1875: 10). In one of his lectures, Banerjea told his audience: 'Embracing Christ, you will find in Him a strength and comfort which your ancient *Rishis* would have regarded as a most valuable treasure had they lived in these days. You will find in Him everything worthy of your lineage, worthy of your antiquity, worthy of your traditions, and worthy of your education, and at the same time just to your children and to your successors in life' (Philip 1982: 201). Christianity, for Banerjea, was Vedic doctrine 'in its legitimately developed form'. He writes: 'The relation between Vedic doctrine and Christianity is indeed so intimate that you can scarcely hold the one without being led to the other, much less can you keep hold on the one while resisting the claims of the other' (Philip 1982: 200). He was able to show that God had been active not only through brahminical traditions but also through Christ, and the Christian gospel as a maturation of and climactic finale of the Vedic hope. By endowing Vedic texts with crypto-Christian ideas, these Brahmin converts challenged the missionary view that Hinduism was unfit to bring about a healthy national rejuvenation. More importantly, they argued for a historical continuity between Christianity and Hinduism whereas missionaries were advocating a complete break with the latter. Unlike the missionaries, they were not interested in contrasting Hinduism with Christianity but perceived Christianity as the fulfilment of Hinduism. Whereas missionaries used Christ and Christian experience as a benchmark to expose the defects of Hinduism, these converts used Hindu texts and Hindu experience to elucidate the meaning and purpose of Christ.

In these Hinduized theologies national redemption was sought not so much by advancing political strategies but by placing faith in the Christian gospel as a remedy for India's problem. They believed that Christianity could provide the solid basis for Indian nationhood. All these thinkers were true patriots and believed in the nationalist cause and uplifting of India from its misery, but their teleological aim was to make India Christian. For instance, Banerjea, who was politically active during the colonial era, and notwithstanding his status as a true patriot, believed that national redemption lay in 'adopting the religion of the present rulers with all its temporal and spiritual blessings' (Banerjea 1851: 70). For him, the answer to India's moral welfare and economic progress was to be found in the Christian faith. He wrote:

> Christianity alone has resisted the bewitching charms of the goddess, and thrown down her altars. Christianity alone has quenched the Brahmin's fire and the ignited darts of Shiva. Christianity alone has destroyed caste, educated females, stopped the marriage, or

rather the prostitution, of infants, relieved widows, and proclaimed due liberty to the captives of the Zenana. Christianity, wherever it has got a footing, has transformed the Hindu's house from a scene of idolatry, female debasement, ignorance, and idleness, into one of rational worship, of moral energy, intellectual advancement, and female aggrandizement. (Banerjea 1851: 75)

Brahmabandhab Upadhyay, another Christian who was caught up in the national politics during the colonial era, exhibited a similar attitude, and saw his task as bringing his people to what he called the Hindu-Catholic faith.[13] The high-caste nineteenth-century converts sought to identify a Hindu textual basis for Christianity by delving into the most ancient Hindu texts. Far from being imitations of Western modes, these intertextual studies, produced within the colonial contexts, were not only complex transformations and transgressions of existing native conventions, but also disrupted and invigorated conservative Christian modes of the time by integrating native idioms. This was the Hinduism of the elite and high culture in which dalits hardly figured. Notwithstanding his disapproval of the caste system, Banerjea's main theological focus was the Brahmins. In one of his lectures he made it clear who the natives were: 'I use the term, however, in a *restricted* sense, meaning thereby the descendants and successors of the Aryan emigrants who occupied the country in the earliest ages of which we have any history or tradition, and formed that great community of scholars, heroes, artisans, and merchants which willingly placed itself under the spiritual guidance of Brahmins and Rishis. To the descendants and representatives of that great family, I now address myself' (Philip 1982: 160).

For some Indian Christians in the earlier twentieth century, inspired by Gandhi, national freedom was of supreme importance, British rule to be opposed as exploitative and corrupting. These Gandhian Christians were a relatively small but important group, among them S. K. Rudra, S. K. George and J. C. Kumarappa. More

---

[13] This was a common view later also. Pandipedi Chenchiah, who threw himself into the cause of national liberation, also spoke in terms of Jesus as the answer to India: 'India needs the living and the present Lord. We offer to India the Jesus of history, the founder of Christianity, as the way to salvation . . . We present Jesus as an exemplar, ideal and model – that is, as a tonic to the soul; India wants him as a perpetual life-giver, renewer of her youth . . . We have offered new lamps for old, God for God, religion for religion, temple for temple' (D. A. Thangasamy, *The Theology of Chenchiah*, Confessing the Faith in India, 1, Bangalore: Christian Institute for the Study of Religion and Society, 1966, pp. 216–18).

accommodating theologically, slightly later was the internationally known and respected M. M. Thomas. For him, the empire was part of the divine ordering of structures and powers. Echoing Marx's double vision of the British in India, one destructive and the other regenerative, Thomas wrote that God used British imperialism 'first to judge and correct traditional Indian life and put India on the path of progress' (Thomas 1959: 7). For him, colonialism was like 'St. Paul in Romans 13, where he says that the Roman power is ordained of God for "your good"' (Thomas 1960: 23). While acknowledging the exploitative nature of colonialism, Thomas saw it as God using 'one evil to correct other evils' (Thomas 1960: 24). Interestingly, in his correspondence with Max Warren, referred to above, Thomas agreed with Warren's main proposal, but he differed from him on three counts. One, like Warren, Thomas, too, saw British rule as God's providence and British imperialism in India as laying the foundation for political unity and social progress. But, unlike Warren, Thomas added Indian nationalism as part of a continuous act of Divine Providence in India. Later, when a virulent form of Hindu communal nationalism emerged as an alternative resolution to colonialism, Thomas became less enchanted with it. Secondly, Thomas redefined God's providence in the light of God's redemption. He wrote: 'It means seeing providential ordering and reordering of power and structures of power in political history as different from and at the same time related to the divine work of redemption in Christ' (Thomas 1959: 8). People who imagine themselves to be agents of God's providence and conscious of God's call, end up as self-righteous and become destructive of their fellow human beings. Thirdly, along with the positive cultural impact of the West, colonialism has also introduced to India new gods such as materialism, secularism, rationalism and communism, which not only vie with other existing gods in India, but also pose a threat to the Christian gospel. Thomas's critique of nationalism in some respects resonates with the fears of national leaders of the time like Rabindranath Tagore. Whereas Tagore wanted to replace Indian nationalism with Indian civilization with its 'demonstrated capacity to live with and creatively use contradictions and inconsistences' (Nandy 1994: 83), Thomas proposed the Christian gospel and the Kingdom as viable alternatives. Thomas believed in nationalism as a preparation for the gospel: 'It is from that angle, I would say that nationalism and nation-building are a divine preparation for the Gospel. It is creating a situation in which Christian social thought and action and the preaching of the Gospel are as integral to each other as raising the Question and giving the

Answer' (Thomas 1960: 26). For him, in any national struggle and in any cultural transformation, people are 'led to a decision for or against Jesus Christ' (Thomas 1960: 25). In an ironic way, Thomas's solution was another form of colonialism – conquering Indians for Christ.

M. M. Thomas and Western-educated liberals paid less attention to critical rereading of Hindu texts than their forebears, though they recognized their importance. Their strategy was synthetic and accumulative rather than a question of reforming, or purifying Hinduism. They relied on insights drawn from biblical theology, evangelical piety and a selective appropriation of secular ideologies such as Marxism, socialism and humanism.

Postcolonial Cogitations

Theologies in India arose as a result of responding to colonialism and later in the cause of nation building. It was the compelling business of national independence, and the re-articulation of nationhood after colonial occupation and its ravages which principally shaped Indian theologies, rather than ecclesiastical practices, doctrinal beliefs, or philosophical or rational concerns. Undergirding their theological concerns was the fundamental issue of relating to the way one constructs and characterizes one's own identity. It was primarily their endeavour to establish a self and national identity as minorities living in communities shaped by a variety of textual and oral traditions both sacred and secular, and by the ongoing socio-political process, which influenced the questions these Indian theologians put to the gospel. When the colonial rulers wondered whether a country like India with a multiplicity of cultures and a diversity of languages could ever become a viable and cohesive nation-state, the emergence of a Western-educated elite was able to lay a basis for a pan-Indian nationalism. They were able to achieve this by reinventing, restoring and reconfiguring some of their religious and cultural symbols.

One may not find in these discourses many of the theoretical issues, theological vocabularies or textual forms we often see in Western theological writings. These theologies are mainly about belonging and identity and how Indian Christians have negotiated and continue to negotiate an Indian-Christian identity in a country which is inured to perceiving Christians with suspicion and prejudice. Any comparative enterprise is likely to discredit Indian Christian theology. Indian theology is either appreciated as pukka theology in the Western scholarly sense, or it is not. If it is not, then it is seen as inchoate and bankrupt by Western standards. These theologians, though, were not interested in measuring up to alien standards. They set up their own parameters by naming and identifying hermeneutical concerns which were relevant to their context, and set out to ask questions which were not addressed elsewhere, and went on to solve the problems they set for themselves. I think there is a lesson here for the current theological enterprise in India, which desires only to 'catch up' with the West.

One of the incongruities of postcolonial discourse is that its proponents hailed from a number of Islamic societies but rarely took account of the potency of religion in these regions. The pioneer theoreticians who investigated colonialism came from the Arabic world – Albert Memmi from Tunisia, Frantz Fanon from Algeria and Edward Said from Palestine. But religion rarely gets into their theoretical agenda. Rae, one of the characters in Leila Aboulela's *The Translator*, is spot-on when he remarks: 'Even Fanon, who I have always admired, had no insights into the religious feelings of the North Africans he wrote about. He never made the link between Islam and anti-colonialism' (Aboulela 1999: 97). Said's own preference for secular criticism over theological did not help either. Since the Enlightenment, the secular has been favoured and the spiritual and theological have been denigrated as signs of primordial urges and as unmodern. The treatment of Islam in the popular media is a conspicuous case in point. After September 11, many have pointed out how Islam is a faith trapped in a medieval time-warp, and is yet to go through an eighteenth-century-style enlightenment. Linking Islam to medieval savagery may serve for theological point-scoring, but such a proposition assumes that barbarism died as the Renaissance emerged in the Christian West. Even a casual reading of history will reveal that the real masters of evil, who even managed to turn genocide into a mundane reality, all lived in the last century and most of them came from the Christianized West. Postcolonial criticism, which was influenced by Marxism, post-structuralism and psychoanalysis, and which is now thriving in modern, secular and liberal cultures, has sadly paid little attention to the potency of religion and theology among Third World peoples.[14] The secular bias and assumptions of

---

[14] There are books on Hinduism, Islam, Buddhism and Confucianism dealing with postcolonial concerns such as orientalism and representation of these religions, but they do not come up with postcolonial theories or strategies to understand religions. See Anouar Majid, *Unveiling Traditions: Postcolonial Islam in a Polycentric World*, Durham, N.C.: Duke University Press, 2000; Richard King, *Orientalism and Religion: Postcolonial Theory, India and 'The*

postcolonial discourse have not only increased the gap between theory and religions, but have also failed to acknowledge alternatives rooted in religion. There is a considerable distance between the theoretical interests of postcolonialism and the hermeneutical interests of postcolonial societies. Religion and religious symbols have been used successfully in both colonial and postcolonial societies as a way of surviving, subverting and challenging colonialism and Christendom. The future legitimacy of postcolonial criticism depends on paying attention to this issue.

In a postcolonial context, geography is no longer an arbiter in defining what theology is. It appears that a theological imagination need not be in harmony with a specific geographical terrain. The idea of India can be invented elsewhere, away from the subcontinent, as is happening in the novels of Salman Rushdie, Jhumpa Lahiri, Rohinton Mistry and Bharati Mukherjee, to name a few. Amy Tan, Le Ly Hayslip and others have wrestled to integrate Chinese and Vietnamese heritage into their new immigrant experience.[15] In theological discourse, too, this is happening, but it is at a nascent phase. Peter Phan (Phan and Lee 1999), Jung Young Lee (Lee 1999) and Eleazar Fernandez (Fernandez 2001) have tried to articulate a theology away from their Vietnamese, Korean and Filipino homes. At a time when national boundaries are becoming blurred, and attachment to a particular locale is being disturbed through displacement of peoples, what is the task of contextual theologies which have invested so much in locations, roots, indigenous resources and soil? There are a couple of options in the offing.

One would be to search for answers in the vernacular and in the ancient heritage which colonial education taught us to sneer at. It would be a painless rebuff to globalization and its tendency to devour vernacular modes. Jettison the larger cosmopolitan canvas for a smaller rural one. Two characters in novels, one written during the colonial time and the other in the postcolonial context, typify such an option. *Thillai Govindan*, written at the height of colonialism by Madhaviah, is an engrossing account of the eponymous hero, a Tamil Brahmin's loss and recovery of self and identity under the impact of British rule, Western education and Christianity, and his finally

Mystic East', London: Routledge, 1999; and J. J. Clarke, *Oriental Enlightenment: The Encounter Between Asian and Western Thought*, London: Routledge, 1997.

[15] The literature on Asian-American literature is too vast to be listed here. A convenient entry point to the subject is Qun Wang, 'Border Crossing, Cultural Negotiations, and the Authenticity of Asian American Voices', *Passages: Journal of Transnational and Transcultural Studies* 1(2) (1999): 278–89.

finding peace and consolation in an indigenous text – the *Bhagavad Gita*.[16] The other, *The House of Blue Mangoes*, a postcolonial look at colonial India, is a novel chronicling three generations of a family from South India, but this time a Christian one. Daniel Dorai, the second-generation head of the family, is a Christian from a non-brahminical class. Typical of his generation, he lionized the work of the missionaries and looked forward to centuries of British rule. This proclaimed appreciation is deceptive. It appears that in spite of his ardent Christian faith and gratitude to the British, at a time of personal and national upheaval and uncertainty, he, too, like Thillai Govindan, found spiritual refuge in the *Bhagavad Gita* and the *Upanishads*. Some weeks after his death, a family member found among his belongings well-thumbed and neatly underlined in blue ink a copy of the *Brhad-aranyaka Upanishad*.[17]

The second option would be to follow the new global nomads depicted in Hwee Hwee Tan's futuristic novel, *Mammon Inc*. This is about the new generations who have 'no fixed cultural identity' and who embrace the cosmopolitan culture enthusiastically and wallow in the possibilities it offers. They are the 'cosmopolitan citizens of the world, equally at home in a 212 or 0207 area code, equally well versed in the work of George Lucas and Joseph Campbell to be able to analyse the mythological arches in Star Wars' (Tan 2002: 143).

Or, there might be a third option, namely to blend creatively cosmopolitan and vernacular cultures. It is not blending into someone else's culture which the globalizers blindly advocate and which will inevitably lead to destruction of one's own identity and history, but the blending into one's own culture some of the liberative elements of someone else's. This is not a particularly original idea. The nineteenth-century converts mentioned above – K. M. Banerjea, Upadhyay and others from Southern India such as Krishna Pillai and Vedanayagam Sasthriyar – have cleverly and creatively combined Bengali and Tamil with Christian ideas. The blending I have in mind differs notably in three aspects from these earlier experiments. (1) It should go beyond identity hermeneutics. Self-affirmation and restoring the lost pride and emasculated dignity of an alienated people are fine and worthy causes in themselves. But to hold on to them, and to reiterate them uncritically when the context out of which these issues arose has moved, is to risk turning them into theological clichés. (2) It

---

[16] Madhaviah 1944: 128. The page number refers to the Tamil version. The English version published by T. F. Unwin, London, appeared in 1916.

[17] David Davidar, *The House of Blue Mangoes*, New Delhi: Viking, 2002, p. 345.

should move beyond its high-caste moorings and take into account the legends and myths of the dalits and tribals. (3) It should shed its overtly Christian superiority and smugness. The earlier attempts at assimilation suffered from Christian triumphalism. What I envisage is a form of vernacular cosmopolitanism, like that advocated by Homi Bhabha, which is not constrained by old boundaries and entrenched positions but allows transgression. Vernacular cosmopolitanism is a cultural act and translation which is 'not simply appropriation or adaptation; it is a process through which cultures are required to revise their own systems of reference, norms and values, by departing from their habitual or "inbred" rules of transformation' (Bhabha 2000: 141). Vernacular cosmopolitanism is about an appropriation and transformation of cultures which resist any simplified binary under-standing. This latter all too often tends to glorify the local and dis-credit the global. It is a discursive practice which anticipates a complicated negotiation requiring an exchange of ideas in all direc-tions, and keeping a constant vigilance over the predatory nature of Western values and treating circumspectly the immaculate qualities of the vernacular. It is in this multi-directional swirl of cultural ideas that I foresee the emergence of postcolonial theology.

References

Aboulela, Leila, 1999. *The Translator*, Edinburgh: Polygon.

Baago, Kaj, 1965. *A History of the National Christian Council of India 1914–1964*, Nagpur: The National Christian Council.

Banerjea, K. M., 1851. 'Hindu Caste', *Calcutta Review* 15: 36–75.

Banerjea, K. M., 1875. *The Arian Witness: Or the Testimony of Arian Scriptures in Corroboration of Biblical History and the Rudiments of Christian Doctrine, includ-ing Dissertations on the original and early adventures of Indo-Arians*, Calcutta: Thacker, Spink & Co.

Bhabha, Homi, 2000. 'The Vernacular Cosmopolitan', in Ferdinand Dennis and Naseem Khan (eds), *Voices of the Crossing: The Impact of Britain on Writers from Asia, the Caribbean and Africa*, London: Serpent's Tail, pp. 133–42.

Elliott-Binns, L. E., 1952. *The Development of English Theology in the Later Nineteenth Century*, London: Longmans, Green & Co.

Fernandez, Eleazar S., 2001. 'Exodus-toward-Egypt: Filipino-Americans' Struggle to Realize the Promised Land in America', in Eleazar S. Fernandez and Fernando F. Segovia (eds), *A Dream Unfinished: Theological Reflections on America from the Margins*, Maryknoll, N.Y.: Orbis Books, pp. 167–81.

Lee, Jung Young, 1999. 'A Life In-Between: A Korean-American Journey', in Peter C. Phan and Jung Young Lee (eds), *Journeys at the Margin: Toward an Autobiographical Theology in American-Asian Perspective*, Collegeville: Liturgical Press, pp. 23–39.

Lipner, Julius, and George Gispert-Sauch (eds), 1991. *The Writings of*

Brahmabandhab Upadhyay including his life and thought, vol. I, Library of Indian Christian Theology, 6, Bangalore: United Theological College.

Madhaviah, A., 1944. *Thillai Govindan*, Madras: Tinamani Press.

Mascall, E. L., 1960. 'Anglican Dogmatic Theology, 1939–60', *Theology* 63(475): 1–7.

Nandy, Ashis, 1994. *The Illegitimacy of Nationalism*, Delhi: Oxford University Press.

Neill, Stephen, 1966. *Colonialism and Christian Missions*, London: Lutterworth Press.

Niebuhr, Reinhold, 1959. *Nations and Empires: Recurring Patterns in the Political Order*, London: Faber & Faber.

Phan, Peter C., and Jung Young Lee (eds), 1999. *Journeys at the Margin: Toward an Autobiographical Theology in American-Asian Perspective*, Collegeville: Liturgical Press.

Philip, T. V., 1982. *Krishna Mohan Banerjea: Christian Apologist*, Confessing the Faith in India Series, 15, Bangalore: Christian Institute for the Study of Religion and Society.

Sen, Keshub Chunder, 1901. *Keshub Chunder Sen's Lectures in India*, London: Cassell.

Stone, Ronald H., 1981. *Reinhold Niebuhr: Prophet to Politicians*, Lanham: University Press of America.

Storr, Vernon F., 1913. *The Development of English Theology in the Nineteenth Century 1800–1860*, London: Longmans, Green & Co.

Tan, Hwee Hwee, 2002. *Mammon Inc.*, London: Penguin Books.

Tharoor, Shashi, 1989. *The Great Indian Novel*, New Delhi: Penguin Books.

Thomas, M. M., 1959. 'Indian Nationalism: A Christian Interpretation', *Religion and Society* 6(2): 4–26.

Thomas, M. M., 1960. 'Some Notes on a Christian Interpretation of Nationalism in Asia', *South East Asia Journal of Theology* 2(2): 16–26.

Warren, M. A. C., 1955. *Caesar: The Beloved Enemy: Three Studies in the Relation of Church and State. The Reinecker Lectures at the Virginia Theological Seminary, Alexandria, Virginia, February 1955*. London: SCM Press.

10

Textual Takeaways

Third World Texts in Western Metropolitan Centres

The scramble for Africa may be over, but the struggle for her history, her art, her literature and her children rages on unabated.

Maraire 1996: 79

In this chapter I wish to share some of my experiences in introducing, teaching and analysing theological texts that originate from what is known as the Third World in 'First World' metropolitan centres. In doing so I would like to narrate how texts from other cultures are smoothed out of their primary contexts, concerns and contestations, travel across borders and become objects of analysis and scrutiny within an alien secondary context. I would also like to explore the role of a Third World academic in presenting such texts to Western audiences when the presenter is seen as both subject matter and a reliable guide to the subject.

Let me begin with an anecdote. Henry Louis Gates Jr, the African-American cultural critic, went to Cambridge for his doctoral studies. On arrival he told his supervisor that he wished to work on black literature for his dissertation. The supervisor's reaction was intriguing. He responded with great disdain: 'Tell me Sir . . . what *is* black literature?' (Gates 1992: 88, italics original). Similarly, when I say that I lecture in Third World theologies, I am often asked in tones varying from the paternalistic to sheer astonishment, 'Do tell me, what are Third World theologies?' Like Gates, I too am not quite sure whether the question is asked with the serious intention of obtaining information or whether it is merely rhetorical. Even before I can provide a list of names, books and topics, a second question is directed at me: 'Do you mean to say that you manage to cover all these things?'

What then are Third World theologies? Third World theologies, like the British term curry, are a fabricated entity. British curry is a colonial invention. No Indian cook would identify it as the genuine stuff. The variety of spicy meat and vegetable dishes that Indians make using local ingredients are not called curry but have specific names in each language. When the English incorporated curry into their cuisine, imagining it was Indian food, they were incorporating the 'other' on their own terms as a unified whole replacing the variety of local spicy dishes. Those who have tasted Indian balti dishes or curries in British homes will know that though they try to make them taste Indian, they are essentially anglicized to suit the British palate. Likewise, 'Third World theologies' is a fabricated term. It is an invented response to cover a network of textual production and theological articulation of a vast array of people having diverse religious, cultural and linguistic backgrounds. In other words, the contextuality and historical process of their development are neglected and/or homogenized. This is evident in their being christened with collective names such as 'Third World Theology' or 'Liberation Theology'. Theologies from different continents, cultures and constituencies are drained of their territorial focus and are often clubbed and blended together into a coherent whole. Just as the earlier oriental scholarship viewed the 'other' as a unified whole, the former colonial metropolis tends now to respond to this wide textual spectrum in all-embracing and totalizing terms. The adjectives Black, Asian and Latin American are more important than the quality of the theology they espouse. Assigning a collective identity enables the academy to view these theologies as a separate 'other' and an 'object' to be studied and assessed.

A Postcolonial Puzzle

Gonzalo Arroyo, a Chilean Jesuit, once asked a group of North American theologians, 'Tell me, why is it that when you speak of *our* theology you call it "Latin American theology", but when you speak of *your* theology you call it "theology"?'[1]

The question then is, what sort of Third World theological curries are available to Western audiences? At the risk of over-generalizing, Third World theological texts fall under two categories, namely, *liberation-focused* and *culture-sensitive*. While the former privileges a liberation hermeneutic as key, the latter mobilizes indigenous cultural nuances for the theological enterprise. I should make it clear that these are not neatly demarcated entities, of course, but often interact and are mutually dependent.

---

[1] See McAfee Brown 1990: xix, emphasis original.

Currently the most popular and accessible to Western audiences is the liberation-focused Latin American theology. To this one could add South African liberation theology, which owes its popularity to the Kairos Document. The sensational presentation of Chung Hyun Kyung, the Korean feminist, at the Canberra Assembly of the WCC brought to light the existence of feminist theologies in non-Western cultures. Recently, there has been an explosion of interest in Indian *dalit*, Japanese *burakumin* and other indigenous peoples' theologies. In spite of the adversarial and partisan nature of these theologies, the reason for their popularity in Western circles in general, and particularly in scholarly guilds, is that they share assumptions with metropolitan academic culture. The intellectual structure of these theologies, the way they mobilize the grandmasters of Western discipline, the overtly Christocentric framework with which they operate, and the theoretical tools they employ, make them easy targets for Western absorption, even colonization. While espousing and retaining grass-roots interest, the theologies of Gutiérrez, Boff and Sobrino largely fall within the Western academic syntax, which makes them easy to incorporate. Kosuke Koyama's observation on the Kairos Document is an apt one. He says that the content is so thoroughly Western that as a result it is better known in Germany than to Zulus (Koyama 1993: 101).

This dominant presence of liberation theology has tended to overshadow and conceal context-sensitive vernacular texts, and has also silenced the pioneering and often daring efforts of an earlier generation of theologians. The vernacular theologies, which privilege indigenous culture as an authentic site for doing theology and focus more on native characteristics and ideas, do not rank as high as liberation theologies that are able to straddle different cultures. These vernacular theologies are context-sensitive and are concerned with and draw heavily on particular language traditions or cultural insights. They are hardly heard in Western academies because they seek to acquire and celebrate their identity by delving into their indigenous resources. They naturally reject the superintending tendencies of Western intellectual tradition. Hence the theological reflections of Vedanayagam Sasthriyar or Krishna Pillai or Vaman Tilak are relatively unknown. Even where they are available in translations, they are deemed not to be addressing the weightier theological issues and are treated as devotional or spiritual texts. The unpopularity of these theologies in Western circles is not due to the fact that they are done in vernacular languages or are non-translatable or incomprehensible, but rather because they employ a different set of ground-rules to fashion their theologies from the protocol set by the academy.

Moreover, the dominance of liberation theology has been instrumental in causing the editing out of some of the earlier Third World attempts at theologizing. Since liberation theology is applauded as the coming of age of the 'younger churches', the tendency has been to overlook their long tradition of theological discourse. I have in mind some of the efforts of Indian theologians during the colonial days. I am sure there are comparable examples in other countries as well. For instance, well before Albert Schweitzer embarked on his celebrated search for the historical Jesus, Raja Rammohun Roy was engaged in such a task, although he did not identify his investigation in those terms. In his *Precepts of Jesus: The Guide to Peace and Happiness* (1820), employing his own version of the narrative criticism which is currently in vogue in biblical scholarship, he was indeed searching for the historical Jesus. Faced with the question of revelation, Nilakanta Sastri (Nehemiah Goreh) was talking about general and special revelation long before these ideas came to be associated with Karl Barth. The 'inclusive' approach to other faiths which is advocated by recent Vatican documents and in the theology of Karl Rahner, was mooted by Indians way back in the early nineteenth century. K. M. Banerjea and Upadhyay were among the first to espouse these ideas. Long before Latin Americans raised the issue of the inappropriateness of European ideals and values for their theology, Indians, who were trying to articulate their faith during the colonial days, had realized this. Brahmabandhab Upadhyay spoke for many when he wrote:

> The Hindu mind is extremely subtle and penetrative, but is opposed to the Graeco-scholastic method of thinking. We must fall back upon the Vedantic method of formulating the Catholic religion to our countrymen. In fact, the Vedanta must be made to do the same service to Catholic faith in India as was done by the Greek philosophy in Europe. (Baago 1969:13)

I recall these theologians and their theological efforts as a sample of the wealth of theologies available. My intention is not to be jingoistic and say we have them all, but just to point out that there is a long tradition of theological discourse in India and other countries but these have been eclipsed by the presence and dominance of liberation theology. Unfortunately, when these texts are studied even in India they are not seen as authoritative theological documents but instead are relegated to church history, and not offered their proper place in systematic theology.

From Contextual Affiliations to International Wanderings

What I would like to do in the rest of this chapter is to discuss the reception of liberation theologies in the former colonial metropolis. What happens when theological texts leave their primary context and move into a secondary context? What sort of reactions do they generate? What Edward Said says in his essay 'Travelling Theory' is equally applicable to theological texts. He writes that when an idea gains this sort of currency, there is 'every likelihood that during its peregrinations it will be reduced, codified, and institutionalised' (Said 1991: 239).

I list below some of the ways in which these texts are received.

Commoditization

When liberation texts are wrested from their native contexts and introduced into the comfort of a First World environment, they become commodities. Though Arjun Appadurai fails to include texts in his study of the social life of commodities, what he says of them is true of texts as well.

> Of course, the best examples of the diversion of commodities from their original nexus is to be found in the domain of fashion, domestic display and collecting in the modern West. These are all examples of what we might call commoditization by diversion, where value, in the art or fashion market, is accelerated or enhanced by placing objects and things in unlikely contexts. It is the aesthetics of decontextualization (itself driven by the quest for novelty) that is at the heart of the display in highbrow Western homes, of the tools and artefacts of the 'other': the Turkman saddlebag, Masai spear or Dink basket. In these objects, we see not only the equation of the authentic with the exotic everyday object, but also the aesthetics of diversion. (Appadurai 1986: 28)

In this double process, which Appadurai identifies as 'commoditization by diversion' and the 'aesthetics of decontextualization', texts which are liberative in their original context become a theology about liberation. Thus the sting is taken out of the text. Liberation theologies are not just a collection of neutral texts. Their intention is to subvert the system that marginalizes people. When such theologies are introduced neglecting the historical and political circumstances of their production and the contextuality of their development, then liberation becomes a commodity which can be theorized, talked about, traded and exchanged among many other interesting theological commodities that are on offer. In describing the function of English intellectuals, Bryan S. Turner sees their role as conduits of ideas rather than creative innovators. He writes, 'If England has been a nation of shopkeepers, then its own intellectuals have been passive traders . . . interpreters and purveyors of "foreign" ideas' (Turner 1994: 144). When liberation becomes a commodity, involvement is kept at a minimum and a cloak of neutrality is maintained without the need to take sides. In other words, the vocabulary of liberation is appropriated devoid of its liberative content, treated as an object to be studied and categorized.

A modern parable

Williams, a Guyanese artist, was introduced to Pablo Picasso. Williams was pleased to meet the master. He thought Picasso and he had certain affinities. Both were immigrants and cosmopolitan. Both were fascinated by non-Western art forms. Both employed the vehicle of art in the struggle against racism and fascism. But Picasso's first comment to Williams was interesting. 'You have a very fine African head. I would like you to pose for me.'[2]

Moral: The West sees the other as an object to be exploited. In the same way, Third World texts are regarded as raw materials to be fitted into Western categories of knowledge.

Prescriptivism

When manifestations of injustice are examined in far-away places, the reaction among First World course participants varies from guilt to blaming the victims. When Third World texts talk about the oppression 'over there' the immediate response is that someone should go there and rectify the mess. This conveniently enables them to overlook not only the injustices in their own backyard but also their own governments' role and involvement in reinforcing and colluding with the structures which perpetuate inequality. Helder Camara's advice to the youth of the developed world is:

Instead of planning to go to the Third World to try and arouse violence there, stay at home in order to help your rich countries to discover that they too are in need of a cultural revolution which will

---

[2] I owe this story to Jordan and Weedon 1995: 446.

produce a new hierarchy of values, a new world vision ... (Camara
1969: 111)

The other reaction is to put the blame on the victims for their own
plight and for not pulling their weight. Consider the following
review:

> The trouble with this is that victimhood is terribly seductive, and
> many become addicted to it, with its corollary of abdicating respon-
> sibility for their own unhappiness ... but victim status needs to be
> renounced early in life before it becomes a habit, and to refuse to see
> oneself as a victim is often a very fine form of protection and
> growth.[3]

Ghettoization

By labelling Third World texts as 'fragments', 'political rhetoric',
'minority discourse' or 'theological lamentations' the academy ghet-
toizes these theologies in the curriculum. Ghettoization operates in
two ways. First, it raises the criterion of universality. Liberation theological texts are seen as partial, political allegories, their exegesis one-
sided, thus replacing honest, objective scholarship. They are seen as
lacking Western intellectual rigour and failing to transcend racial,
gender and class boundaries, as any good theology should do. The
criterion of universality is used to justify the claim that Asian, African,
Latin American, Caribbean and Pacific theologies are provincial
and therefore have no direct relevance to the European context. The
Church of England's *Faith in the City* report, discussing the theological
priorities for English inner cities, captures this mood: 'Liberation
theology is a development that has grown out of political and economic conditions radically different from our own' (*Faith in the City*:
64). Liberation theology is therefore inappropriate to Britain because
the conditions which gave rise to its emergence in Latin America do
not exist in Britain. The report seems unable even to imagine what sort
of liberative reading of the gospel might be called for by the specificity
of the British situation, so impressively analysed there.

 The provincial nature of these theologies enables curriculum
developers to append them as an interesting extra on the timetable.
Theological curricula are dominated by a single model of modernity,
based on the experience of a handful of Western nations, which has
little room for plurality or cultural diversity. Thus liberation theolo-

---

[3] *Church Times*, 13 March 1995, p. 13.

gies are simply tagged on or juxtaposed with already existing courses without examining the ideological agendas, power structures and pedagogical practices that these syllabi reinforce. As a result, little of what happens in these classes penetrates the rest of the curriculum. Such exclusion limits any real impact of courses like mine within the timetable. For instance, the class and race scrutiny that the Ethiopian Eunuch goes through, inevitably dealt with in a course on 'Interpreting the Bible in the Third World', is likely to go unnoticed in the 'Acts of the Apostles' class, where students are encouraged to do 'disinterested' reading and apply traditional strategies of exegesis.

Second, under the rubric of ghettoization, the notion of cultural difference is mobilized. Ghettoization encourages a separate status for and separate development of theologies. It suggests that people should affirm, articulate and map out their theologies within and from their cultural, social and political milieu. Such a notion reinscribes ethnic determinism, which supports the idea that the creative abilities of black people can only be realized through and within the limits of their traditional cultures. In other words, creative abilities are fixed and codified.

This emphasis on cultural difference sometimes manifests itself in a different way. Most of the European students in my classes, who will normally be the first to spot and expose gender-biased language and racial nuances in their own European authors, nevertheless keep quiet when they come across these things in Third World writings, or encounter sloppy exegesis. In refraining from criticism, their reticence reinscribes the notion that these negative aspects are part of the culture and therefore no-go areas for criticism. Such circumspection sets up different rules for the evaluation of 'their' work and 'ours'.

A modern proverb: When a metropolitan academic talks about 'the rhetoric of Difference', beware.

Cultural differences are also invoked to reinforce the idea that serious theological work is the domain of Western academics, whereas what Africans, Asians and Latin Americans can offer is their hospitality and their friendly nature. Listen to what a reviewer has to say about African theology:

> After all that, does the book have anything to say? I too rejoice in the experience that African Christians have a lot to teach Europeans about our common humanity, and about the God who created us; and I have no doubt that in the theologians such as the three here studied, Africa is beginning to develop an impressive body of liter-

ature to help in that. But I doubt if it will be greatly advanced by such a bookish approach. This feels more like a dogged scholar burning much midnight oil and relying on his magnifying glass than the open, laughing, often boisterous yet always friendly, mutual challenge that I have known . . . Sorry, but the enlargement and enrichment of a European's faith by friendship with African Christians is endlessly more real and more fun than this![4]

One way to bridge the gap between the texts emanating from the margins and the centre is to engage in contrapuntal reading. This is a reading strategy advocated by Edward Said with the view to encouraging the experiences of the exploited and exploiter to be studied together. To read contrapuntally means to be aware simultaneously of mainstream scholarship and of other scholarship which the dominant discourse tries to domesticate and speaks and acts against. In Said's words, 'we re-read it not univocally but *contrapuntally*, with a simultaneous awareness both of the metropolitan history that is narrated and of those histories against which (and together with which) the dominating discourse acts' (Said 1993: 59). Translating this into theological disciplines, it means to read Kitamori's *Theology of the Pain of God* with Moltmann's *Crucified God*; Karl Barth's *Romans* with Elsa Tamez's *The Amnesty of Grace*; Mosala's *Biblical Hermeneutics and Black Theology in South Africa* with Adam's *What is Postmodern Biblical Criticism?*

By linking such works to each other, juxtaposing neglected texts with the mainstream, we can highlight gaps, absences and imbalances. Such reading will reiterate the fact that many readings are possible and that it is preferable to highlight the diversity than privilege one over the others.

Let me digress here and share with you some of my observations on the somewhat lukewarm response to liberation theology and the reluctance to incorporate it into the mainstream.[5] British theology has

---

[4] See *Modern Believing* 35 (1994): 50, 51. I am grateful to Werner Ustorf for pointing this out to me.

[5] Liberation hermeneutic has had its application in the English context. Christopher Hill, who has done extensive research into seventeenth-century English popular history, sees interesting parallels between the radical religions of the time and the Latin American liberation hermeneutic. See *The English Bible and the Seventeenth-Century Revolution* (London: Allen Lane, 1993), especially pp. 447–51. He writes: 'Like seventeenth-century radicals, Gustavo Gutiérrez, the leading liberation theologian, pays special attention to the sufferings and the needs of the poor, relying on the same biblical texts' (p. 447). For recent attempts at English liberation theology, see Christopher

been done mainly from the victor's point of view. Liberation theology, on the other hand, is about the victims. Despite its history and colonial past, Britain has been very slow to evaluate the theological and moral implications of its role in subjugating other people and their cultures. Max Warren, the mission theologian, claimed that in spite of a few aberrations imperialism was a *preparatio* for 'God's good will for the world', a 'means to a greater end' and a 'vehicle of great good to a subject people' (Warren 1955: 28, 38, 36). Because of its involvement in past oppression and its continued responsibility for injustice, the former colonizer cannot escape the challenges of liberation theology.

Theological discourse in Britain is a class-based activity. It is this class which has been going around the world for over two centuries as civilizing agents, theological educators, moral teachers and spiritual guides, lecturing others on what theology is about. They are good at telling others how theology ought to look, but reluctant to listen. Liberation theology is born out of listening to the cries of the people.

Most British theologians are trained in the classical tradition that revels in the capitalist idea of the division of labour – some think and others work. In contrast, liberation theology is based on action-reflection and hence this demarcation is non-existent. British theologians, because of their training, are keen on methods and on critiquing rather than transforming those systems that produce unjust situations. Their tendency is to place liberation theology in the category of history of ideas rather than relate it to the socio-economic context out of which these theologies emerge. They are reluctant to take any form of economic theory into their theologizing. They largely depend on Scripture, tradition, church pronouncements and the theological works of fellow theologians. Listen to the testimonies of two European modern masters, Bultmann first and then Barth:

> So I do not believe that the war has influenced my theology. My view is that if anyone is looking for the genesis of our theology he [*sic.*] will find that internal discussion with the theology of our teachers plays an incomparably greater role than the impact of the war or reading Dostoevsky. (Georgi 1985: 83)

> We do not always have to bring in the latest and most sensational events. For instance, if a fire broke out in the community last week,

Rowland and Mark Corner, *Liberating Exegesis: The Challenge of Liberation Theology to Biblical Studies* (London: SPCK, 1990); Christopher Rowland and John Vincent (eds), *Liberation Theology UK* (Sheffield: Urban Theology Unit, 1995).

church members are still suffering under its awful impact, we should guard against even hinting at this theme in the sermon. It belongs to the everyday life, but now it is Sunday. (Buttrick 1992: 106)

Barth regretted mentioning World War I in his sermons. He wrote, 'Pastors should aim their guns beyond the hills of relevance' (Buttrick 1992: 101). Their aim is to establish a critical ground through a series of analyses and systems, using texts rather than listening to the stories, lamentations and yearnings of people.

The current theological scene in Britain, according to Oliver Davies (1990: 854), is insular and dominated by Anglican middle-class rationalism whose main aim is to evangelize the secular person who has come of age fed on Enlightenment values such as reason and human progress. The object of English theology is the person who has come of age, whereas that in the case of liberation theology, as Gutiérrez has been repeatedly reminding us, is the person who has yet to become a person. English theology is cautious in its approach and sees keeping the balance as its cardinal mantra. Liberation theology, on the other hand, is not about maintaining balance but rather about how to cope in a context of injustice. Boff writes:

There is no point in saying in theology or ethics, 'on this issue there are five positions'. The people are interested in one, since they are not concerned with knowing but with living. And living means taking a stance, taking a position on issues. Or as Elijah said to all the Israelites and the prophets at Mount Carmel: 'How long will you go limping with two different opinions?' (1 Kgs 18.21). (Boff 1993: 8)

Brokering Third World Theologies: Teacher as Text

In teaching Third World texts, one cannot divorce the text from the teacher. In the classroom, students encounter, along with the texts, the teacher, who is also constantly being studied, exegeted and deconstructed. We are seen as the visible link between Third World texts and Eurocentric master discourses. The words of Indira Karamcheti, the Indian academic, ring bells for all Third World academics who find themselves in Western academia:

. . . after all I am the pukka, the genuine article. As a woman and as an Indian I am simultaneously completely known to my students and an impenetrable mystery. I represent the extremes of glamour and squalor, the exotic woman, the pampered idol of orientalist fantasy; and the eternal victim, the oppressed Third World female . . . (Karamcheti 1993: 277)

We, as interpreters, have a peculiar position – we are both the most reliable guide to the subject and also the subject matter. In this capacity we are expected to fulfil two roles. I am there to challenge and raise consciousness. One often hears people telling us, 'We need to hear voices like yours to make us think.' This means that in Western academic circles I have a role manufactured for me which has been already scripted and assigned. In other words, I become what Gates calls 'the official marginality'. 'Be critical please, you look so cute, when you make us angry' (Gates 1992: 185).

Second, I become an official spokesman for vast continents of peoples and cultures. One is invested with the enormous responsibility of representing and teaching materials from nearly two-thirds of the world. The fact that I am often introduced as 'Third World lecturer' and not 'lecturer in Third World theologies' is also an indication that my credibility is derived not from my academic credentials or my ability to use professional tools but from my otherness, my cultural difference and my geographical situatedness. I would like to use the recent volume that I edited, *Voices from the Margin: Interpreting the Bible in the Third World* (1991), as an example of this perception. The way some of the libraries in and around Birmingham have classified the volume indicates where they place our work. Even though the volume has a subtitle which clearly states, *Interpreting the Bible in the Third World*, and the publishers give the Dewey classification 220 indicating that the book is about the Bible and biblical criticism, the librarians seem to ignore this. For instance, one theological college library classifies it as 261.3, where anything from social theology to inter-faith issues are placed. Two other colleges shelve it under 230, acknowledging it as a theological work, with one giving it an additional .091274 to indicate the contextual nature of the theological reflection. The SCM Press in its periodical listings 'Religion and Theology' places it under multi-cultural theology. It is hard to avoid the conclusion that our works are classified on the basis of what we look like rather than what we are professionally capable of. We appear to be judged by the geographical location from which we originate or the colour of our skin rather than the quality of our work. As Rasheed Araeen said, 'Whatever these artists do, the status and value of their work is already predetermined' (Jordan and Weedon 1995: 445).

The credibility I derive from being an Asian is, of course, a dubious one. We are often asked to put across the Third World point of view, or the Asian perspective, or the African view or the Latin American feminist perspective, on a variety of issues. Such an expectation is misleading on two counts. It is unreasonable to expect 'the view' from any of these locations. Even in India one may find at least 10 different perceptions on any issue. It also suggests that all theological problems faced by Western audiences are resolvable by reference to this elusive Indian or Argentinian point of view. In a heterogeneous class, such a solution would merely replace one monolithic hegemonic dominance with another, this time imported from the former colonies. This assumes the teacher's role not as an interactor but as a transactor – one with exclusive access to a particular reservoir of knowledge handing over to a passive recipient, a commodity. I see my role as interactive rather than simply passing on ideas and concepts.

One final thought. In the early part of the essay, I referred to curry. I would like to end with a curry-related anecdote. It comes from the BBC comedy show *Not the Nine O'clock News*. In a sketch, Rowan Atkinson, speaking as a Tory minister on immigration issues, tells the audience, 'I like curry, I do. But now we've got the recipes . . . is there any need for them to stay?' I leave you to work out the hermeneutical implications of this for Third World texts and especially for the Third World interpreters working in metropolitan centres.

This chapter was originally published in *Black Theology in Britain: A Journal of Contextual Praxis* 2 (1999): 33–46. Reprinted with permission of Continuum.

References

Appadurai, Arjun, 1986. 'Introduction: Commodities and the Politics of Value', in Arjun Appadurai (ed.), *The Social Life of Things: Commodities in Cultural Perspective*, Cambridge: Cambridge University Press.

Baago, Kaj, 1969. *Pioneers of Indigenous Christianity*, Confessing the Faith in India, 4, Madras: Christian Literature Society.

Boff, Leonardo, 1993. *The Path to Hope: Fragments from a Theologian's Journey*, Maryknoll, N.Y.: Orbis Books.

Buttrick, D. G., 1992. 'Preaching, Hermeneutics and Liberation', in P. P. Parker (ed.), *Standing with the Poor: Theological Reflections on Economic Reality*, Cleveland: Pilgrim Press.

Camara, Helder, 1969. *Church and Colonialism*, London: Sheed & Ward.

Davies, Oliver, 1990. 'Between the Lines', *The Tablet*, 7 July.

Faith in the City: Call for Action by Church and Nation. The Report of the Archbishop of Canterbury's Commission on Urban Priority Areas, London: Church House.

Gates, Henry Louis, Jr, 1992. *Loose Cannons: Notes on Culture Wars*, New York: Oxford University Press.

Georgi, D., 1985. 'Rudolf Bultmann's *Theology of the New Testament* Revisited', in Edward C. Hobbs (ed.), *Bultmann: Retrospect and Prospect*, Philadelphia: Fortress Press.

Jordan, Glenn, and Chris Weedon, 1995. *Cultural Politics: Class, Gender, Race and the Postmodern World*, Oxford: Blackwell.

Karamcheti, Indira, 1993. 'The Graves of Academe', in Women of South Asian Descent Collective (eds), *Our Feet Walk the Sky: Women of the South Asian Diaspora*, San Francisco: Aunt Lute Books.

Koyama, Kosuke, 1993. 'Theological Education: Its Unities and Diversities', *Theological Education* 30, Supplement 1.

Maraire, Nozipo, 1996. *Zenzele: A Letter for My Daughter*, London: Weidenfeld & Nicolson.

McAfee Brown, Robert, 1990. *Gustavo Gutiérrez: An Introduction to Liberation Theology*, Maryknoll, N.Y.: Orbis Books.

Said, Edward W., 1991. *The World, the Text and the Critic* (1983), London: Vintage.

Said, Edward W., 1993. *Culture and Imperialism*, London: Chatto & Windus.

Turner, Bryan S., 1994. *Orientalism, Postmodernism and Globalism*, London: Routledge.

Warren, M. A. C., 1955. *Caesar the Beloved Enemy: Three Studies in the Relation of Church and State*, London: SCM Press.

Select Bibliography

Postcolonialism and Biblical Studies

Roland Boer, *Last Stop Before Antarctica: The Bible and Postcolonialism in Australia*, The Bible and Postcolonialism, 6, Sheffield: Sheffield Academic Press, 2001.

Warren Carter, *Matthew and the Margins: A Sociopolitical and Religious Reading*, Maryknoll, N.Y.: Orbis Books, 2001.

Musa W. Dube and Jeffrey L. Staley, *John and Postcolonialism: Travel, Space and Power*, The Bible and Postcolonialism, 7, London: Sheffield Academic Press, 2002.

Richard A. Horsley, *Jesus and Empire: The Kingdom of God and the New World Order*, Minneapolis: Fortress Press, 2003.

Richard A. Horsley (ed.), *Paul and Empire: Religion and Power in Roman Imperial Society*, Harrisburg: Trinity Press International, 1997.

Shawn Kelley, *Racializing Jesus: Race, Ideology and the Formation of Modern Biblical Scholarship*, London: Routledge, 2002.

Michael Prior, *The Bible and Colonialism: A Moral Critique*, Sheffield: Sheffield Academic Press, 1997.

Erin Runious, *Changing Subjects: Gender, Nation and Future in Micah*, Sheffield: Sheffield Academic Press, 2001.

Fernando F. Segovia, *Decolonizing Biblical Studies: A View from the Margins*, Maryknoll, N.Y.: Orbis Books, 2000.

Fernando F. Segovia, *Interpreting Beyond Borders*, The Bible and Postcolonialism, 3, Sheffield: Sheffield Academic Press, 2000.

R. S. Sugirtharajah, *Postcolonial Criticism and Biblical Interpretation*, Oxford: Oxford University Press, 2002.

R. S. Sugirtharajah, *The Bible and the Third World: Precolonial, Colonial and Postcolonial Encounters*, Cambridge: Cambridge University Press, 2001.

R. S. Sugirtharajah, *Asian Biblical Hermeneutics and Postcolonialism: Contesting the Interpretations*, Sheffield: Sheffield Academic Press, 1999.

R. S. Sugirtharajah (ed.) *The Postcolonial Bible*, The Bible and Postcolonialism, 1, Sheffield: Sheffield Academic Press, 1998.

Keith Whitelam, *The Invention of Ancient Israel: The Silencing of Palestine History*, London: Routledge, 1996.

Semeia 75 (1996): 'Postcolonialism and Scriptural Reading'.

Jian Dao: A Journal of Bible and Theology 8 (1997): 'A Postcolonial Discourse'.

Journal for the Study of the New Testament 73 (1999): 'Postcolonial Perspectives on the New Testament and its Interpretation', guest editor R. S. Sugirtharajah.

Postcolonial Theory

Ian Adam and Helen Tiffin, *Past the Last Post: Theorizing Post-Colonialism and Post-Modernism*, Hemel Hempstead: Harvester Wheatsheaf, 1993.

Bill Ashcroft, Gareth Griffiths and Helen Tiffin, *Key Concepts in Post-Colonial Studies*, London: Routledge, 1998.

David Theo Goldberg and Ato Quayson (eds), *Relocating Post-colonialism*, Oxford: Blackwell, 2002.

Ania Loomba, *Colonialism/Postcolonialism*, London: Routledge, 1998.

John McLeod, *Beginning Postcolonialism*, Manchester: Manchester University Press, 2000.

Padmini Mongia (ed.), *Contemporary Postcolonial Theory: A Reader*, London: Arnold, 1996.

Bart Moore-Gilbert, *Postcolonial Theory: Contexts, Practices, Politics*, London: Verso, 1997.

Bart Moore-Gilbert, Gareth Stanton and Willy Maley, *Postcolonial Criticism*, London: Longman, 1997.

Ato Quayson, *Postcolonialism: Theory, Practice or Process?* Cambridge: Polity Press, 2000.

Edward W. Said, *Orientalism*, Harmondsworth: Penguin, 1985.

Edward W. Said, *Culture and Imperialism*, London: Chatto & Windus, 1993.

Henry Schwarz and Ray Sangeeta (eds), *A Companion to Postcolonial Studies*, Oxford: Blackwell, 2000.

Robert J. C. Young, *Postcolonialism: An Historical Introduction*, Oxford: Blackwell, 2001.

Feminism and Postcolonialism

Laura E. Donaldson and Kwok Pui-lan (eds), *Postcolonialism, Feminism and Religious Discourse*, London: Routledge, 2002.

Musa W. Dube, *Postcolonial Feminist Interpretation of the Bible*, St Louis: Chalice Press, 2000.

Meyda Yegenoglu, *Colonial Fantasies: Towards a Feminist Reading of Orientalism*, Cambridge: Cambridge University Press, 1998.

Postcolonialism and Religions

Anouar Majid, *Unveiling Traditions: Postcolonial Islam in a Polycentric World*, Durham, N.C.: Duke University Press, 2000.

Richard King, *Orientalism and Religion: Postcolonial Theory, India and 'The Mystic East'*, London: Routledge, 1999.

Gauri Viswanathan, *Outside the Fold: Conversion, Modernity, and Belief*, Princeton: Princeton University Press, 1998.

Journals

Postcolonial Studies: Culture, Politics, Economy
Interventions: International Journal of Postcolonial Studies

Index of Biblical References

Index of Names and Subjects